Global networks of Indigeneity

Manchester University Press

Global networks of Indigeneity

Peoples, sovereignty and futures

Edited by

Bronwyn Carlson, Tristan Kennedy
and Madi Day

MANCHESTER UNIVERSITY PRESS

Published by Manchester University Press
Oxford Road, Manchester M13 9PL

www.manchesteruniversitypress.co.uk

British Library Cataloguing-in-Publication Data
A catalogue record for this book is available from the British
Library

ISBN 978 1 5261 5697 6 hardback
ISBN 978 1 5261 9162 5 paperback

First published 2023
Paperback published 2025

EU authorised representative for GPSR:
Easy Access System Europe – Mustamäe tee 50,
10621 Tallinn, Estonia
gpsr.requests@easproject.com

Typeset by Newgen Publishing UK

The editors who are all members of The Centre for Global Indigenous Futures would like to dedicate this collection to Indigenous peoples worldwide.

We thank the Wallumattagal clan of the Dharug speaking peoples for the privilege of working on their homelands where Macquarie University is located. This collection includes contributions from numerous Indigenous peoples and we respect and honour our respective ancestors and the Elders who continue to guide us.

Contents

Figures

Contributors

Bronwyn Carlson is an Aboriginal scholar, Head of the Department of Indigenous Studies and Director of the Centre for Global Indigenous Futures at Macquarie University. Her research focuses on Indigenous digital life and the ways in which Indigenous peoples globally make use of social media; colonial commemorations, truth-telling and settler violence, the politics of identity and global Indigeneity. In 2021 she co-edited and contributed to a global Indigenous collection published by Rutgers University Press, *Indigenous People Rise Up: The Global Ascendancy of Social Media Activism*, and co-authored *Indigenous Digital Life: The Practice and Politics of Being Indigenous on Social Media* published by Palgrave Macmillan.

Madi Day is an Aboriginal transgender academic and PhD candidate in Indigenous Studies at Macquarie University. Madi worked on the first offering of Indigenous queer studies in Australia and has published about this work in 'Indigenist origins: institutionalizing Indigenous queer and trans studies in Australia' in *Trans Studies Quarterly* (2020). They specialise in research on the relationship between setter colonialism, heterosexuality and gender and have published research on heterosexualism, gendered violence, online racism, transgender studies, queer studies and sex work.

Dion Enari is Lecturer at the School of Sport and Recreation, Faculty of Health and Environmental Sciences at Auckland University of Technology. He is a PhD Candidate at Bond University, Gold

Coast with a Master of International Relations and Lefaoali'i (high talking Chief) title from Lepa, Samoa. His research interests include Sport Management, Sport Leadership, mental health, Pacific language, Indigenous studies and trans-nationalism.

Andrew Farrell is Lecturer in the Department of Indigenous Studies, Macquarie University. Andrew is a Wodi Wodi descendant from Jerrinja Aboriginal community on the South Coast of NSW. Their research is multidisciplinary with a focus on Aboriginal and Torres Strait Islander LGBTIQ+ (lesbian, gay, bisexual, transgender, intersex, queer) gender and sexualities on social media. They are instrumental in the development and delivery of Australia's first multidisciplinary Indigenous gender and sexuality curriculum in ABST2035: Indigenous Queer Studies at Macquarie University. Andrew is an ongoing board member of the grassroots Aboriginal and Torres Strait Islander LGBTIQ+ community organisation Black Rainbow.

Tim Frandy is a member of the Sámi American community, was born and raised on Anishinaabe lands in northern Wisconsin, and is an Assistant Professor of Nordic Studies at the University of British Columbia. Their research centres around Sámi and Anishinaabe environmental ontologies, traditional knowledge, and public humanities. Frandy is the editor and translator of *Inari Sámi Folklore: Stories from Aanaar*, the first multivoiced anthology of Sámi oral tradition published in English, and co-editor with B. Marcus Cederström of a volume public folklore and the public humanities, titled *Culture Work: Folklore for the Public Good*.

Innez Haua is Aotearoa Māori, a daughter of the Pacific, a descendant of iwi; Ngāti Porou, Ngāi Tāmanuhiri, Rongowhakaata, Te Aitanga-a-Māhaki and Ngāti Kahungunu. She is (currently) gratefully residing on the unceded lands of Biddegal Country. She is a lecturer and PhD Candidate in the Department of Indigenous Studies at Macquarie University, Sydney, Australia. Her research focus includes Indigenous diasporas, Indigenous cultural sustainability and the entangled histories and futures of Indigenous peoples and cultures.

Ellen Marie Jensen is Associate Professor at Sámi Allaskuvla (The Sámi University of Applied Sciences) where she teaches in the Sámi Pathfinder program and in Journalism and Media Studies. She holds a PhD in Humanities and Social Sciences, Literature and Cultural Studies concentration, as well as a Master's in Indigenous Studies and a Master's in English Literature. The child of a coastal Sámi from the Norwegian side of Sápmi and an Anglo-American settler from the American Midwest, much of Jensen's scholarship has addressed the complexities of trans-Atlantic Sámi migration from Indigenous and gendered perspectives. She is currently working on two volumes based on her PhD study on narratives of early twentieth-century Sámi migrant women while also attending to future research on coastal Sámi communities of West Finnmark.

Coro J.-A. Juanena, Kolonialism Osteko Ikasteka Zentroa (KOIZ)/ Center for Postcolonial Studies) and Professor, Rey Juan Carlos I University, Spain and is a sociologist from Euskal Herria, doctor and professor at the URJC and Villanueva universities in Madrid. She is a member of the African Studies Group of the Autonomous University of Madrid and Coordinator of the Kolonialism Osteko Ikasketa Zentroa, KOIZ (Center for Postcolonial Studies) in the Basque Country. Her doctoral dissertation examines research methodologies on the different cultural identities of the Other and of Indigenous Women in international organisations. For more than fifteen years she has attended the forum on Indigenous issues working with Indigenous women in transnational spaces. Her research interests include Indigenous women, extractive industries, knowledge building and the Indigenous African movement.

Tristan Kennedy is Professor and Pro Vice Chancellor (Indigenous) at Monash University. He is an Indigenous researcher interested in the emerging configurations of digital global citizenship and Indigenous peoples' futures in academia. He has conducted research into Indigenous peoples' experiences of harmful content on social media and how Indigenous bands and music fans use digital technology to establish digital communities of resistance. He is currently investigating the affordances of digital technology in relation to Indigenous peoples' innovation and success in higher education in Australia and internationally. Tristan is a member of the Centre for Global Indigenous Futures.

Souksavanh T. Keovorabouth is a PhD candidate at Oregon State University in the Women, Gender, and Sexuality Studies program with a minor in Queer Studies and a certificate in Geographic Information Systems. They are also a PhD candidate at Macquarie University in Indigenous Studies as a Cotutelle Student in Sydney, Australia. Prior to Oregon State University, they received a dual Bachelor's and Master's at the University of Arizona in Sustainable Built Environments and American Indian Studies. Their concentrated area of research is on Indigenous urban experience, Two Spirit wellbeing, Relocation Act of 1950 and Native and Queer urbanisation.

Percy Lezard. I am outma sqilxw, and my relations are the Lezards in Sn'pinkton, the Krugers from Arrow Lakes and the Baptistes from Chopka. I am an Assistant Professor in the Indigenous Studies Program at Wilfrid Laurier University. I am the lead writer for the 2SLGBTQQIA+ Sub-Working Group MMIWG2SLGBTQQIA+ National Action Plan Final report. My family and I are all full status and registered members under the Indian Act and under OUR nations custom membership code, we/I are members of the Penticton Indian Band my people, the sqilxw, have lived on the territory known as the Okanagan Valley since the beginning of people on those lands.

Yi-Chun Tricia Lin (林怡君) is a seventeenth-generation daughter of Taiwan and the Chair and Professor of the Women's & Gender Studies Program at Southern Connecticut State University. She was President of National Women's Studies Association (NWSA), from 2012–2014. As Senior Fulbright Scholar, Lin was visiting professor in College of Indigenous Studies at National Dong Hwa University in 2018. Lin is editor of a special issue on transnational Indigenous feminisms for *Lectora: Revista de dones i textualitat* (2016). Internationally and on Turtle Island, she continues the activist scholar's journey which includes her work with and writing about Taiwan Indigenous feminists' cultural productions as resistance, knowledge production and resurgence. She is co-editor on two volumes in progress: on transnational Indigenous feminisms and on women's and social movements.

Binalakshmi 'Bina' Nepram is an Indigenous scholar whose work focuses on documenting Indigenous histories, constitutions, armed conflicts and women-led peace and conflict resolution processes in Manipur, Northeast India in particular and Asia in general. Bina completed her MPhil in South Asian Studies in the School of International Relations, Jawaharlal University, New Delhi, and has a Master's specialising in Subaltern Studies in Indian Modern History from Hindu College, Delhi University. Bina has authored and edited five books, including *Deepening Democracy, Diversity, and Women's Rights in India* (2019), *Where Are Our Women in Decision Making?* (2016), *Meckley: A Historical Fiction on Manipur* (2004) and *South Asia's Fractured Frontier* (2002) based on her MPhil thesis which looked into the linkages of conflict in Indigenous territories and small arms and narco-trafficking in Indo-Burma border region.

Lou Netana-Glover (Ngā Puhi, Tainui) is a PhD candidate in the Macquarie University Department of Indigenous Studies. Lou's research interests sit primarily with the lawlessness of the colonial state; however, her own identity journey has compelled her to write about the complexities of being a woman whose Māori identity was not revealed to her until age fifty. Lou had previously believed herself to be of Aboriginal (and settler) descent, she still may be. Lou's cultural history, reconnection with her whānau, language and culture, and now being part of a diaspora generates both data and theory for Lou to bring into the academy.

Sandy O'Sullivan is a transgender/non-binary Wiradjuri person and Professor of Indigenous Studies in the Centre for Global Indigenous Futures at Macquarie University. They are a 2020–2024 ARC Future Fellow with the project *Saving Lives: Mapping the influence of Indigenous LGBTIQ+ creative artists* exploring the contribution of queer artists to modelling complex identities contributing to the wellbeing of First Nations' peoples. Since 1991 they have taught and researched across gender, sexuality, museums, the body, creativities and First Nations' identity. In addition to academic work, Sandy has been a musician, performer and sound artist since 1982 holding national and international residencies.

Jo Anne Rey is a Dharug Aboriginal community member and Indigenous Research Fellow with Macquarie University. Her current post-doctoral research weaves three Dharug sites located in western, central and northern areas of Dharug Sydney. In 2021, the NSW Department of Planning and Environment offered the historic opportunity to undertake a Dharug women's cultural burn at the northern site of Brown's Waterhole, Lane Cove National Park. Together, with Dharug community, her Ancestors, family and allies, Jo's journey weaves cultural knowledges across Dharug Ngurra/Country.

waaseyaa'sin Christine Sy, University of Victoria, Canada is a poet, mother and Assistant Professor in Gender Studies at the University of Victoria. Her research amplifies Anishinaabe womxn's relationships with the natural world within Anishinaabeg territories through an Anishinaabe historical feminist lens that centres Indigeneity and gender while also considering governance, class, subsistence, materiality, political and social economic relations. She is presently working on a book project tentatively entitled *At the Boiling Place: Anishinaabe Stories of the Sugar Bush*, through which she demonstrates the historically formidable, complex and shifting nature of Anishinaabeg womxn's relationship with, and arising from, the sugar bush.

Maggie Walter is a palawa scholar, sociologist and Pro Vice Chancellor Aboriginal research at the University of Tasmania. Maggie's scholarly obsessions centre around Indigenous inequalities and Indigenous methodologies, especially Indigenous statistics to change the narrative (and the policy focus) on that inequality. She has published extensively in the field of race relations, inequality and research methods and methodologies.

Alex Wilson is Professor of Educational Foundations and Director of the Aboriginal Education Research Centre at the University of

Saskatchewan. Her research and community work span a wide spectrum, from Two Spirit people and 'coming in', to Indigenous land-based education, to sustainable housing. She is an organiser with the Idle No More Movement, integrating radical education movement work with grassroots interventions that prevent the destruction of land and water.

Foreword

Maggie Walter

This volume asks the critical question: what does it mean to be Indigenous in an increasingly connected and globalised world? This question assumes a greater importance in the current era of global Indigenous resurgence and reclamation. The increasing prominence of Indigeneity identity is significantly driven by the work of global networks of Indigenous scholars, advocates and activists. The United Nations Declaration of the Rights of Indigenous Peoples, for example, released in 2007 and finally adopted by Anglo-settler nation-states in 2009, was, and is, manifestly driven by Indigenous leaders coming together in shared purpose.

The question 'what does it mean to be Indigenous?' has multiple facets and answers. Until recently, the primary answer was that to be Indigenous is to be marginalised, impoverished and disregarded minorities within our own lands. Now, an increasingly frequent answer is that to be Indigenous means being able to draw on the strength, experiences and successes of other Indigenous Peoples. This impact of this solidarity cannot be overstated. As an Indigenous scholar (Palawa), for example, attending global conferences such as those held by the Native American and Indigenous Studies Association (NAISA) where Indigenous scholarship IS the topic, rather than a peripheral disregarded stream, has been foundational in inspiring and motivating my scholarship over the last decade.

But the trend to global Indigenous identity is not without risks. Indigenous communities across the globe, resist, appropriately, having their First Nation identities subsumed into the mega-category of Indigenous. But it is not a case of being one or the other. I am Palawa, Aboriginal and Indigenous and retain the right to assume each identity as appropriate to the circumstance. I also retain the right to be all three concurrently. Claiming an Indigenous identity does not diminish or dim my embodied Palawa connection to Country and family and First Nation.

The three editors of this work are all Indigenous scholars. And it shows. As demonstrated throughout these chapters, despite the many cultural, colonising historical, geographical and language differences, there exists an instantly recognisable and distinctive Indigenous relationality between peoples, place and Country. This way of being and knowing unites us without detracting from who we are as individual First Nations and Peoples.

Acknowledgements

Everyone who we've worked with throughout the years, who have informed our research in productive ways; the Forum for Indigenous Research Excellence (FIRE), now the Centre for Global Indigenous Futures (www.globalindigenousfutures.com), the global symposia that have come out of FIRE, and everyone who participated in them: Cultured Queer/Queering Culture: Indigenous Perspectives On Queerness (2015); Reterritorialising social media: Indigenous people rise up (2015); Decolonising Criminal Justice: Indigenous Perspectives on Social Harm (2016); Indigenous Peoples Rise Up: An International Symposium on the Global Ascendancy of Social Media Activism (2019); Indigenous Futurisms (2019) and many more to come. To all the members of the Centre for Global Indigenous Futures who share the vision of a world in which Indigenous people are thriving. We are looking forward to all the possibilities and collaborations this global network will bring.

Bronwyn: I want to thank my partner, Mike, for being so supportive of all that I do and who never fails to make me a lovely cup of tea and provide countless statements of support. I am thankful for the distractions my grannies provide me, Scarlet, Jack, Aurora, Evie, Phoenix, Isaac and Grace. I want to thank my colleagues in the Department of Indigenous Studies who are truly the best mob that someone could ever hope to work with: Sandy O'Sullivan, Madi Day, Andrew Farrell, Tetei Bakic, Jo Rey, Zac Roberts, Innez Haua, Tamika Worrell and Terri Farrelly. When you get to work with such inspirational people work becomes productive and enjoyable. A bunch of big dreamers, schemers and networkers who I am thankful to know.

Tristan: My friends and colleagues in the Department of Indigenous Studies at Macquarie University have provided a most enjoyable space to write, research and develop ideas. Working with such future thinking Indigenous scholars is a privilege and an honour. Thanks to Evie and Audrey, Jo and Mark, you keep me grounded and offer endless support for my work. Thanks also to our amazing network of Indigenous scholars and allies across the globe. Indigenous research continues to face challenges but thanks to the ground-breaking knowledge work and immeasurable generosity of this community the future is immensely promising.

Madi: Foremost I would like to thank my colleagues Bronwyn Carlson, Sandy O'Sullivan and Percy Lezard for their care and leadership. It's a dream come true working with you mob. Thank you to my teammates in the Department of Indigenous Studies at Macquarie University including Tetei Bakic, Jo Rey, Andy Farrell, Souksavanh Keovorabouth, Innez Haua, Tamika Worrell and Zac Roberts who are all brilliant, generous and hilarious. Thank you to my siblings and sisters including Ellie, Cassi, Karina, SG and Aims who took care of my chihuahua so I could get on with it. Finally, thank you to my grandparents, Jim and Bev, who taught me to speak up, cook stew and think big.

1

Global Indigenous futures: a new research agenda

Madi Day, Tristan Kennedy and Bronwyn Carlson

Indigenous lives are exponentially more complex, connected and dynamic than settlers can imagine. And, they do imagine Indigenous peoples – more often than not, as limited, solely local people of a romanticised past. Both actual and imagined elimination of Indigenous peoples are cornerstones of settler colonialism (Veracini 2008). Such a violent structure, inherently concerned with securing land for settler populations, rests tenuously on cultures of denial and negation – that which Patrick Wolfe (2006) calls the logic of elimination. Settler colonial nations and societies rely on racialised discourses that position Indigenous peoples as ill-suited to Western conceptions of humanity and modernity; as inferior, uncivilised and pre-modern. Even in places where legal and political fictions of *terra nullius*[1] are overturned, romantic narratives of national identity and peaceful settlement prevail, referencing Indigenous peoples either in myths of retrospect or reconciliation (Behrendt 2003). When settler–colonisers do observe Indigenous cultures as acceptable, they are romanticised and celebrated in ways that pose no threat to the continued hegemonic negotiation of settler colonial dominance. The settler gaze relegates Indigenous people to strictly physical and cultural domains, revelling in sporting cultures and certain artistic pursuits, and imagining us as incompatible with technology, politics, society and economy (Carlson & Frazer 2021).

As settler colonial narratives are continuously defined and redefined, Indigenous peoples are ever innovating ways through, around and beyond colonial impositions and limitations. In spaces and narratives of our own making, we are people of the now, of the future and of the world. Globally, Indigenous thinkers, activists, knowledge holders and scholars identify, reject and respond to epistemic violence with acts of self-determination and sovereignty. Social media has been a powerful tool for change particularly in challenging symbolic annihilation and (mis)representation of Indigenous peoples worldwide (O'Sullivan 2022). Transnational movements of resistance and activism are proliferating building on relationships as old as and older than colonisation, and forging new connections based in shared recognition of struggle and sovereignty (Carlson & Berglund 2021). From Idle No More (INM)[2] to #NoDAPL[3] to the Missing and Murdered Indigenous Persons (MMIP) movement,[4] there is ample will and cause to fight as Indigenous peoples survive systemically violent settler colonial nation-states whose continuation depend on the extinguishing of Indigenous lives and sovereignties (Perera & Pugliese 2021). Social media and the internet are also tools of settler colonial violence as sites where hate speech and white supremacist cultures abound (Carlson & Frazer 2021; Kennedy & Frazer 2021). Yet, in the face of settler colonial efforts of elimination, Indigenous and anti-colonial thinkers and scholars cultivate international cultures of counter-discourse that collectively challenge colonial violence and hegemony.

This edited volume speaks into these cultures and into conversations about what it means to be Indigenous in an increasingly connected and globalised world. Certainly, these conversations are fraught and complex. As Kim Tallbear (2013a, p. 511) writes the term Indigenous itself 'helps facilitate networking and mutual recognition between peoples from across the globe, even while the category intersects with different regimes of race, ethnicity, and class in different parts of the world'. Tallbear's (2013b) scholarship highlights some of the challenges and complications of negotiating Indigeneity in a globalised context where technologies like DNA testing reference Indigeneity disconnected from relationships and place. As a framework to study these complexities, Chadwick Allen (2012) offered 'Trans-Indigenous' originally for comparative Indigenous studies between Indigenous peoples in English-speaking settler colonial nations, primarily in Canada, the United States, Australia and New Zealand. Allen himself acknowledged the limitations of this including concerns that 'there is so much work still to be done within specific, distinct traditions and communities' and so the local risks becoming 'engulfed (one again) in the name of the global' (Allen 2012, p. iiiv). These concerns remain relevant particularly in the South Pacific and in African and South Asian countries where globalisation is synonymous with neo-colonialism and imperial expansion (Patnaik & Patnaik 2016). Simultaneously, there are shared experiences among Indigenous and colonised peoples in formerly and currently Commonwealth countries, and as such there is cause for shared anti-colonial scholarship, resistance and critique.

The title of this volume *Global Networks of Indigeneity: People, Sovereignties and Futures* denotes shared solidarity, activism and envisioning amongst Indigenous peoples – we are jointly invested in futures liberated of colonialism and settler colonialism where we are free to enjoy our own lands and lives in conditions of our own making. Leonie Pihama (2021, p. 164) refers to this in Māku Anō e Hanga Tōku Nei Whare (I myself shall build my house) as she advocates for Mana Wāhine theory – a means by which Māori women can draw on ancestral and relational teachings to shape sovereign and self-determined futures. Grace Dillon has named this collective investment Indigenous Futurism and describes this kind of praxis and envisioning in Anishaanaabe as Biskaabiiyang (Returning to Ourselves) (2012; 2016). In this way, Indigenous futures are connected global efforts to articulate and enact threats to colonial fantasies of a world where settlers have successfully eliminated and assimilated Indigenous peoples and replaced us on our lands. In Aboriginal English, Mykaela Saunders declares 'this all come back now' to insist that restoration of our lands, lore and governance is both inevitable and imminent (2022a). Saunders also invokes Indian author Arundhati Roy's words to this end: 'Another world is not only possible, she is on her way. Maybe many of us won't be here to greet her, but on a quiet day, if I listen very carefully, I can hear her breathing' (Roy in Saunders 2022b).

Adding voices to this conversation, this edited volume forms a global network in and of itself of writers, thinkers and scholars connected by common investment in Indigenous futures.

This book assembles collective visions of Indigenous futures, contemplations of the potential of digital technologies towards these ends, and considerations of Indigenous intimacies, relationalities and manners in which we locate ourselves in an increasingly global and connected world. Together, we present possibilities and the practicalities required to bring Indigenous futures to fruition. In Chapter 2, Bronwyn Carlson continues her scholarship on nomenclature and the politics of terms like Indigenous and Indigeneity. She presents and analyses data from online survey respondents on the Australian continent, North America and Aotearoa (New Zealand), some of whom report using 'Indigenous' and 'Indigeneity' in global settings to describe precedence and ancestral connections, and to position themselves in relation other Indigenous peoples. Others find these terms simplistic and homogenising, and prefer more specific descriptors. Many respondents describe involvement in global relationships and networks with other Indigenous peoples including academic conferences, political movements and cultural festivals. In Chapter 3, Tristan Kennedy considers the potential of social media for circumventing colonial borders and forming translocal solidarity. He observes the uses of social media for Indigenous political mobilisation around and against settler colonial nation-states as assertions of sovereignty.

In Chapter 4, Andrew Farrell explores how settler colonial heteropatriarchy results in displacement and migration for Indigenous LGBTIQ+ peoples globally. They identify urban spaces as liminal sites where Indigenous LGBTIQ+ peoples seek refuge while they renegotiate connections to and conceptions of home. In Chapter 5, Lou Netana-Glover reflects on their own experiences of displacement and finding home. Netana-Glover shares a complex story of relations between Ngurra (Country), Tūpuna (Ancestors), Wairua (spirit) and people connected by Te Moana-nui-a-Kiwa (the Pacific Ocean). In Chapter 6, Innez Haua and Dion Enari continue thinking through Pasifika connections and the meaning of whānau (family). They contemplate distinctly Indigenous notions of relationality as ways of being that both expand and query what it means to be in relationship with people, place and tangata whenua (the people of the land). Movement, connection, home, peoples, identity and place run as a common thread through these chapters, which are also linked geographically by the Pacific Ocean.

Chapter 7 begins with a journey of Sámi migration across another ocean – the Atlantic. Ellen Marie Jensen and Tim Frandy grapple with diasporic–Indigenous identity and what it means to be Sámi away from Sápmi. Speaking to contexts of both Nordic settler colonialism and settler colonialism in North America, Jensen and

Frandy raise important questions about Indigeneity, community, relationality, resurgence and reclamation. In Chapter 8, Jo Anne Rey invokes relationality to combat human-centric, patriarchal, hierarchical and colonising governance on Dharug Ngurra (Sydney, Australia). In doing so, she calls into question the legitimacy and legality of colonial sovereignty on Dharug lands. In Chapter 9, Bronwyn Carlson considers the role of social media in asserting Indigeneity and sovereignty. She draws on her extensive body of work investigating Indigenous digital lives reflecting on the political and social uses of social media for subverting settler colonialism with humour, ingenuity and style. Community-building, political innovation and global networks of sovereignty and relationality are common to each of these chapters.

In Chapter 10, Percy Lezard, Madi Day and Sandy O'Sullivan engage in an intergenerational, transnational discussion of what it is like to be Indigenous and non-binary in academic institutions, and in broader settler colonial societies. The chapter outlines complex trajectories of activism, resistance, and resilience, which shape the current and future terrain in Indigenous Studies for Indigiqueer thinkers. In Chapter 11, Binalakshmi Nepram offers an intricate analysis of state-sanctioned and state-ordered violence against women in Manipur, India. Nepram recounts non-violent protest from women of Manipur since the 1970s including Meira Paibis (women with bamboo torches), the hunger strike of Irom Sharmila, and a nude protest by the mothers of Manipur who continue sustained efforts of resistance. Chapter 12 begins with a poem where Souksavanh Keovorabouth describes their experience of being a Diné and Laotian person engaged in the academy and living in an urban location. Their chapter contains a series of deliberations on anti-Asian violence in the United States of America, and the future of being queer, Indigenous and multi-racial in a white supremacist settler colonial society. In the final chapter, Yi-Chun Tricia Lin joins four prominent Indigenous feminists, Bronwyn Carlson, Coro J.-A. Juanena, waaseyaa'sin Christine Sy, and Alex Wilson and they present four narratives of global Indigeneity. The chapter is based on a roundtable at the National Women's Studies Association (NWSA) chaired by Lin and that highlights Indigenous feminist and queer movements as some of the most successful and enduring global collaborations between Indigenous peoples. Lin, Carlson, Juanena,

Sy and Wilson show us glimpses of the future – of what is possible when living and thinking beyond colonial borders and settler colonial heteropatriarchy and, instead, making worlds based in relations, reciprocity and mutual responsibility.

Notes

1 *Terra nullius* means 'nobody's land'. This doctrine has existed in the law of nations throughout the development of Western democracy. See www.fedcourt.gov.au/digital-law-library/judges-speeches/justice-jagot/jagot-j-20171020

2 Idle No More (INM) is a movement beginning in Saskatchewan in 2012 started by four Indigenous women who raised awareness of the Canadian government's attempts to deteriorate treaty rights to protect land and water. With the use of social media, INM is now a decentralised, international movement dedicated to protecting Indigenous sovereignty and land rights. For more on INM please see Wilson and Zheng (2021).

3 The #NoDAPL movement was an Indigenous-led movement resisting Energy Transfer Partner's plans to build an oil pipeline running across four states in the USA: North Dakota, South Dakota, Iowa and Illinois. The movement culminated in a Water Protector camp in 2016 on Standing Rock Sioux reservation lands in North Dakota where Indigenous peoples and allies from around the world came to prevent the pipeline crossing the Missouri River. #NoDAPL is credited as one of the largest protest movements resisting colonial policies and protecting Indigenous sovereignty (Estes 2019) as it successfully engaged a critical following and international support via social media. For more on #NoDAPL please see (Deschine Parkhurst 2021).

4 The Missing and Murdered Indigenous Persons (MMIP) movement stems from the Missing and Murdered Indigenous Women and Girls (MMIWG) movement, which resulted in a National Inquiry from the Canadian government from 2015. The inquiry showed that Indigenous women and girls were overrepresented in missing persons cases, and instances of homicide and violence that were both racialised and gendered (Moeke-Pickering et al. 2021). Since then there has been international pressure to identify how gendered violence in Anglo settler colonial nations including the USA, Canada, New Zealand and Australia is disappearing not only Indigenous

women and girls but also queer and transgender Indigenous persons. Social media, particularly Twitter, has been instrumental in this push. For more on the origins of MMIP please see Lezard et al. (2021).

References

Allen, C. (2012). *Trans-Indigenous: Methodologies for Global Native Literary Studies* (Vol. 10). Minneapolis: University of Minnesota Press.

Behrendt, L. (2003). *Achieving Social Justice: Indigenous Rights and Australia's Future*. Annandale: Federation Press.

Carlson, B., & Berglund, J. (Eds). (2021). *Indigenous Peoples Rise Up: The Global Ascendency of Social Media Activism*. New Brunswick: Rutgers University Press.

Carlson, B., & Frazer, R. (2020). 'They got filters': Indigenous social media, the settler gaze, and a politics of hope. *Social Media+ Society*, 6(2), 2056305120925261.

Carlson, B., & Frazer, R. (2021). *Indigenous Digital Life: The Practice and Politics of Being Indigenous on Social Media*. London: Palgrave Macmillan.

Dillon, G. L. (2012). *Walking The Clouds: An Anthology of Indigenous Science Fiction*. Tucson: University of Arizona Press.

Dillon, G. L. (2016). Indigenous futurisms, Bimaashi Biidaas Mose, flying and walking towards you. *Extrapolation*, 57(1/2), 1.

Estes, N. (2019). *Our History Is the Future: Standing Rock versus the Dakota Access Pipeline, and the Long Tradition of Indigenous Resistance*. London: Verso Books.

Kennedy, T., & Frazer, R. (2021). Indigenous people and the varieties of colonial violence on social media. *Journal of Global Indigeneity*, 5(2), 31063.

Lezard, P., Prefontaine, N., Cederwall, D. M., Sparrow, C., Maracle, S., Beck, A., & McCleod, A. (2021). 2SLGBTQQIA+ Sub-Working Group MMIWG2SLGBTQQIA+ National Action Plan Final report. https://scholars.wlu.ca/indg_faculty/1/

Moeke-Pickering, T., Rowat, J., Cote-Meek, S., & Pegoraro, A. (2021). Indigenous social activism using Twitter: Amplifying voices using #MMIWG. In *Indigenous Peoples Rise Up* (pp. 112–124). New Brunswick: Rutgers University Press.

O'Sullivan, S. (2022). Challenging the colonialities of symbolic annihilation. *Southerly*, 79(3), 16–22.

Pankhurst Deschine, N. (2021). How the# NoDAPL movement disrupted physical and virtual spaces and brought Indigenous liberation to the forefront of people's minds. In Carlson, B. & Berglund, J. (Eds), *Indigenous Peoples Rise Up: The Global Ascendency of Social Media Activism* (pp. 32–47). New Brunswick: Rutgers University Press.

Patnaik, U., & Patnaik, P. (2016). *A Theory of Imperialism.* New York: Columbia University Press.

Perera, S., & Pugliese, J. (Eds). (2021). *Mapping Deathscapes: Digital Geographies of Racial and Border Violence.* London: Routledge.

Pihama, L. (2020). Māku Anō e Hanga Tōku Nei Whare: I myself shall build my house. In Hokowhitu, B. et al. (Eds), *Routledge Handbook of Critical Indigenous Studies* (pp. 162–74). London: Routledge.

Saunders, M. (Ed.). (2022a). *This All Come Back Now: An Anthology of First Nations Speculative Fiction.* Brisbane: University of Queensland Press.

Saunders, M. (2022b). Everywhen: Against 'the power of now'. *Griffith Review,* 76, 115–25.

TallBear, K. (2013a). Genomic articulations of Indigeneity. *Social Studies of Science,* 43(4), 509–533.

TallBear, K. (2013b). *Native American DNA: Tribal Belonging and the False Promise of Genetic Science.* Minneapolis: University of Minnesota Press.

Veracini, L. (2008). Settler collective, founding violence and disavowal: The settler colonial situation. *Journal of Intercultural Studies,* 29(4), 363–79.

Wilson, A., & Zheng, C. (2021). Shifting social media and the Idle No More movement. In Carlson, B., & Berglund, J. (Eds), *Indigenous Peoples Rise Up: The Global Ascendency of Social Media Activism* (pp. 14–31). New Brunswick: Rutgers University Press.

Wolfe, P. (2006). Settler colonialism and the elimination of the Native. *Journal of Genocide Research,* 8(4), 387–409.

2

Global perspectives on Indigeneity: Indigenous perspectives on global Indigeneity

Bronwyn Carlson

Introduction

The title of this chapter assumes that perspectives can be formulated to enhance an understanding of Indigenous experiences and to provide an understanding of some of the nuances that accrue around terms such as 'Indigenous' and 'Indigeneity'. I commence, therefore, from language itself. I ask: what do these terms imply? How do they differ, are they interchangeable with other appellations such as 'Aboriginal' and 'Aboriginality', 'First Nations' and so on? If language can provide a conduit for collective consciousness or some means of comprehension, does 'Indigenous' simply mean, as defined by Macquarie Dictionary online, 'originating and characterising a particular region or country' or does it have a vast complexity of signification specific to individuals, groups, locations, those who identify as Indigenous and those who don't? The problem with definitions is that they often defy the very act of defining. Definitions often do not correlate to any kind of specificity but rather provide a sense of meaning that may or may not be recognisable or collective. For example, the term 'Indigenous' often fails to signify varying Indigenous histories, movements, changes, shifting identities or, indeed, the multitudinous shifts in the English language, for example, capitalisation, pronunciation, changes in spelling, dialect, vernacular and so on.

This chapter begins, therefore, by noting its own limitations within the very domain of language. For many Indigenous peoples, this is crucial because it is English that is primarily used, particularly in the academy, to describe, understand and give voice to

Indigenous peoples globally. The chapter is thus an exploration of terms such as 'Indigenous' and 'Indigeneity'. It considers how several Indigenous groups understand and use the terms. The objective is to draw from research and see what emerges rather than have a clear roadmap of what 'Indigenous perspectives' might signify while at all times keeping in mind the dynamism of language as it has been applied to Indigenous peoples since the imposition of English as a means of conveying meaning.

In this chapter I draw on data collected from an online social media driven survey that asked participants about their preferred terminology and the way in which they identify themselves locally, nationally and internationally. The survey specifically asked participants about the terms 'Indigenous', 'Indigeneity' and 'global Indigeneity'. Responders identified themselves as belonging to one or more of the Indigenous nations across this continent (colonially referred to as Australia[1]), Aotearoa (New Zealand), Canada and the United States, which some Indigenous groups refer to as Turtle Island (North America). I note that these nation-states cannot simply imply a global coverage but Indigenous peoples from these locations comprise hundreds of self-identifying groups and see themselves as peoples connected to other Indigenous peoples globally. As Māori scholar Roger Maaka and settler scholar Augie Fleras (2005, p. 7) observe:

> The world is in the midst of a profound transformation because of 'people' politics. In the space of a generation, indigenous peoples have leaped from the margins of society to become key contestants in a rapidly evolving global order. An international movement of indigenous peoples has evolved because of shared experiences and common realities.

Language as a system of naming

In previous publications, I have argued that language matters (Carlson et al. 2014; McGloin & Carlson 2013). As a scholar of Indigenous Studies, the importance of language is given weight so that all students are aware that naming is crucial and not just some kind of nod to the politically correct furphy (Roberts et al. 2021). How we are named by others and ourselves dictates how we are seen as descriptors change over time. For example, there was a time when certain names, now considered by many to be derogatory, identified us quite commonly to colonisers but I won't give those space here. It was the case, however, that those names originated from a long history of white supremacy that could only endure through violence: the physical violence endured by Indigenous peoples and the violence of the language that supported it. In order for colonisation to succeed, the colonised must 'become' synonymous with the names they are accorded; thus, colonial power remains *in situ*. This chapter is ultimately about language. Language is a system of naming. When we speak of Others, we name them. Although language is always changing and is a dynamic force in culture, it is not a neutral conduit for expression. In saying language is 'not neutral', I mean that it carries meaning that allows us to understand culture, life and the world we live in. In other words, language is not just a series of marks on the page or words that have no value or meaning – language allows us to make meaning of the world. As articulated by cultural critic Henry Giroux (2004, p. 59), 'language is more than a mode of communication or a symbolic practice that produces real effects; it is also a site of contestation and struggle'. Imposed languages, in particular, are a site of struggle as they delete the frames of reference colonised people once used to describe themselves and their existence.

Blanket terms

When googled, the term 'aborigine' is defined as being 'a person, animal or plant that has been in a country or region since the earliest of times'. The term is also defined in many online dictionaries such as Merriam-Webster as 'an aboriginal inhabitant of Australia'.[2] It has its origins in Latin and means 'from the beginning'. Similarly, across Turtle Island now known as North America, blanket terms were imposed. All of the tribal nations across the now United States were defined as 'Indian' and across Canada as 'Aboriginal' and at times 'Indian'. Over the past five centuries, there have been a range of terms used to refer to the peoples of Turtle Island. 'Indigenous', 'Native American', 'First Nations', 'Aboriginal', 'Eskimo', 'Inuit', 'Native Alaskan', 'Natives' and so forth. Some terms have become more acceptable to those being named than others. Like here, Indigenous people around the globe generally prefer to be referred to by their tribal, clan or local names. However, despite the existence of hundreds of self-identifying and named autonomous groups across this content colonially referred to as Australia, the original inhabitants have always been understood and named by colonisers as a singular group (Carlson 2016). The term 'aborigine' was applied to us here to simplify the situation for colonisers – there was them and there was us. This neat bifurcation underscored the relationship between us and the policies that ensued from it. 'Aborigine' thus became an antonym of 'Australian', a term encoded with meaning that was shared and understood by colonisers. It named us, defined us and gave meaning to our experience as colonised people while opposing us to settlers in every way possible.

As I write this chapter, I am collaborating with Native American colleagues in the United States on an international grant opportunity that aims to facilitate knowledge exchange between Indigenous peoples in the United States and Australia. The grant is entitled 'First Nation Fellowship' and is a joint offering with the US Department of State and the US Embassy in Canberra. The first thing that was raised when we were reading the guidelines was terminology. The Native American contingent commented that they do not generally use the term 'First Nations' in the United States. Terms such as 'Native American' and in some instances 'Indian' were more common. The term 'Indian' was discussed and it was noted that some organisations or groups, such as the 'American Indian Movement' or the 'National Museum of the American Indian', use this term but, in general, in the everyday, people don't use it and it is considered outdated. My colleagues stated that term 'First Nations' is generally associated with Indigenous peoples of Canada. It does not apply to all people who are Indigenous and who are from the lands now referred to as Canada; Métis or Inuit are excluded, for example. The term 'First Nations' came into popular use in Canada in the 1970s and 1980s replacing 'Indian'. However, First Nations peoples in Canada are still defined as 'Indian' in the settler legal framework via the Indian Act of 1876.[3]

The term 'First Nations' is becoming more common across this continent in recent years. Colonially, we have been referred to collectively in a range of terms as described by settler scholar Bruce Reece (1987, p. 14):

Partly for the sake of convenience, partly out of ignorance of these differences, Europeans referred to them collectively as 'Indians', 'aboriginal natives', 'Australians', 'black natives', 'blacks', 'blackfellows' and finally, 'Aborigines' or 'Aboriginals'. So, the aboriginal peoples or Indigenes of Australia became the 'Australian Aborigines' or simply 'the Aborigines'.

Indigenous people globally have long been identified under umbrella terms; this was and remains convenient for colonisers. Blanket terms are handy. They remove the inclination or need to think critically about terminology and act as 'safe' descriptors for those who are either unsure or not in the habit of asking subjects how they would like to be categorised in relation to the specificity of their Indigenous identity. As Reece argues, 'So the Aborigines were invented as a convenient, if fictitious, entity or category' (1987, p. 15). Blanket terms serve settlers and their aspirations to steal land and eliminate the Indigenous populations (Wolfe 2006). It is also the case that blanket terms can 'move' with the times as language changes to include more acceptable (usually to colonisers) nominal signifiers. This is not a cynical standpoint; it is the truth. If naming were politically motivated towards a shift in power relations, colonisers would seek collaboration to identify Indigenous language frames of reference. In this schema, colonial naming would be abolished and the entire continent would undergo a significant change where roads, towns, buildings, monuments and the like would all be renamed according to Indigenous language preferences. Current 'shifts' in terminology, therefore, while nodding to some 'politically correct' inclination, are invariably signifiers of the colonisers' making and not motivated by a desire for real change.

Online survey

To supplement the scholarly literature, I also conducted a short online survey created using SurveyMonkey and promoted via Facebook (n=45). Respondents to the survey identified as Indigenous to this continent, Aotearoa and across Turtle Island. The survey asked respondents how they describe their cultural identity and what communities they belong to. It also asked if respondents used the term 'Indigenous' or 'Indigeneity' to describe themselves and whether they have a sense of belonging to a global Indigenous community. Additional questions were asked if the respondent attended any global Indigenous events or connected with Indigenous peoples outside of their own cultural group. All respondents identified with one or more Indigenous groups other than one respondent who identified as British and was therefore disqualified.

The survey garnered a broad array of responses, likes and dislikes. They serve as a testimonial to the inappropriateness – and laziness – of a lot of blanket terminology, but also disclose the preferences of some of these terms as identifiers. When asked 'how do you usually describe your cultural identity?', respondents used general terms or very specific terms. For example, several responded using more general and collective terms such as 'Aboriginal' (n=10), 'Indigenous' (n=5), 'First Nations' (n=3), Māori'(n=5) or Torres Strait Islander' (n=3), while others used more specific terms. For example, very local, clan or tribal affiliations such as 'Wiradjuri' (n=4), 'Trawlwulwuy' (n=1), 'Noongar' (n=5), 'Cree' (n=4), 'Bidigal/Dharawal' (n=1), 'Cherokee' (n=3), 'Biripai' (n=2), 'Métis' (n=7), 'Algonquin' (n=1), 'Anishnaabe' (n=2), 'Tharawal and Yorta Yorta' [and] 'Yamatji' (n=1), 'Karuk' (n=1) and 'Dharug/Dharawal' and 'Te Atihau nui a paparangi te iwi' (n=1).

They were then asked, how they usually describe the Indigenous communities they belong to. Respondents chose mostly collective terms, such as 'Indigenous' (n=9), 'Aboriginal' (n=6), 'First Nations' (n=6), 'Native American' (n=9), 'Indian' (n=1), 'Métis' (n=7) and 'Māori' (n=7). Some offered multiple terms that they identify with such as 'First Nations/Indigenous/Aboriginal', 'First Nations/Torres Strait Islander', 'Indigenous/Māori/Pasifika' and 'First Nations/Indigenous/Aboriginal/Torres Strait Islander', which could indicate more than one Indigenous heritage or it might show how collective or blanket terms can be lacking when speaking about complex identities as one respondent replied 'my clanal countries of cameragal, warmuli, kamay and gweagal in the Sydney basin'.

A few of the respondents listed more colloquial terms, such as 'Blackfulla', 'mob' or 'iwi'. 'Iwi' is a te reo Māori word that, when translated to English, can mean people or nation (Moeke-Pickering 1996). 'Blackfulla' or 'Blackfella' is a term like 'mob', which we have reappropriated (Carlson et al. 2014; Latimore 2021). The spelling can differ but generally the meaning is the same. 'Blackfella' was a term non-Indigenous colonials used to describe us. In the resistant act of appropriation, they are the 'whitefellas'. Aboriginal and Torres Strait Islander people have reassigned this term and use it in a defiant way (Carlson & Frazer 2021). The English language, while doing immeasurable harm to us, also offers opportunities for our intervention: regardless of all the efforts to eliminate us, we are still here. The term 'Blackfulla' then, is a political statement. We use it to describe ourselves and, in doing so, we are saying regardless of how non-Indigenous people describe or see us we are Black/Indigenous. As Arrernte writer Celeste Liddle (2014: para. 7) puts it: 'the term "Black" carries a lot of political weight. It is word that has power and a term that we've reclaimed. After years of removal policies and stolen generations based on the tone of one's skin and their alleged blood quanta, to state that you are "Black" regardless is defiant.'

Similarly, 'mob' is a term now used commonly by Aboriginal and Torres Strait Islander people to refer to us as a collective. You will often see statements like 'us mob' or 'for mob only', which signals that whatever is being discussed does not invite non-Indigenous involvement. However, Torres Strait Islander scholar Martin Nakata wrote of how he remembers a time when the term 'mob' was used by pastoralists to refer to their livestock, which included Aboriginal people (see Carlson et al. 2014, p. 68). Appropriation and the re-assignment of colonial terminology to our own ends is a deeply political act of resistance precisely because it often goes unnoticed and betrays an ironic (to us) act of insubordination: *we* reapply positive meaning to terms that identify us negatively.

Qualitative responses

To elicit more qualitative responses, the survey provided a space for respondents to specify more details about their identities. They were asked: what does it mean to belong to the communities which they listed as belonging to? Many articulated strong feelings of connection and belonging, making statements about their bloodlines, kinship and being part of a collective:

My bloodline, my DNA, my ancestry. (Aboriginal)

It's very important. To have shared experiences, identities and struggles. It makes us who we are. (Wiradjuri)

It is the core of who I am, my connection to my country and to my language, people and cultural practice. It is my kinship. (First Nations)

I feel that it explains me and who I am, why I am. It gives me a sense of pride and belonging. (Māori, Pasifika)

A sense of security and care wherever I go. I feel calm knowing other Blackfellas will care for me. A national understanding of what life is like and how I experience the world. Being part of a powerful minority. (Blackfulla/Noongar)

A strong sense of responsibility and obligation was also articulated:

Belonging to mob means I feel connected and loved, but it has responsibilities too. My identity and my integrity to culture is intertwined – what I do is tell, write and relate stories of power and pass on what information or wisdom I gain to those in community who may wish to accept it. It is all about raising up, stepping firmly into a space, and sometimes stepping out of the way for others to occupy. But always with respect. (Mob)

Learning and practising traditions, culture and ways of being. (First Nations)

That I have a homelands & people that claim me. I have protocol, language & relations to the land. (First Nations)

Ensuring that I walk in a good way that focuses on the next generation being healthier than the previous. (Indigenous)

It defines who I am and how I am placed in the world. It also details my rights, responsibilities and accountabilities. It tells others where and how I belong. It also gives me a deep sense of who I am as a person. (Aboriginal)

Being 'Indigenous'

All but three respondents stated they use the term 'Indigenous'. They were then asked about the context in which they would refer to themselves as 'Indigenous'. There were several who commented that they generally use terms such as 'Indigenous' in relation to communicating with those who are non-Indigenous or as required in their workplace. For example:

> Any time I am communicating with non-Indigenous peoples. (Māori)

> In professional terms only because we are required to, I personally don't like any of our labels other than our nations. (Wiradjuri)

> Largely among white folks and non-Indigenous folks. (Cree)

> Mostly in contexts where institutions seem to want it more. Sometimes with writing there is a tendency to use it because of editors and word count. My university has not got a protocol regarding the wording of culturally diverse peoples as yet. (Mob)

Some indicated that they love the term and use it all the time to identify themselves and others. One explained that after a long history of racist terms, 'Indigenous' was much preferred:

> I am always Indigenous, even when I am not standing on my land. (Cherokee)

> In all contexts, social, political and academic. (Māori)

> With other Indigenous folks. (Cree)

> I use it all the time – my Elders use it proudly after being called every racist name under sun when they were growing up. I think it's offensive now to be told by other Indigenous people I shouldn't use that term – it's quite offensive. (Aboriginal)

Several stated they used the term 'Indigenous' in a global sense that connects all first peoples as a collective:

> I tend to use Indigenous within a global context. (Torres Strait Islander)

> I use it in the UNDriP [sic] context, as meaning first peoples with a historic history to land and place, before the arrival of a colony. (Māori)

> It can sometimes homogenise the diversity of Indigenous peoples; however, I do think the global Indigenous collective needs a 'pronoun'. (Aboriginal)

> I don't love it. But I use it. I prefer the term First Nations to describe larger collectives, but I think Indigenous helps in the international space. (First Nations)

Several were not keen on the term 'Indigenous' and felt it homogenised diverse peoples. In general, they only used it when they felt they had little choice or lacked a more appropriate term for many nations as a collective:

> Typically in settings where I might be talking about things with non-Indigenous people. Teaching students or colleagues and knowing there is limited awareness or knowledge about Indigenous people. Or in global health contexts and referring to things like UNDRIP. If I'm talking to other Indigenous people, I will be specific and who I am and the community I belong to. (Métis)

> I was using the word when speaking about the first peoples globally and Aboriginal Peoples within Canada. I get as specific as possible about individual nations. The new use of Indigenous is problematic. It denies our group differences and pan-Indigenizes us into a homogeneous group palatable for white audiences. I refer to myself as Indigenous in classrooms and articles but not in many Indigenous spaces. (First Nations)

> I don't use it for others, I refer to the region and how they might refer to themselves.

> I don't use Aboriginal – it's context is Kkkanada using for me (and Métis, Inuit peoples), colonisation is the continued naming of us original people. (First Nations)

There were several comments that discussed the limitations of language more broadly and particularly English terms that have been used to homogenise collectives in simplistic ways:

> They all are terrible in some way or another aren't they? I have no real issue with it. (Māori)

> Flattens specificities, but opens up international connections. (Torres Strait Islander)

> Indigenous, Aboriginal, First Nations, First Peoples, Original Inhabitants are all labels using the oppressor's language, and personally I feel arguments about these labels are often petty distractions. Any person in authority must be flexible to what the local community may use (and also respectfully negotiate the tensions around these imposed labels). (Dharawal)

> It's an umbrella term that in a way erodes our identity as individual communities and humanity. (Wiradjuri)

Yes, I don't think it's an appropriate descriptor of my peoples. (First Nations)

It's a bit 'clinical'? Like seems to be a political attempt at using a more scientific word to describe us? It's also homogenising. I don't have a problem with the connotations of being native/first to an area because that's what I am. (Blackfulla/Noongar)

Yes, it is a politically temporal term that has limits. It means something now in a way it didn't 5 years ago. This will be the case in 5 years. It's also decontextualising. (Cree)

The term 'Indigenous' in recent years has acquired some kind of affirming self-identity among many who are not Indigenous. There are instances where settlers have used the term 'Indigenous' to affirm their 'right' to a national identity and also others who have made false claims to an Indigenous heritage (see Learn's 2018 discussion in relation to 'Pretendians'[4]). These issues are complex and would easily comprise a book or many books to do justice to the topic. This chapter does not discuss these issues in any detail. Rather, this chapter is focused on people who are Indigenous and how they engage with terms used to describe their identities. Several people who responded to the survey raised the issue of non-Indigenous peoples making the claim to be Indigenous to Australia when they are actually settlers. Notably they mentioned people like Australian political party One Nation's senator Pauline Hanson, who has on numerous occasions made the claim to be 'Indigenous' to Australia because she was born in Australia. In 2019, for example, Hanson was filmed confronting a group of young Aboriginal people, telling them, 'I'm Indigenous, I was born here, I'm native to the land. So, you know, I'm Australian as well, and I'm Indigenous.' Hanson then asked, 'Where's my land if not Australia?' to which one of the young people responded by telling Hanson that her land was England.[5] Settler colonialism as noted by scholars such as Eve Tuck and Wayne Yang (2021) is a distinct form of colonialism that seeks to remove Indigenous populations from their lands and replace them with settlers who then claim to be Indigenous to that land. Participants articulated these concerns:

It can be misused. Pauline Hanson and the likes use the word to reinforce possessiveness of land. (Aboriginal)

> Indigenous refers to a broad spectrum. (ie) British could be considered as Indigenous to their country of origin. (Torres Strait Islander)

> Yes – it is a colonial term that is used to describe anyone born on this land, which can mean white people who have no connection or relationship with country. (Aboriginal)

The notion of being 'Indigenous' as a form of appropriation secures ownership in the colonial mindset; to be 'Indigenous' now carries cultural capital that is unique to first peoples and, along with land and much cultural expression, it is a much-coveted identifier for those seeking affirmation *and* for those seeking to remove Indigenous sovereignty based on prior ownership and occupation of the land. Such are the previously mentioned 'shifts' that often serve the colonial mindset while perhaps changing, to a small degree, the ways we can perceive ourselves through the collective eyes of colonisers.

Indigeneity

All respondents to the survey stated they are familiar with the term 'Indigeneity' and, for many, it was preferred over 'Indigenous'. Indigenous connotes 'I am' whereas 'Indigeneity', for many connotes 'I have'. Settler anthropologist Francesca Meran (2009, p. 304) suggests, 'Indigeneity' 'connotes belonging and originariness [the quality of being ordinary] and deeply felt processes of attachment and identification, and thus it distinguishes "natives" from others.' For many mixed heritage Indigenous people, in particular, 'I have' is not only inclusive of other possibilities but also foregrounds 'Indigeneity' as the focal point of one's cultural heritage. One respondent stated, 'I'm much more comfortable with Indigeneity than I am with Indigenous. I think it means what it is to be a First Nations person' (Wiradjuri). Others thought of the term as a way of describing 'being Indigenous', for example:

> Indigeneity is the state or an element of being Indigenous. My iwi seldom use the term to define themselves. For them and in context of being on their Country they are Māori or even more applicable Naati. Indigenous is a word I use as I do not live on my lands and it is much widely understood. (Māori)

Similar to 'Aboriginality' – a term used to discuss cultural ways of being and identity. (Birripi)

A classifier of one's state of being Indigenous. (Torres Strait Islander)

Participants were also asked about the context in which they would use the term 'Indigeneity' and many suggested that they use the term when articulating what it means to *be* 'Indigenous'. For example, one replied, 'To describe a state of being Indigenous' (First Nations). Another stated:

> My Indigeneity lies in the theoretical framework of my ancestors, their cultural, spiritual and sense of place and history. It embraces contemporary growth as well as aspirations of self-determination and sovereignty, it is alive and thrives, means it's not in the distant past, it is useful today and tomorrow. (Māori)

'Indigeneity' was often used in relation to international or global context: 'When I am talking about Indigenous ways of being in, and seeing the world in a global context' (Māori/Pasifika). Another respondent stated, 'When referring to Indigenous peoples on a larger general scale' (Cree) and another, 'in reference to a shared collective of diverse First Peoples facing the ongoing onslaught of colonisation' (Dharawal).

Survey participants were asked if they felt they were part of a global Indigenous community. Many answered yes but generally as a result of their employment or due to the affordances of social media such as Twitter or Facebook. For example, 'I always link with International Indigenous scholars both at conferences and or research and writing partnerships. It means I am supported and endorsed by my academic Indigenous peers, they are who I look to for confirmation and affirmation of my Indigeneity in academia' (Dharawal). Another commented, 'I have connections through my work to other Indigenous mobs and it's a wonderful thing to share our collective experiences' (Aboriginal). In relation to social media one responded, 'It allows for connection and to share ideas and understanding and also importantly provides a support system of people you can reach out to. People who understand what you're experiencing' (Métis), and another stated, 'Twitter allows me to instantly connect with Indigenous people and have short discussions about issues that we are facing in different parts of Canada and globally' (Algonquin).

Indigenous peoples are avid social media users (Carlson & Frazer 2021; Carson & Berglund 2021) and often post about terminology. In response to a number of settlers who were posting about whether white should be capitalised in reference to 'white people' in the same way Black and Indigenous is capitalised, Māori scholar Dominic O'Sullivan tweeted: 'I'm quite happy being Māori – Indigenous is not an ethnicity it is an homogenising colonial construct. Much better politically and more culturally authentic to have a nationhood' (@indigpolitics 9 July 2022).

While hosting the rotating Twitter account @IndigenousX, Amy Creighton tweeted:

> I was born in the 50's and YT governments have named me native aborigine Aboriginal ATSI Indigenous First Nations. A powerful tactic to stop mob from being grounded in identity and strength. I AM GOMEROI MURRI AlwaysWasAlwaysWillBe. (@AmyCreighton123 for @IndigenousX 14 July 2022)

These posts and many more like them highlight not only the complexity of terminology but also the violence of colonialism which has used nomenclature as a way to dehumanise, homogenise and eliminate Indigenous peoples.

Global networks

Many respondents spoke of the way Indigenous peoples in settler–colonial states, such as Australia, New Zealand, Canada and the United States, have and continue to experience similar issues and, as such, saw the value in a global collective:

> I am currently meeting with Indigenous scholars around the globe every two weeks to build an Indigenous scholars network. We need to stand united. (Algonquin)

> I think Indigenous peoples, while different across the world still share some common values, beliefs as well as experiences with colonisation. As such we are bound together in many ways despite different languages cultures and traditions. (Anishinaabe)

> Many FN people experience the same effects of colonisation and marginalisation, i think that unfortunately brings us together in a common struggle. (Torres Strait Islander)

Participants spoke of global Indigenous conferences and festivals that they attended and of the importance of getting together with other Indigenous peoples and sharing knowledge and experiences. Conferences included World Indigenous Peoples Conference on Education (WIPCE); Native American and Indigenous Studies Association (NAISA); Ngā Pae o te Māramatanga; Lowitja Conference and university conferences that included cultural events, such as 'Cultured Queer/Queering Culture: Indigenous Perspectives on Queerness' Symposium; Two Spirit gatherings; powwows and the Yirramboi Festival. The majority expressed feeling a sense of global Indigenous solidarity with one stating; 'We all face colonisation and all the horrors it brings such as racism, discrimination etc so I do feel a bond' (Cherokee), and another stated, 'similar struggle to topple power structures' (Noongar). Indigenous people are often defined in terms of our relationship to colonisation. However, being Indigenous is not just about struggle as Maaka and Anderson explain (2006, p. 247), 'Indigenous people are determined not to simply survive, but also to prosper and to see their cultures and societies grow and flourish on their own terms' as articulated by many respondents, 'I think we share more than colonisation. Though I do think we have an opportunity to extend our understanding of First Nations' contributions and unique experiences'(First Nations) and another expressing a sense of global connection, 'we have a global kinship' (Trawlwulwuy) and another, 'It feels like we share common insights and ways of being that don't need to be explained' (Algonquin).

Global Indigeneity

As 'being Indigenous' is increasingly acquiring a more globalised focus, terms such as 'Indigeneity' are becoming more popular (Meran 2009). According to Meran, 'Indigeneity' has come to presuppose a sphere of commonality among those who form a world collectivity of 'Indigenous peoples' (2009, p. 303). Similarly, Maaka and Fleras (2005, p. 20) argue that, while Indigeneity has traditionally implied a relationship or tension between Indigenous peoples and politics, and colonial governments, the term also now encompasses connections between Indigenous peoples through shared experiences of colonialism. Māori scholar Dominic O'Sullivan argues that the 'Indigeneity' provides 'membership of an international Indigenous community that affords intellectual opportunities unrestrained by the often antagonistic political and policy climates of their own nation-states' (2006, p. 3).

The work carried out so far is merely a starting point in terms of the way (English) language drives perception, reality – and government policies that pertain to pre-colonised peoples everywhere. Respondents tell us quite clearly how language frames their identities and self-perceptions. We can see shifts, appropriations and marked differences in preferences that vary according to the application of colonial naming systems. Overall, however, what this research tells us is that we – First Nations, Indigenous, Blackfullas, Inuit, Aboriginal, Mob, Native, Indian and so on – are in an ongoing process of defiance and of self-assignation that will continue to affirm our right as sovereign peoples. Language is messy, untidy, contested. But we will continue to bear responsibility for our naming as a reaffirmation of identity.

Notes

1 I make the point that this is a continent not a country. 'Australia', as it is now referred to, was built on a legal fiction of *terra nullius* (nobody's land) and claimed for the British Crown, despite being home to hundreds of self-identifying nations. Day (2021) uses the term 'so-called Australia' to draw attention to the falsehood of the claim.
2 www.merriam-webster.com/dictionary/aborigine
3 See https://indigenousfoundations.arts.ubc.ca/the_indian_act/
4 'Pretendian' is a term used to describe a settler who has claimed an Indigenous identity, generally referring to a Native American or First Nations identity when indeed they have no Indigenous ancestry. The term is gaining some traction in so-called Australia as are terms such as 'race shifters' or 'box tickers'.
5 Watch the video of Pauline Hanson harassing young Aboriginal people, www.youtube.com/watch?v=myngWhgRTg4

References

Carlson, B. (2016). *The Politics of Identity: Who Counts as Aboriginal Today?*. Aboriginal Studies Press.

Carlson, B., & Berglund, J. (2021). *Indigenous Peoples Rise Up: The Global Ascendency of Social Media Activism*. Rutgers University Press.

Carlson, B., & Frazer, R. (2021). *Indigenous Digital Life: The Practice and Politics of Being Indigenous on Social Media*. Palgrave Macmillan.

Carlson, B., Berglund, J., Harris, M., & Poata-Smith, E. (2014). Four scholars speak to navigating the complexities of naming in Indigenous Studies. *Australian Journal of Indigenous Education*, 43(1), 58–72.

Creighton, A. (2022). I was born in the 50's and YT governments. Twitter post, 14 July. https://twitter.com/IndigenousX/status/154754145249 4086144

Day, M. (2021). Remembering Lugones: The critical potential of heterosexualism for studies of so-called Australia. *Genealogy*, 5(3), 71.

Giroux, H. (2004). *Terror of Neoliberalism: Authoritarianism and the Eclipse of Democracy*. Routledge.

Latimore, J. (2021). Blak, Black, Blackfulla: Language is important, but it can be tricky. *The Sydney Morning Herald*. www.smh.com.au/national/blak-black-blackfulla-language-is-important-but-it-can-be-tricky-20210826-p58lzg.html

Learn, M. (2018). *Elizabeth Warren's DNA and What It Means for Indigenous Folx*. The Texas Orator Blog Entries.

Liddle, C. (2014). Why I prefer the term 'black'. *The Stringer*. https://thestringer.com.au/why-i-prefer-the-term-black-6733#.Ylzb-S8Rrs0

Maaka, R., & Andersen, C. (Eds). (2006). *The Indigenous Experience: Global Perspectives*. Canadian Scholars' Press.

Maaka, R., & Fleras, A. (2005). *The Politics of Indigeneity: Challenging the State in Canada and Aotearoa New Zealand*. Otago University Press.

McGloin, C. & Carlson, B. (2013). Indigenous studies and the politics of language. *Journal of University Teaching and Learning Practice*, 10(1), 1–10.

Moeke-Pickering, T. (1996). *Maori Identity within Whanau: A Review of Literature*. Hamilton: University of Waikato.

Merlan, F. (2009). Indigeneity: Global and local. *Current Anthropology*, 50(3), 303–333.

O'Sullivan, D. (2006). Needs, rights, nationhood, and the politics of Indigeneity. *MAI Review LW*, 1(1), 12.

O'Sullivan, D. (2022). I'm quite happy being Maori. Twitter post, 9 July. https://twitter.com/search?q=I%27m%20quite%20happy%20being%20Maori&src=typed_query

Reece, B. (1987). Inventing Aborigines. *Aboriginal History*, 14–23.

Roberts, Z., Carlson, B., O'Sullivan, S., Day, M., Rey, J., Kennedy, T., Bakic, T., & Farrell, A. (2021). *A Guide to Writing and Speaking about Indigenous People*. Australia Macquarie University. https://researchers. mq.edu.au/en/publications/a-guide-to-writing-and-speaking-about-indigenous-people-in-austra[

Tuck, E., & Yang, K. W. (2021). Decolonization is not a metaphor. *Tabula Rasa (38)*, 61–111.

Wolfe, P. (2006). Settler colonialism and the elimination of the Native. *Journal of Genocide Research*, 8(4), 387–409.

3

Translocal Indigenous communities: global Indigeneity and networks of political activism

Tristan Kennedy

Introduction

Globalisation has presented unique challenges for Indigenous peoples with regard to the maintenance of sovereignty in the face of direct and resource capitalism, global colonisation and environmental catastrophe. Indigenous peoples not only face the persistent threat from settler–colonial nation-states, they now face the added intrusion from multinational corporations as capitalist interests sweep the globe. Today, we are considering less the benefits of industrialisation (global travel, communication technology, resource production) and more the potential destruction caused by advances in technology (pollution, nuclear disaster, climate change). For Indigenous populations across the globe already facing existential threats presented by ongoing colonisation, the shift toward what Beck called a 'risk society' (1992) caused by global industrialisation has seen further impetus for the establishment of global networks of solidarity and resistance.

Amidst the global flows of information, Indigenous peoples continue to face oppression and marginalisation as settler–colonial nation-states shuffle for position in volatile global marketplaces. The preferred narrative of the Western world and particularly settler–colonial nation-states is one which places colonisation as an uneasy relic of the past. However, colonisation continues unabated and in varying configurations despite this narrative. Indigenous peoples continue to be excluded from the formation and negotiation of new nation-state alliances; the management of public infrastructure; and face disproportionate impact and intrusion from the resource industry – often backed by settler–colonial governments. In many cases, Indigenous peoples' exclusion is maintained through exertion of economic, ideological and physical violence. History proves, however, that Indigenous peoples have never shied away from vocal opposition and staunch resistance to existing and future threats of colonisation. In this chapter, I propose that digital technology facilitates the establishment of translocal Indigenous communities that respond to and challenge the very foundations of colonisation, and the current and future threats to Indigenous communities and their sovereignty. A central task in this chapter is to position 'translocal' as a viable and necessary theoretical departure from transnationalism. That is, in deploying social media technology to mobilise and enact resistance, Indigenous peoples establish translocal communities that transcend nation-state boundaries and fortify global networks of solidarity across vast geographies and with increasingly complex avenues of connectivity.

This chapter initially points to early globalisation theorists Arjun Appadurai and Nico Carpentier whose work canvassed the impacts of globalisation on migration and community building. These foundational approaches, combined with notions of community, set out the departure point and what must be achieved in order to arrive at a truly translocal network. I then outline the efficacy of more recent assertions from Katherine Brickell and Ayona Datta whose conceptualisation of 'translocal' enables the configuration of diverse, dispersed but connected communities. Appadurai and Carpentier's theorisations respond to the impacts of industrialisation and globalisation on marginalised and migrant communities across the globe. Appadurai considered the emergent flows of people, nations, news and information around new global channels. His conceptualisation of 'ideoscapes' – 'a concatenation of ideas, terms and images, include "freedom", "welfare", "rights", "sovereignty" [and] "representation"' (Appadurai 1990, p. 299) – allows an initial understanding of the emergence of translocal Indigenous networks; however, it still places a great deal of emphasis on transnationalism and thus, the modern nation-state. Carpentier deploys Appadurai's concept of the translocal as 'the moment when the local is stretched beyond its borders, whilst still remaining situated in the local' (2007, p. 6). The movement across borders in Carpentier's theory is a fundamental idea in the establishment of translocal Indigenous networks. However, its continued reliance on nation-state boundaries renders it a step short of a meaningful conceptualisation of Indigenous translocal communities that must reject boundaries imposed by settler–colonial nation-states.

Brickell and Datta, writing more recently however, outline the need to move away from transnationalism as a concept and toward 'translocal geographies as a simultaneous situatedness across different locales which provide ways of understanding the overlapping place-time(s) in migrants' everyday lives' (2011, p. 4). Useful for their discussion of situatedness and their openness to multiple incarnations of local spaces, the focus on migrant mobility in Brickell and Datta's work will be adapted to show that migration is not necessarily key to establishing translocal communities in the context of global Indigeneity and digital communication technology. In moving away from migration as a core feature of translocal communities, this chapter will propose that *connection*, such as that provided through digital technologies, is a more appropriate prerequisite. Indigenous peoples establish communities and mobilise politically through digital connectivity without the need to traverse geographical boundaries. The concept of the translocal thus remains appropriate to theorise the emergence of connections within and outside of nation-state geographies that facilitate Indigenous global solidarity on colonised lands. Moving away from nation-state boundaries is both a political as well as methodological tactic. First, the imposition of colonial nation-state boundaries serves only to reify colonial hegemony and further delegitimise Indigenous cultures. Second, to understand Indigenous mobility and connection, one must dismiss the imposed colonial borders and recognise the significance of Indigenous concepts of nationhood, identity and community.

The working definition of 'translocal' in this discussion of global Indigenous translocal communities centres on the conceptualisation of digital technology facilitated networks of Indigenous peoples who share common political goals in the face of colonisation outside, but still connected to, local geographies. That is, Indigenous peoples, as enthusiastic users of digital media (Carlson & Dreher 2018), are establishing global networks of solidarity among Indigenous citizens from hundreds of sovereign Indigenous nations. Looking toward the future where the bounds of social and digital media technologies are unforeseen, it remains important to understand the establishment and reflexive reestablishment of networks of solidarity that transcend nation-state boundaries and emerge in online as well as on-Country spaces. Conceptualising these networks as fluid, ever-changing networks reflects the bridging of temporal and geographical distance simultaneously.

Nowhere is the establishment and reestablishment of translocal Indigenous communities more visible than in the arena of Indigenous political mobilisation. Through a purposeful utilisation of digital technology, a global Indigeneity has evolved in response to myriad challenges from colonisation. In 2019, in Flagstaff Arizona, dozens of Indigenous scholars, community members and knowledge holders from around the globe met to discuss the affordances of digital technology for Indigenous peoples' collaborative efforts towards political action (Carlson & Berglund 2021). This symposium itself was an example of the establishment of a translocal community of Indigenous peoples facilitated through the affordances of digital technology. A key outcome of this meeting, aside from further establishing a network of Indigenous scholars and communities, was an interrogation of the rise of global Indigenous political activism and resistance facilitated through digital translocal networks. This chapter was inspired by the work being done by Indigenous scholars and community members to foster and promote these networks of solidarity and political activism as well as the introspection of the group on the import of creating yet another global network of Indigenous activists.

In the previous ten years, Indigenous peoples across the globe have mobilised through social media platforms. They have engaged in resistance to the intrusion and existential threat of the Dakota Access Pipeline construction on Turtle Island, they have responded to police brutality and Black and Indigenous deaths in custody in the United States and Australia, and they have mobilised a global response to the forced closure of Indigenous communities in Western Australia. Each of these movements will be looked at as signs of a growing global translocal Indigenous community. These translocal Indigenous communities and networks exemplify a new and highly effective grassroots mobilisation or globalisation from below (Appadurai 2000). Global

Indigenous networks of solidarity, with increased reach and efficacy of Indigenous voices in response to both local and global colonial processes, is achieved through the affordances of digital communication technology.

Community building on a global scale

While the advances in digital communication technology have presented a far greater reach thirty years on from Appadurai's writing in the 1990s, it remains appropriate to consider the key theoretical elements of community building. Ferdinand Tönnies famously differentiated between *Gemeinschaft* (community) and *Gessellschaft* (society) (Tönnies & Loomis 2002). Gemeinschaft refers to a group of individuals who maintain close connections and ties to each other. In this conceptualisation of community, individuals work together, formally or informally, for the production and reproduction of communal bonds. Society, for Tönnies, conversely refers to larger groups of individuals who maintain no strong or close communal bonds like kinship but rather are connected through wider social structures. Citizens within nation-states for instance often have these looser or wider reaching social ties without the necessity of close communal bonds. There appears to be a reliance on geographical proximity in these conceptions of community and society. With the evolution of global digital technology, notions of community especially reliant upon particular geographical boundaries, are no longer adequate.

This theorisation of community and society favours a Western ideological standpoint. Tönnies wrote about a Western conceptualisation of industrialised nations and not about nations of Indigenous peoples who were at once diverse in national identity and experiencing forced homogenisation by settler-colonisers (Tönnies & Loomis 2002). Indigenous peoples are often compelled to accept their marginalisation and classification as a single homogeneous community positioned in opposition to modern Western ontology. Dominant narratives of settler–colonial nation-states reinforce this positioning through institutions such as education and media. While maintaining an awareness of the value of *Gemeinschaft* and *Gessellschaft*, it is appropriate that this chapter move toward a conceptualisation of translocal that is not tied to settler–colonial ideology.

In pondering the notion of 'locality' in an increasingly globalising world, Appadurai conceptualised locality as being of a 'complex phenomenological quality' (1995, p. 208). In doing so, he suggested that: 'Locality is an inherently fragile social achievement. Even in the most intimate, spatially confined, geographically isolated situations, locality must be maintained carefully against various kinds of odds' (1995, p. 209). The odds against which locality is achieved and maintained are never more notable than when considered in relation to Indigenous communities. The very essence of colonisation relies upon the dismantling and eradication of Indigenous peoples' and communities' legitimate connection to space and place. As Wolfe famously noted the 'logic of elimination not only refers to the summary liquidation of Indigenous people ... it strives for the dissolution of native societies' (2006, p. 388). The maintenance of geographical and cultural boundaries that facilitate the very existence of Indigenous localities is facilitated through the routine reinforcement of Indigenous cultures, knowledges and ways of being that are constantly under threat of destruction by settler–colonial society. The establishment and maintenance of Indigenous communities, thus, is itself a political act of resistance.

The task then becomes to theorise the complex context producing communities tied to what has become a deterritorialised locality – that is, a translocal Indigenous community facilitated by digital technology, which transcends geographical boundaries. Escobar offers a particularly expedient springboard from which to move past geographical neighbourhoods in suggesting that neighbourhoods or communities are 'produced by complex relations of culture and power that go well beyond local bounds' (Escobar 2001, p. 146). That is, the contextual production and reproduction of local subjects in deterritorialised space. This then leads us to a conceptualisation of a technologically mediated translocal community constituted through shared language, imagery and text produced and reproduced by individuals who share a common interest and may or may not share common geographical space.

Geographies are important for Indigenous peoples. Connection to Country and land is a core cultural element for many Indigenous peoples across the globe. Many scholars suggest that relational ontologies based on connection to, among everything else, Country, is shared by global Indigenous peoples (Wilson 2008). Indeed, maintaining a connection to Country or Land is central to Indigenous resistance to colonisation. From an Aboriginal–Australian perspective, all resistance to colonisation is about land precisely because colonisation centres on the logic of elimination (Wolfe 2006). The establishment of translocal Indigenous communities does not overlook nor dismiss such a connection. Translocal Indigenous networks of resistance are about solidarity that transcends Western conceptualisations of nation-state boundaries that bear little resemblance to Indigenous geographies. As our working definition suggests, translocal Indigenous networks are established through the affordances of digital communication technology outside of but still linked to ontologically significant geographical space.

Disintermediated, deterritorialised, translocal

The future of Indigenous resistance to colonisation is translocal and is specifically reliant upon two key affordances of digital technology: disintermediation and deterritorialisation. Disintermediation has arisen predominantly through the capacity of digital technology to bypass intermediaries and gatekeepers through swift and far-reaching self-publication. The affordance of disintermediation presented by digital communication technology has presented drastic changes to the global flows of information. The music industry has seen the decline in importance of record distribution and production companies as digital technology has offered opportunities for 'decentralisation and accelerated spread of music' (Munro & Thanem 2018, p. 74). Global economists are grappling with the question of sovereignty raised through disintermediated monetary systems such as blockchain-enabled cryptocurrencies like Bitcoin (Malherbe et al. 2019). Modern diplomacy and international relations scholars too, are grappling with variations to nation-state diplomatic channels, once seen as trusted national ministries, that are now facing an increase in contestation and stigmatisation (Cooper 2019). The digital communication industry itself is wrestling with the very technological affordances that undergird its own existence as platforms scramble to develop artificial intelligence (AI) and moderation processes to combat the exponential rise in misinformation and disinformation that permeate our digital civic spaces (Tandoc et al. 2020).

For future-focused groups and individuals across the globe, disintermediation presents considerable benefit. As Cooper notes, large multinational corporations, philanthropic and non-government organisations are benefitting from this particular aspect of twenty-first century hyper-globalisation (2019, p. 799). Through the global reach of digital technology, organisations and individuals can now transcend nation-state boundaries in the pursuit of capital, philanthropy and network building. For Indigenous peoples, whose citizenship has been persistently undermined, challenged and marginalised, there exist significant opportunities to transcend the oppressive colonial boundaries of the modern nation-state. As Cooper suggests, disintermediation permits 'hyper-empowered individuals to represent themselves as the flag bearers for the frustrations of ordinary and often left behind citizens through freewheeling tactics [such as] the use of referenda and social media' (2019, p. 802). Indigenous voices and opportunities for network and community building, political action and mobilisation, and self-determination were once at the mercy of government and corporate-mediated media and policies. Disintermediation presents Indigenous peoples with the opportunity to bypass these oppressive structures and operate as global digital citizens.

Deterritorialisation is a parallel affordance of globally connected digital technology. In geographically vast countries such as Australia, individuals were once at the mercy of the limited reach of government and media messaging and communication. Local issues necessarily remained geographically isolated and struggled to gain attention on wider national and international scales. One's identity was in many ways tied to the bounds of one's geographical reach. Digital technology, as it has developed over the past forty years, has provided new opportunities for both physical and metaphysical travel and relationship building. It is now possible to remain connected through synchronous communication technology, such as video conferencing, to communities and networks across the globe irrespective of geographical limitations.

Digital communication technology, through affordances of disintermediation and deterritorialisation, permits the establishment of new translocal Indigenous networks as part of the global flow of people and culture across nation-state boundaries. For Appadurai, the flows that characterise these translocal networks are complex deterritorialisations where ideas, identities and connections are disconnected from geographies and reproduced in another locale dependent upon 'the cultural, class, historical, and ecological setting' in which they re-emerge (1995, p. 225). In terms of a translocal Indigeneity, what emerges is a global Indigenous community that transcends colonial nation-states; allows for the establishment of new shared cultural goals, norms and values; and, by its very existence, demonstrates resistance to colonial regimes. A community that, once emerged as translocal, does not homogenise Indigenous experiences but acknowledges and benefits from similar but diverse experiences of colonisation.

Translocal

Anthropologists pursued the concept of transnationalism to understand human movement across nation-state boundaries. Brickell and Datta suggest that 'transnationalism became more nuanced and sophisticated through attention to its situatedness, by articulating a notion of translocality that was based on local-local connections across national boundaries' (2011, p. 10). A useful starting point to understand migratory movement across and around nation-state boundaries as was used by early proponents. For Brickell and Datta (2011) however, the issue with such a marriage of nation-state boundaries and translocalism was that the concept could not account for internal migration or movement outside and around nation-states. For Brickell and Datta then, 'translocal geographies' presented a more useful approach as it:

> includes migration in all its forms; it includes highly mobile and elite transnationals as well as those who are 'immobile' and often viewed as parochial; and it includes a focus on local-local movements that are part of a continuum of spaces and places related to migration. (2011, p. 10)

The concept of translocal, whether it includes reference to geographies or not, is properly suited to an analysis of global Indigenous networks and collaborations which, in a decolonial vein, must theoretically transcend or reject the colonial nation-state's boundaries in order to fully understand local and global mobilities associated with Indigenous solidarity and resistance.

Translocalism then, permits an interrogation of digital technology, particularly that which enables disintermediated self-publication and connection between localities simultaneously outside of, but still meaningfully connected to, geographical space. With an increasing focus on digital technology, the theory of translocal accommodated for: 'virtual neighbourhoods ... able to mobilise ideas, opinions, monies, and social linkages which often flow directly back into lived neighbourhoods in the form of currency flows, arms for nationalisms, and support for various positions in highly localised public spheres' (Appadurai 1995, p. 223). That is, translocal communities of resistance can mobilise community members from outside of geographical localities in pursuit of political action and resistance that is specifically tied to space and place such as incursions on Country by nation-state-sanctioned mining and resource industry activity.

Migration should not, however, be considered a prerequisite of translocal communities as much of the literature suggests (Brickell and Datta 2011; Appadurai 1995; Carpentier 2007). The establishment of global Indigenous communities, especially for the purposes of engaging in resistance to settler–colonial power, does not necessarily require migration. With the affordances of deterritorialisation and disintermediation presented by global digital networks, a translocal Indigenous community may be established through digital connections. These connections include the sharing of stories, ideas, images and text that serve to raise awareness and challenge settler–colonial hegemony in its varying forms across the globe. In response, these connections also permit the political mobilisation of allies, both Indigenous and non-Indigenous, from First Nations communities around the world.

Global colonisation

Global colonisation is an important aspect of a digitally mediated global society and marketplace. Colonisation, often conveniently conceptualised as representing a static point in history, remains an ongoing mechanism to assert dominance of the colonising group. While colonisation was once about the expansion of the British Empire, for example, today it is configured through various channels and flows of settler capitalism, which necessarily involves the 'disappearance of Indigenous polities and agency' (Veracini 2013, p. 323). While state-sponsored violence and institutional racism continue to threaten Indigenous peoples and our ways of life, the recent expansion of a multinational global resource industry poses a critical threat to Indigenous land, people and culture. While the settler–colonial narrative has shifted away from the expansion of empire, there remains a continued struggle to retain and reclaim stolen lands and protect the interests of Indigenous communities across the globe in response to the spread of global capitalism. Translocal Indigenous networks of solidarity are being established in response to this nuanced global threat.

Mining companies present perhaps the most salient examples of global colonisation through capitalist ventures. Rio Tinto in 2020 made headlines for the blatant disregard for Indigenous Australian culture and the destruction, through detonation, of Juukan Gorge a 46,000-year-old sacred site. The company conducted an internal review of the events leading to the detonation of Juukan Gorge and admitted that internal processes were not sufficient to prevent the destruction of sacred sites (Kemp et al. 2021). The same company attracted further attention from Indigenous peoples a year later when they proposed a copper mine at Chi'chil Bildagotee (or Oak Flat) Arizona (Al Jazeera.com 2022). In response, Apache Stronghold, a not-for-profit organisation, held a virtual rally via video conferencing technology (Apache Stronghold 2022). The spread of global mining interests, the extraction and exportation of minerals and land from Indigenous peoples' land and Country, is the face of global colonisation today.

Banerjee reminds us of the current trend toward 'neoliberal globalization where business firms have taken on roles once the purview of governments' (2021, p. 132). Banerjee highlights the immense danger of this shift, particularly in the extractive sector where 'corporations and their industry associations are powerful players in … state politics, often giving them de facto political authority to negotiate with states and communities impacted by mining' (2021, p. 133). The task now for Indigenous political activists is to counter the voices of multinational corporations, who often have the ear of state governments, by engaging in deliberate and impactful translocal political mobilisation. While these multinational corporations are still technically bound by the policy and processes that accompany nation-state boundaries, through negotiation and lobbying they tend to sidestep boundaries to the point they can assume 'de facto political authority' (Banerjee 2021, p. 133) which they then deploy to their advantage in negotiation with local Indigenous communities.

These risks differ from those faced during the initial intrusion from settler–colonial arrivals. They have far greater reach. Climate change, air pollution, rising sea levels, and destruction of sacred sites by the expansion of global corporations are above the individual level of impact. However, as globalisation has pushed us into a 'risk society' that poses unique challenges for colonised communities, it also presents opportunities for collaboration, network building and political mobilisation. Disintermediated and deterritorialised digital media technology provides significant possibilities for Indigenous peoples to mobilise and engage in political action and resistance. Increasingly, Indigenous peoples are innovative political activists (Carlson & Berglund 2021) and more and more, we see the establishment of translocal networks of solidarity by Indigenous peoples from across the globe. Through digital communication technology, Indigenous knowledges and voices transcend colonial nation-state boundaries and contribute to growing measures of resistance toward the impacts of settler colonialism. Indigenous peoples, as avid users of digital technology, are active translocal citizens mobilising to fight the next waves of local and global colonisation.

Translocal Indigenous resistance

In 2014, the Standing Rock Sioux Nation began protesting the construction of the Dakota Access Pipeline (DAPL) on the basis that 'the pipeline is endangering the water supply of the reservation, and its construction has and will continue to destroy sacred sites' (Johnson 2017, p. 157). The Oceti Sakowin was established in 2016 as a 'centre for cultural preservation and spiritual resistance to the Dakota Access Pipeline' (Johnson 2017, p. 157). In 2016, the United States Army Corps of Engineers relocated the proposed pipeline from upstream of Bismarck, North Dakota, to just north of Standing Rock. According to Estes 'Standing Rock had no say in this proposed reroute and stridently opposed the pipeline … [However], as it had in previous years, the Corps simply ignored Standing Rock's concerns, claiming sole jurisdiction over the parts of Oceti Sakowin treaty territory' (2017, p. 115). As Estes notes, such action on the part of the settler coloniser on Turtle Island was common. The DAPL was constructed on lands West of the Mississippi River that were unwillingly 'sold' as part of the Louisiana Purchase (Estes 2017). This land carries a history of forced relocation and environmental vandalism on the lands and waters by settler colonisers. It is also land that has seen staunch and continued resistance by Native Americans over the last 400 years.

Oceti Sakowin resistance had previously been successful in halting the Keystone XL (KXL) pipeline. Lessons learned from a history of resistance provided the Oceti Sakowin with a viable method of resisting the proposed pipeline at Standing Rock. Estes recalls 'Our nation is made up of some of the poorest people in the Western hemisphere organising to oppose a fossil fuel industry made up of some of the most powerful and wealthiest people on the planet. Despite these odds KXL was defeated on November 6, 2015' (2017, p. 119). Importantly, the immense strength and successful resistance against the KXL pipeline came from the growing number of alliances between Indigenous and non-Indigenous peoples from around the United States and the world. Estes attributed 'The power of multinational unity between Natives and non-Natives [as] one of the movement's successes' (2017, p. 119). These alliances were drawn upon and grown by the Oceti Sakowin and their supporters in resistance to the DAPL through the creation of the simple hashtag #NoDAPL. Indigenous peoples from across the world sent messages of solidarity in their own languages and from their own viewpoints by including #NoDAPL in their social media posts. These messages were picked up and strengthened the resolve of those protesting on site. The awareness raised via social media also resulted in the mobilisation of Indigenous peoples from all over the world who travelled to stand in solidarity and physical proximity with the Oceti Sakowin.

As Johnson points out, the history of Native American representation in mainstream media is one framed by negative assumptions and disinterest (2017). The #NoDAPL protests were not fully covered by mainstream media, at least initially, because of a lack of reporters in the geographically isolated location. Despite patchy connectivity on the ground, activists would successfully post content to 'Facebook or other social media platforms to get images, videos, and first-person accounts out to the world about what was transpiring at Standing Rock' (Johnson 2017, p. 162). Disintermediated social media platforms easily sidestepped the traditional frames of negativity through which Native American content was portrayed in mainstream media. Additionally, deterritorialised social media technology meant that these unfiltered messages of resistance were received across the globe.

While the protest at Standing Rock is seen as one of the most visible social media campaigns that brought Indigenous peoples together across the globe, there are many others. The Black Lives Matter (BLM) movement routinely gathers worldwide attention across a multitude of social media platforms. #BlackLivesMatter emerged on social media in 2013 following the murder of African American teenager Trayvon Martin in Florida (Mourão & Brown 2021). The social media movement has experienced fluctuating levels of attention in response to several violent incidents involving the deaths of Black people across the United States. Following the 2020 murder of George Floyd in Minnesota, Black Lives Matter movement regained considerable momentum across the world via social media. In Australia, #BlackLivesMatter was deployed to reignite Indigenous and allied resistance to ongoing colonial violence and Indigenous peoples' deaths in custody (Fredericks et al. 2021). Mundt et al. (2018) demonstrated how 'social media … simultaneously facilitates *strengthening* the movement, specifically by enabling local BLM groups to form coalitions and to amplify and disseminate non-dominant discourse about police brutality and Black liberation' (2018, p. 1). Mundt et al. further observe, 'the role of social media in collective action … mobilization, coalition building, and collective meaning making' (2018, p. 1). Such utilisation of social media signals the latest avenues for the establishment of translocal Indigenous communities of resistance.

In Australia, #SOSBLAKAUSTRALIA gained international attention in 2015 after the then Premier of Western Australia announced the intended closure of remote Indigenous communities on the basis that it was too expensive for the state to continue to provide services to remote locations. This proposition led Aboriginal activist Sam Cook and others to establish the social media-based movement. In the months that followed the initial posting, support was gathered through retweets and sharing of images and messages of support between activists and celebrities from around the world. International protests were held in Canada, the United Kingdom, New Zealand and parts of Europe (Cook 2015). Today #SOSBLAKAUSTRALIA's Facebook page titled 'Stop the Forced Closure of Aboriginal Communities in Australia' retains over 60,000 followers. A community of Indigenous peoples and their allies, geographically distanced, who together engage in resistance, coalition building and collective meaning making (Mundt et al. 2018).

The #SOSBLAKAUSTRALIA movement highlights the value of disintermediated social media technology for global Indigenous community building and political action (see Carlson & Frazer 2016). In the days that followed the establishment of the movement, protests were held in major cities in Australia. The *Herald Sun*, a mainstream newspaper in Melbourne, Australia, dedicated its front page to an image of the protesters with the headline 'Selfish Rabble Shut City' (*Herald Sun* 2015). This mainstream media outlet followed the colonial narrative that Indigenous peoples were ungrateful, disorganised and uncivilised in their behaviour. Through this headline on the front page, the newspaper aimed to drown out Indigenous voices as they spoke of the threats to Indigenous lives and homes in remote areas of Western Australia. The accusation was swiftly redeployed by activists via disintermediated social media channels and with humour to highlight the hypocrisy of a mainstream news service that supports similar rallies and sporting events that temporarily close the very same city streets.

Mainstream media were slow to cover the Standing Rock protests. Historically, many (Bacon 2020; Moeke-Pickering et al. 2018; Wilkes et al. 2010) have argued that mainstream media coverage tends to be published within a 'dominant frame that can minimize the message [protesters] are trying to communicate' (Johnson 2017, p. 163). Social media presented an innovative avenue to mobilise global support and actively resist the incursion on and threat to Native American land. The coverage of George Floyd's death began with the posting of a bystander's video footage on Facebook. For Dixon and Dundes, 'the widespread distribution of video plainly showing nearly eight minutes of police brutality against Floyd resulted in widespread consternation' (2020, pp. 1–2). Self-publication that bypassed mainstream media was key to awareness-raising of the planned closure of Indigenous communities in Australia. According to Johnson, 'In today's hyperconnected society, social media provides a tool that historically disenfranchised groups can utilize to bypass mainstream media and have their voices and stories heard by a larger population of people' (2017, p. 157). In all of these examples, it is clear that Indigenous peoples harness digital communication technology to facilitate the establishment of translocal networks of resistance in the face of continued flows of global colonisation.

Conclusion

Deterritorialised and disintermediated digital technology and the associated flows of information and connection that occur through social media facilitate the emergence of a translocal Indigenous community in which individual Indigenous peoples and communities collaborate, connect and engage in solidarity in the face of global colonial expansion. Connections and knowledge-sharing across communities through trade, conferences, and inter- and intra-community collaboration have been a feature of Indigenous civilisation for centuries. Indigenous peoples have also been swift in their adoption of new and innovative technologies. Digital communication technology, a key catalyst for the spread of capitalism, has likewise been embraced by Indigenous peoples and communities. While these new channels and media present new challenges regarding exploitation and violence, they also offer innovative and valuable opportunities for Indigenous peoples to build communities and engage in solidarity. The mobilisation and swift global connection to digital technology facilitated resistance such as #NoDAPL, #BlackLivesMatter and #SOSBlakaustralia are prime examples of the establishment of disintermediated and deterritorialised translocal Indigenous networks of resistance. The results of these collaborations are varied but, more and more, we are witnessing an accelerated production of knowledge, knowledge-sharing, and expression of Indigenous voices. This is a vital outcome of the incorporation of digital technology in our lives, one that responds to the concurrent and new threat to Indigenous peoples' cultural survival.

References

Al Jazeera. (2021). Native Americans try to block US move to give land to Rio Tinto. www.aljazeera.com/economy/2021/1/15/native-americans-try-to-block-us-move-to-give-land-to-rio-tinto

Apache Stronghold. (2022). *Call to Action: Virtual Rally for Sacred Site of Oak Flat w/ Apache Stronghold.* Indybay. www.indybay.org/newsitems/2020/12/21/18839037.php

Appadurai, A. (1995). The production of locality. In Fardon, R. (Ed.), *Counterworks.* Abingdon: Routledge.

Appadurai, A. (2000). Grassroots globalization and the research imagination. *Public Culture, 12*(1), 1–19.

Appadurai, A. (2010). Disjuncture and difference in the global cultural economy. *Theory, Culture & Society, 7*(2–3), 295–310.

Bacon, J. M. (2020). Dangerous pipelines, dangerous people: Colonial ecological violence and media framing of threat in the Dakota access pipeline conflict. *Environmental Sociology, 6*(2), 143–153.

Banerjee, S. B. (2021). Transnational power and translocal governance: The politics of corporate responsibility. In *The Routledge Companion to Corporate Social Responsibility* (pp. 129–149). Abingdon: Routledge.

Beck, U. (1992). *Risk Society: Towards a New Modernity* (Vol. 17). Thousand Oaks: SAGE.

Brickell, K., & Datta, A. (2011). *Translocal Geographies.* Farnham: Ashgate Publishing.

Carlson, B., & Berglund, J. (2021). *Indigenous People Rise Up: The Global Ascendency of Social Media Activism.* New Brunswick: Rutgers University Press.

Carlson, B., & Dreher, T. (2018). Introduction: Indigenous innovation in social media. *Media International Australia, 169*(1), 16–20.

Carlson, B. & Frazer, R. (2016). Indigenous activism and social media: The global response to #SOSBLAKAUSTRALIA. In McCosker, A., Vivienne, S., & Johns, A. (Eds), *Rethinking Digital Citizenship: Control, Contest and Culture* (pp. 115–130). Lanham: Rowman and Littlefield International.

Carpentier, N. (2007). Translocalism, community media and the city. www.researchgate.net/profile/Nico-Carpentier/publication/242659670_Translocalism_Community_Media_and_the_City/links/02e7e53885c7ecb510000000/Translocalism-Community-Media-and-the-City.pdf

Cook, S. (2015). #SOSBLAKAUSTRALIA: Stop the forced closure of Aboriginal communities – IndigenousX (1 April 2015). *Guardian.* www.theguardian.com/commentisfree/2015/apr/01/sosblakaustralia-stop-the-forced-closure-of-aboriginal-communities-indigenousx

Cooper, A. F. (2019). The disintermediation dilemma and its impact on diplomacy: A research agenda for turbulent times. *Diplomacy & Statecraft, 30*(4), 799–807.

Dixon, P. J., & Dundes, L. (2020). Exceptional injustice: Facebook as a reflection of race- and gender-based narratives following the death of George Floyd. *Social Sciences, 9*(12), 231.

Escobar, A. (2001). Culture sits in places: Reflections on globalism and subaltern strategies of localization. *Political Geography, 20*(2), 139–174.

Estes, N. (2017). Fighting for our lives:# NoDAPL in historical context. *Wicazo Sa Review, 32*(2), 115–122.

Fredericks, B., Bradfield, A., Nguyen, J., & Ansell, S. (2021). Disrupting the colonial algorithm: Indigenous Australia and social media. *Media International Australia, 183*(1), 158–178.

Herald Sun. (2015). The *Herald Sun* has dismissed 4,000 Indigenous rights protesters as a 'selfish rabble' (11 April 2015). Junkee. https://junkee.com/the-herald-sun-has-dismissed-4000-indigenous-rights-protestors-as-a-selfish-rabble/54833

Johnson, H. (2017). # NoDAPL: Social media, empowerment, and civic participation at standing rock. *Library Trends, 66*(2), 155–175.

Kemp, D., Owen, J., & Barnes, R. (2021). Juukan Gorge inquiry puts Rio Tinto on notice, but without drastic reforms, it could happen again. *Chain Reaction, 139*, 8–9.

Malherbe, L., Montalban, M., Bédu, N., & Granier, C. (2019). Cryptocurrencies and Blockchain: Opportunities and limits of a new monetary regime. *International Journal of Political Economy, 48*(2), 127–152.

Moeke-Pickering, T., Cote-Meek, S., & Pegoraro, A. (2018). Understanding the ways missing and murdered Indigenous women are framed and handled by social media users. *Media International Australia, 169*(1), 54–64.

Mourão, R. R., & Brown, D. K. (2022). Black Lives Matter coverage: How protest news frames and attitudinal change affect social media engagement. *Digital Journalism, 10*(4), 626–646.

Mundt, M., Ross, K., & Burnett, C. M. (2018). Scaling social movements through social media: The case of Black Lives Matter. *Social Media + Society, 4*(4), 2056305118807911.

Munro, I., & Thanem, T. (2018). Deleuze and the deterritorialization of strategy. *Critical Perspectives on Accounting, 53*, 69–78.

Tandoc, E. C., Lim, D., & Ling, R. (2020). Diffusion of disinformation: How social media users respond to fake news and why. *Journalism*, *21*(3), 381–398.

Tonnies, F., & Loomis, C. P. (2002). *Community and Society*. Courier Corporation.

Veracini, L. (2013). 'Settler colonialism': Career of a concept. *The Journal of Imperial and Commonwealth History*, *41*(2), 313–333.

Wilkes, R., Corrigall-Brown, C., & Ricard, D. (2010). Nationalism and media coverage of Indigenous people's collective action in Canada. *American Indian Culture and Research Journal*, *34*(4), 41–59.

Wilson, S. (2008). *Research is Ceremony: Indigenous Research Methods*. Nova Scotia: Fernwood.

Wolfe, P. (2006). Settler colonialism and the elimination of the native. *Journal of Genocide Research*, *8*(4), 387–409.

4

Connecting back home: globalising conversations on Indigenous LGBTIQ+ peoples, migration and social media

Andrew Farrell

Introduction

This chapter explores the trajectories of Indigenous LGBTIQ+ (lesbian, gay, bisexual, transgender, intersex and queer) peoples as they navigate identity, belonging and home. Through the broader theme of migration, Indigenous LGBTIQ+ people inform globalising conversations on Indigeneity and contemporary life. Included within that scope is the individual and intersubjective experiences of gender, sex and sexuality, which produce a more complex understanding of why Indigenous people migrate. I will foreground these examples through relevant Indigenous queer scholarship and available testimonies that locate heteropatriarchal settler colonialism and its various manifestations and effects on queer Indigenous bodies and Indigenous communities.

In the history of LGBTIQ+, Indigenous and queer Indigenous community developments, there exists an ongoing push for recognition for Indigenous LGBTIQ+ lives. Indigenous LGBTIQ+ experiences explored in this chapter include themes of home, relationships, and identity through resonant characteristics across settler–colonial geographies, including North America, Australia, and nations of the Pacific nations. This chapter centres relationships between Indigenous peoples. By unpacking instances of queer-targeted violence, othering, and relational fractures, we can observe how LGBTIQ+ Indigenous kin are subject to heteropatriarchal settler–colonial mechanisms that attempt to suppress and erase gendered and sexual difference. This chapter counteracts settler–colonial heteropatriarchy through an anti-colonial Indigenous ethics of relationality across Indigenous communities globally. This will include strategies of resistance on social media that fortify inclusive approaches to relationality and self-determination towards LGBTIQ+ reconnection, belonging, and resurgence.

Settler–colonial heteropatriarchy and queer Indigenous migration

The history of the dispersal of Indigenous peoples is tied to empiricism and settler colonialism. To recognise Indigenous LGBTIQ+ migratory patterns, we must recognise the role of settler–colonial heteropatriarchy in the occupation of places such as United States, Canada, nations of the Pacific, and Australia that continue to represent permutations of Western settler colonialisms. Across these locations, Indigenous populations have experienced significant dispossession and displacement. Beginning with first contact, abject frontier violence was followed closely by dispersal, confinement, segregation and assimilation across hundreds of years in recent history. Indigenous peoples globally have emerged from this history to resist colonial structures that have been set in place to attack articulations of Indigeneity. To contextualise complex Indigenous queer histories into the present day, Clark (2015, p. 386) argues that 'we must understand the underlying relationship between sexuality and the racialised white nation, and how that relationship has travelled through all [settler colonial] frontiers and into the present'. To fully understand Indigenous LGBTIQ+ peoples' experiences of displacement, we must consider the role of normative and settler ideas about gender and sexuality, and how they continue to impact Indigenous peoples in the present.

Globally, there is increasing recognition of the experiences of Indigenous peoples under colonial regimes of gender, sex, and sexuality from the perspective of gender, sex, and sexually diverse Indigenous peoples. The transformative work of Indigenous academics, activists, and communities has been to critically reexamine settler colonial histories. Queer Indigenous Studies has emerged as a multidisciplinary field of study from this. It speaks to settler–colonialism while also being heavily invested in Indigenous resurgence. Scholars, both Indigenous and non-Indigenous, have argued that Western understandings fundamentally fail to translate Indigenous genders and sexualities and, in doing so, reproduce the inherent violence of settler colonialism through the symbolic and material elimination of Indigenous peoples (Driskill 2004; 2011; Morgensen 2011; Wilson 1996). Across settler–colonial landscapes, Indigenous peoples were met with forms of violence that explicitly targeted their genders and sexualities. Ohlone-Costanoan Esselen Nation and Chumash scholar Deborah A. Miranda (2010) identifies that colonial violence took shape through gendercide, which she identifies as acts of violence committed against a victim's primary gender identity. Miranda builds on non-Indigenous interpretations of gendercide as one that fails to encompass Indigenous genders and sexualities beyond the binaries of male and female, heterosexual and non-heterosexual. Gendercide underlines that the attempted genocide of Indigenous peoples did not merely target men and women. Gendercide also encompasses the waves of violence that attempted to assimilate Indigenous communities into shifting Eurocentric norms. Morgensen (2012, p. 10) argues that Indigenous 'elimination proceeded through [the] regulation of Indigenous sexual relations, gender identity, marriage, reproduction, and genealogy, and all similar means for restricting resistant Indigenous national difference'.

As argued by Driskill (2004, p. 52), 'our erotic lives and identities have been colonised along with our homelands'. The importing and installing of Eurocentric sexual and gendered epistemologies and ontologies is recognised as settler–colonial heteropatriarchy – a system of power that facilitates hierarchies of social, cultural and sexual domination led by white, cisgendered, heterosexual men over others. It particularly locates those whose wealth is extracted and exploited through colonialism as well as settler beneficiaries. Settler–colonial heteropatriarchy also prescribes the role of those it controls such as women, people of colour, and LGBTIQ+ peoples. The imposition of settler–colonial heteropatriarchy on Indigenous peoples evolved across the colonial landscape in response to their diverse practices of gender, sex and sexuality. Across the European empire, its outposts, settlements and colonies, Indigenous peoples experienced a range of policies that outlawed their social and intimate practices. In India, the British introduced the *Criminal Tribes Act (1871)*, which called for the 'registration, surveillance and control of certain tribes and eunuchs' or appearing dressed or ornamented like a woman in a public street or place, or in any other place, with the intention of being seen (Roy 2015, para. 5). In Hawai'i, sodomy laws outlawed and policed mahū identity to submit to the western gender binary and across Polynesian societies, such as Samoa and Tonga, female impersonation was criminalised as a form of soliciting and sexual deviancy (Kashay 2008; Zanghellini 2013). In the United States, the *1887 Dawes Act* Citizenship law granted citizen status and land ownership under the provision that natives would adopt and abide by heterosexual monogamy through state-sanctioned marriage and conform to settler norms by adopting white clothing and ways (Gustafson 2019). Hundreds of years of colonial occupation has attempted to deplete Indigenous societies of their ancient and self-determined genders, sex, and sexualities. While gendercide was endemic, settlers also sought to nativise themselves to entrench ownership and settler sovereignty over Indigenous' lands. This is identified through the creation of distinct settler identities through the processes of settler nativism and settler sexuality described by Morgensen (2010, p. 106) as 'a white national heteronormativity that regulates Indigenous sexuality and gender by supplanting them with the sexual modernity of settler subjects'. Heteropatriarchal settler colonialism is an integral feature of settler colonialism across the globe. It has further evolved in the production of settler homonormativities as settler states claim progressiveness through modern queer rights movements (Picq 2020).

Competing vocabularies and definitions within migratory studies discursively inform how we come to know and recognise Indigenous LGBTIQ+ migrations. Queer/LGBTIQ+ Indigenous migrations are largely framed through displacement and diaspora rather than migration and mobility. This is predicated on the segregation of these terms; whereas the LGBTIQ+ Indigenous movement is characterised by forced migration, their inclusion within discussions of chosen migration is often absent or in the periphery. This interplay is exacerbated by the broader disengagement of Indigenous LGBTIQ+ peoples as a central theme. The centralising definitions of supposedly contradictory terms, between Indigeneity, queerness and diaspora/migration is foregrounded by tensions caught between

Indigeneity and migration, as well as those between Indigeneity and queerness. Indigenous LGBTIQ+ migrations have recently emerged in scholarly and grey literatures explicitly addressing a dearth in qualitative and quantitative data and knowledge (Gopinath 2018; Harris 2015; Lezard et al. 2021; Ristock et al. 2010). Much of this burgeoning literature has been established in Turtle Island (US and Canada) where data has emerged to address the exclusion of Indigenous LGBTIQ+ peoples. In the global context, minimal data is unsurprising from my perspective working in the field of Indigenous Queer Studies in Australia. The field suffers from a distinct lack of rigorous data on a range of topics relating to LGBTIQ+ Aboriginal and Torres Strait Islander peoples, as well as inclusion across literatures which prescribe knowledge about Aboriginal and Torres Strait Islander peoples.

The continued domination of introduced racial, gendered and sexual categories in settler–colonial societies fails to capture Indigenous people who sit outside of dominant definitions. Rarely do we see the prioritising and centralising of diverse Indigenous standpoints as they're often filtered through narrowing and homogeneous ontologies and epistemologies that reinforce settler–colonial heteropatriarchal knowledge (O'Sullivan 2019). As argued by Gopinath (2018, p. 87), the incongruity of Indigeneity and migration originates from foundational definitions where 'the concepts of diaspora and Indigeneity are, more often than not, situated in a binary or oppositional relation to one another: by its very definition, diaspora seems to privilege mobility, hybridity, and uprootedness, while Indigeneity seems to privilege belonging, authenticity, and rootedness.' Gopinath (2018) contends that if someone is mobile, then they cannot fulfil the defining categories of what it means to be an Indigenous person. This erasure is active across migration studies, which considers Indigeneity redundant. The absence of Indigenous inclusion also exists because migration studies has yet to face a 'genuine reckoning with the role played by diasporic formations within this settler colonial project' (Gopinath 2018, p. 89). This means we must address the ways that migrant populations become settlers through their occupation of Indigenous lands. The migrant subject is thus positioned as not from here, and not Indigenous here or elsewhere. This fundamentally evades critical work on migration that observes movement within and across settler colonial borders, with little complexity around sovereign borders that have all but been erased from mobility discourses.

Indigenous LGBTIQ+ migrations are further destabilised by arguments that attempt to separate and disassociate LGBTIQ+ identities from Indigeneity, that is, the existence of Indigenous gender, sex and sexually diverse peoples. The politics that surrounds Indigenous queer bodies and identities is embedded in discourses of Indigeneity and how it is defined through the exclusion and inclusion of LGBTIQ+ Indigenous peoples. Carlson (2016, p. 151) notes the layered and competing tensions and complexities that arise from debates about who is and who is not Aboriginal, where matters of identity are implicated and questioned based on arbitrary definitions, including phenotypical characteristics such as skin colour. Across many settler–colonial nations, these arguments persist through a legacy of eugenicist policies aimed at defining and controlling Indigenous populations. The boundary-making and gatekeeping of Indigenous identity extends towards gender and sexual identities such as those across the LGBTIQ+ spectrums. As argued by O'Sullivan (2021, p. 3), globally 'not all First Nations' communities connect diverse gender and sexuality, nor do they have names that articulate these connections or this divergence from the colonial binary'. Conceptualisations of tradition used in a way to define and affirm contemporary Indigenous gender and sexual diversities is problematic, essentialist and racist. LGBTIQ+ exclusions undermine the survival of Indigenous societies while reinforcing proponents of settler–colonial heteropatriarchy.

Contemporary forms of community building between Indigenous LGBTIQ+ peoples has reframed how their genders and sexualities are known. They have also invested in Indigenous LGBTIQ+ rights and justice as recent studies reveal the silent displacement of queer Indigenous peoples by observing their experiences of LGBTIQ+ discrimination and violence as contributing to their displacement and migration (Ristock et al. 2010). Emerging research centring Indigenous LGBTIQ+ lives against the ongoing denial of gender and sexual diversity in Indigenous research. This is led by grassroots activists and queer Indigenous scholarship, which continues to fight for the recognition of all of us rather than the dominant categories ascribed to us, even from within. Globalising discussions against settler–colonial heteropatriarchy, as it persists, is validated by globalising criticisms that locate settler–colonial heteropatriarchal occupation across the globe, moving towards solidarity with Indigenous LGBTIQ+ causes elsewhere.

Historically, Indigenous peoples have been defined and redefined by waves of displacement. The creation of Indigenous communities such as missions, reservations, bands, and various institutions such as boarding schools and children's homes extended out of ongoing colonial occupation and control. These institutions further entrenched settler colonialism through quarantine and surveillance, which enforced western domesticity, gender roles and family structures. In tandem, colonisers criminalised ancient cultural practices, such as language and ceremony. which they justified through ideas about protection, paternalism and prevailing beliefs about the imminent extinction of Indigenous peoples. The coding of Western norms in Indigenous lands produced settler–colonial identities that continue to assume non-Indigenous ownership and belonging (Morgensen 2015). These histories have only recently included Indigenous LGBTIQ+ experiences of displacement, which have, for much of history, been ignored and erased. Discourses of dispersal underpin current perceptions of where Indigenous people live and exist. Indigenous peoples have been instrumental in resituating Indigenous populations who live in all settings from urban to rural and remote. Fredericks (2013) notes that more than 70 per cent of Australia's Indigenous peoples live in urban locations, and urban living is just as much part of a reality for Aboriginal and Torres Strait Islander people as living in remote discrete communities. In the US, census data shows that approximately 71 per cent of the native population lives in urban areas (Urban Indian Health Institute 2013). The conflation of historical perceptions and evidence-based data has done well to service the shifting needs and desires of settler societies. In response, Indigenous LGBTIQ+ voices continue to push for recognition. When mobilised, their experiences have become powerful antidotes to settler–colonial heteropatriarchy and tools of anti-colonialism broadly.

Identity, belonging and liminality

Testimonies of LGBTIQ+ peoples suggest a trend in migration where binaries of urban and non-urban reinforce stereotypes of acceptance and non-acceptance. Anecdotally, for Indigenous LGBTIQ peoples urban spaces underpin a great deal of acceptance for LGBTIQ+ identity. Muruwari and Gomeroi Aboriginal journalist Allan Clarke reflects:

> It wasn't until I moved to Sydney that I found freedom among the concrete towers and in the loving embrace of older staunch gay black men, women and sistergirls. They taught me I was exactly how I was meant to be, that we have existed in our beautiful culture since the very beginning. (Clarke 2017, para. 10)

Clarke's experience of acceptance is expressed through urban connections between LGBTIQ+ Aboriginal and Torres Strait Islander peoples. These alignments locate enclaves of networks that converge and centre complex intersections of Indigeneity and queerness. Urban living, and the trajectory between urban and rural/remote binaries, will be explored in this section through global examples that follow Indigenous LGBTIQ+ migrations, its benefits and pitfalls.

In transit, cultural continuity is difficult to replicate elsewhere. As connections to country evolve, adaptive strategies are employed to fulfil and reinforce cultural continuity. Indigenous LGBTIQ+ stories of migration have largely been extrapolated from the way individuals find themselves having connections in urban communities that support their identities – particularly connections with other Indigenous people and allies. These relationships attempt to secure safety around gender and sexual diversities in what gender studies scholar Qwo-Li Driskill terms the sovereign erotic: 'a sovereign claim to not only land but of subjectivity, desire, and the right to self-determination through culturally embedded practices of sexual and gender diversity' (Driskill 2004, p. 52). Driskill argues that claiming ourselves is a process of 'erotic wholeness healed and/or healing from the historical trauma that First Nations people continue to survive, rooted within the histories, traditions, and resistance struggles of our nations' (2004, p. 52). In the US and Canada, this has emerged through the naming of gender and sexual diversities as 'Two Spirit'. In Australia, terms such as Sistergirl and Brotherboy recognise Indigenous trans identity (Farrell 2017). Across Pacific countries, Indigenous terms such as 'takatāpui', 'fa'afafine', and 'māhū' are used in Aotearoa (New Zealand), Samoa and Hawai'i, respectively. These terms have served as anchors to complex and fluid social and cultural spaces that constitute individual and shared identity and community that, in part, secure sovereign relationships when not 'on Country'.

Waitt and Gorman-Murray (2011) identify settler heteronormativity in queer migrations. They argue that settler conceptions of gender and sexuality are uniquely entrenched in areas with smaller populations. Under such conditions, queer subjects are often cast out. Through this, queer people experience precarious relationships to home through 'unidirectional migrations from small rural towns to large urban centres, reliant upon aligning smallness and rurality as purgatory for non-normative sexualities, and bigness and urbanity as qualities necessary for sexual liberation' (Waitt and Gorman-Murray 2011, p. 1380). Home is redefined as an 'outcome of embodied and material practices – a space that offers safety' (Waitt and Gorman-Murray 2011, p. 1381). Whittaker (2016) illuminates these complexities by identifying the liminality of traversing geographic binaries, moving as a queer Indigenous person from a rural place to the city. Her path is experienced through complicated feelings relating to identity and belonging:

> The train was the only place I thought I, in all my complicated parts, could live. It was an in-between space that seemed like nowhere and made me no-one: free to be at once queer and Aboriginal and everything ... the suggestion that queerness is inherently incompatible with Aboriginality and the bush is fuelled by racism and colonisation. It's also what motivated me in earlier days, dripping with self-loathing, to move to what I thought was queer utopia: Sydney. (Whittaker 2016)

Buchanan (2013) describes 'liminality' as a ritual space or phase of transition in which a person is no longer what they were while not yet what they will be. For Indigenous LGBTIQ+ peoples, the interplay of binaries between Indigenous/non-Indigenous, queer/non-queer and urban/rural/remote geographies necessarily complicate understandings of liminal identity formations that prioritise intersectionalities grounded in Indigenous sovereignty and relationality. The notion of home and belonging, through the lens of sovereignty and relationality, is fundamental to conceptualising Indigenous LGBTIQ+ identity formations. Wilson (1996, p. 305) argues that for the Native people of North America, identity is inextricably tied to land and that Indigenous people are also 'bound to each other in an intimately spiritual way' in a shared existence. Under settler–colonial heteropatriarchy, these relationships are suppressed and divided through modes of difference. These fractures continue to threaten and deteriorate ancient and inclusive relationalities across Indigenous peoples' intimate landscapes. The threatening of sovereign selfhood is deeply impacted by the perpetuation of settler–colonial norms around identity which cast out family members, thereby contributing to genocide. The securing and maintenance of sovereign relationalities, as discussed by Dharug scholar Jo Rey (2019, p. 59), builds collectives and communities through caring and belonging where 'strong communities are better able to support families, and strong families are better able to raise individuals that feel they are strong in belonging, caring and connecting to the presences, places and practices' that they belong to, which has sustained cultural diversities for thousands of years.

In his youth, Daniel Browning, a Bundjalung and Kullilli gay-identified man, recalls: 'I can't say that I knew exactly what my difference was, but I knew it was something to be ashamed of' (Browning, n.d., para. 1). In recalling his experiences of difference as a flamboyant youth, Browning importantly locates the role of homophobia in reinforcing heteronormativity through the abjection of queerness. Browning (n.d., para. 10) states that bonds between abusers are solidified as 'they pour their contempt on a shared, common enemy', LGBTIQ+ people and are further validated by 'a critical mass of people who silently harbour the same contempt'. Those who do not intervene in homophobic violence are complicit through their silence and inaction. The prevalence of homophobia and transphobia in the family home is particularly toxic. As described by Kurnai/Gunai, Gunditjmara, Wiradjuri and Yorta Yorta person Nayuka Gorrie, disagreements about gender and sexuality in the home constitutes a kind of symbolic death of familial relationships characterised by the passive and active exclusion of family members based solely on their gendered and sexual differences (Gorrie 2019).

It is not true to say that Indigenous LGBTIQ+ peoples' experiences of home are uniformly violent towards them. Doing so would only reinforce racist tropes of social disunity of Indigenous peoples rampant across settler–colonial societies (Pearson 2016; Simpson 2017). As processes of queer othering occur, so do substantive experiences of support, community buffering, and the maintenance of relationality through acceptance and inclusion. As argued by Mississauga Nishnaabeg scholar Leanne Betasamosake Simpson (2017, p. 85), the 'negative beliefs we carry within ourselves were planted in us and the generations that came before us for a very specific reason: the dispossession of our lands'. Healing from homophobia and transphobia, for example, must be achieved to reassert the collective sovereignty of Indigenous peoples by challenging settler binaries and norms.

Indigenous LGBTIQ+ peoples continue to lead the way on acceptance and inclusion. An example of this can be seen in the documentary film *A Place in the Middle* (Hamer & Wilson 2014). The film, set in Honolulu, Hawai'i, explores the relationship between a Native Hawaiian teacher, who identifies as transgender and māhū wahine (transfeminine), Kumu Hina and her student Ho'onani, who identifies as māhū kāne (transmasculine). Māhū identities are a traditionally recognised third-gender category that encompasses feminine and masculine traits, wahine and kāne respectively. Through the role modelling and guidance of Kumu Hina, Ho'onani can join in cultural activities aligning with their gender identity rather than the gender assigned to them. While centred on this relationship, the documentary also makes it apparent that acceptance for Ho'onani is also extended to and dependent on the community around them. With community support, Ho'onani can thrive.

Acceptance is the foundation of belonging. However, it does not always alleviate the pain of displacement. Support services for LGBTIQ+ peoples are sparse but sometimes necessary, particularly for trans affirmations of identity, including medical transition. Two Spirit sqilxʷ scholar Percy Lezard and colleagues (2021, p. 32) argue that structural change is vital 'in every context of culture, governance, ceremony, health, education, and community development for cultural continuity. The resurgence process can only be successful if systemic shifts are made in those areas' for the health and wellbeing of Indigenous LGBTIQ+ peoples. All social and cultural structures and institutions that fortify and embed heterosexism and cast out gender and sexual difference has an impact on Indigenous LGBTIQ+ peoples throughout their lives. It is especially dire when LGBTIQ+ people are entangled in punitive state apparatus, the prison-industrial complex, which oppresses trans populations with great severity (Young 2011). Acceptance and belonging remain precarious as shown by reports such as the Aboriginal Two Spirit and LGBTQ Migration, Mobility, and Health Research Project in Canada (Ristock et al. 2010), which indicated that a third of Aboriginal/Métis LGBTIQ+ identified participants had been forced out of their community because of their sexual or gender identity. In Western Australia, the Breaking the Silence Report (Hill et al. 2021, p. 19) identified that 'a third of participants stated they felt "invisible" within their community because of their sexual and/or gender identity, and twenty one percent of participants did not feel accepted by their community'. Joshua Whitehead, an Oji-Cree member of the Peguis First Nation in Manitoba, describes home as being 'full of hope and ghosts'. He continues:

> All my life I wanted to leave the rez – and every time I was about to, I stopped myself. It hurt. Leaving hurts … I can't eat anything other than fried bologna or Klik for breakfast … even in the twenty-first century, two brown boys can't fall in love on the rez. (Whitehead 2018, p. 15)

Arrival in new places, those that are perceived to be safer, is no guarantee. Cree scholar Alex Wilson recounts how her experience of both racism and homophobia across rural and urban binaries persist in certain ways. Speaking of urban queer communities, Wilson discusses racism and cultural stereotypes in queer urban spaces:

> I had looked for affirmation by immersing myself in the minority cultures to which I belonged. Most significantly though, when I sought support in the mainstream lesbian and gay community, it simply wasn't there … Two Spirit [identity] is rarely recognised in mainstream community unless it is accompanied by romantic notions that linger from [the past]. (Wilson 1996, p. 313)

Wilson (1996) describes the relationship with queer communities as one in which Indigenous people must employ short-term survival strategies to fulfil and negotiate identity across their own and settler–colonial spaces of community. In urban spaces, Indigenous

LGBTIQ+ people often seek and find each other in ways that combat urban disparities.

Urban community spaces have served as vital for Indigenous LGBTIQ+ peoples in recent history. For Indigenous LGBTIQ+ populations, their experiences of community have emerged through kinships built out of historical social and cultural advocacy between Indigenous and LGBTIQ+ communities. Globally, from north America to the Pacific, Australia and beyond, Indigenous LGBTIQ+ communities shaped in response to the globalising crisis of HIV/AIDS. Morgensen (2011, p. 211) notes that the Pacific Sexual Diversity Network (PSDN) mobilised 'AIDS organizers from Fiji, Tonga, Vanuatu, Cook Islands, and Papua New Guinea, many of whom practiced what they defended as traditional nonheteronormative social roles'. In Australia, Indigenous LGBTIQ+ health workers were mobilised to establish the Anwernekenhe conference, which represented the diversity and needs of Aboriginal and Torres Strait Islander LGBTIQ+ peoples (Farrell 2021a). In the context of native health sovereignty, Morgensen (2011, p. 195) argues that Indigenous AIDS 'activisms provided a model of transnational modes of naming and defending Native sovereignty and inflected global alliance to target and critique the biopolitics of settler colonialism in state and global health governance'. Indigenous LGBTIQ+ people globally experienced the double burden of racism and homophobia. While facing racism, Indigenous LGBTIQ+ peoples faced increasing homophobia within their own communities. Goudie recalls: 'The truth, I observed back then, was that a lot of people 'blamed the gays' for bringing this 'disease' of HIV/AIDS. This only seemed to heighten the homophobia that already existed in the entire community and especially within the Aboriginal local community, where people also tended to blame the gays' (Goudie 2015, p. 213).

Sexual health worker and advocate Edward John Milera identifies the pervasive stereotype of homosexuals as dirty, deviant child molesters across the country (in Hobson 1993). Stigmas associated with the queer community were also to the detriment of the broader Indigenous community. Goudie argues that the Aboriginal population was disproportionately at risk from the virus at the height of the epidemic (2015, p. 214). Despite this, communities carried on with spirit and determination. While facing barriers such as racism, homophobia and a decline in morale, Indigenous LGBTIQ+ communities globally have established and contributed to events that are now cultural institutions. Pageants, balls, Indigenous' presence at pride parades, and smaller discrete and intimate social contexts underpin the contemporary lives of Indigenous LGBTIQ+ peoples. Importantly, the formation of Indigenous LGBTIQ+ networks and communities provided the safety that Waitt and Gorman-Murray (2011) call 'home'. Home is where you can feel safe and secure within your identity. Milera highlights this through the safety he felt with his chosen family:

> If you are with your group, like in Adelaide we had a fairly strong network – the Aboriginal gays down there – we socialised a lot ... but once you're removed from that ... you don't camp it up as much ... in Adelaide we'd go to a lot of the gay functions, like sports days, or the bowling, the baths. Go to the hotel, like the Colonel Light, and play pool and stuff. So we lived gay every day. But in Alice Springs it's a lot different [for me]. (In Hobson 1993)

Connecting back home

In a *TEDx* talk, Selasi (2014) argues that 'we can never go back to a place and find it exactly where we left it. Something, somewhere will always have changed, most of all, ourselves.' Following dislocation, notions of home adapt. Where we find ourselves may not be our custodial lands, but they fulfil our desires to live and exist as completely as we can manage or achieve. As demonstrated in the previous section, connections between resettled and local Indigenous communities often form the basis of local recognition in which Indigenous LGBTIQ+ people can achieve a sense of belonging and safety. This section will continue to examine strategies of cohesion as they evolve and persist online through social media platforms that provide new experimental avenues of community building.

Digital spaces can be fraught, violent, and dangerous spaces for Indigenous peoples. Carlson and Frazer (2018; 2021) argue that racism and discrimination online are all too common experiences for Indigenous Australians. Between high-profile and publicly generated forms of racism and interpersonal and intimate forms of racism,

Indigenous users are subject to abject treatment across many popular social media platforms (Carlson 2013; Carlson 2021; Carlson & Frazer 2018; 2021). This is further evident as the discriminatory and violent experiences of social media is extrapolated through scholarly work which includes and centres Indigenous LGBTIQ+ experiences of social media and dating apps (Carlson 2020; Farrell 2021c). This research locates layered and conflating forms of violence including racism, homophobia, queerphobia and heterosexism. These interactions inform the shifting nature of settler–colonial heteropatriarchy in the contemporary landscape upon which Indigenous people reconstitute dynamic and inclusive forms of resistance.

Counter to the violence that persists online is the resilience and resurgence of Indigenous peoples who have formed critical activisms around various issues affecting their communities globally (Carlson & Berglund 2021; Farrell 2021a). There is a foundation of support mechanisms developed out of important intracommunity support and allegiances that bolster Indigenous presence globally. Farrell (2021c) highlights from a small sample of surveys that many Aboriginal and Torres Strait Islander LGBTIQ+ peoples live in cities. The everyday expression of diverse gender and sexually on social media demonstrate that Indigenous LGBTIQ+ erotic lives are not distinct or separate to our cultural identities (Farrell 2021a). As Monaghan (2015, p. 309) writes: 'I cannot separate the queer parts of me from the Aboriginal ... I cannot bracket the queer when I am doing decolonising work, and I cannot bracket the brown and black and Indigenous when I am resisting the heteropatriarchy.' This is demonstrated online through various strategies of self-representation employed by Indigenous LGBTIQ+ peoples.

Social media sites, such as Facebook, played a significant role in my life as I migrated from a regional coastal community to a larger city. Social media sites serve as an environment where I continue to maintain my connection between the place I grew up, the people who I still regularly communicate with (most of whom are people who accept my queer identity), and the new and evolving social and work environments that I am now embedded in. Before the period of COVID restrictions in my area – relative to my very introverted and stationary personal life – mobility is a fact of my existence as I commute between Sydney and Wollongong, as well as nationally and internationally as part of my career. Importantly, social media has provided a space in which I can identify as queer on my own terms. I have written about my experience of drag, race, and identity as it has evolved across both online and offline contexts (Farrell 2016; 2020). My universe continues to be tethered by social media activity through comments, messages, statuses, memes and personal photos. Over time, I have also been involved in global conversations on Indigenous queer identity as I have utilised social media to reach out and connect with Indigenous peoples worldwide. As I relate outward, my internal world is contained in my social media history. Even as social media continues to be advantageous for my current circumstance, it does not satisfy my desire for my cultural lands; the sand at my feet, salt air and the bubbling brine of oysters hitting ash. Some days, social media shows me exactly what I am missing while I am not living on my Country.

As I romanticise my past, I am also cognisant of the realities that I have experienced as a queer person. My displacement from Country is a web of tepid acceptance and estrangement undergirded by difference; my separation was a natural progression of my unwillingness to conform. My estrangement and displacement is only exacerbated by the negative spaces in my social media where my large family are not fully accounted for, some for the mere fact that they do not use social media or are not interested in a digital connection. Through these dissonances, I experience a kind of limbo of belonging. Luckily, I am privileged enough to be able to physically return home with little trouble or danger to my safety. For some LGBTIQ+ mob, this is not the case. Chosen migration is a luxury few can afford, but for some it is the only option for survival (Riggs & Toone 2017).

Social media platforms are utilised to scrutinise heteropatriarchal colonialism through the recognition of sovereign gender and sexual diversities. Everyday reminders of 'our erotic knowledge empowers us, becomes a lens through which we scrutinize all aspects of our existence, forcing us to evaluate those aspects honestly in terms of their relative meaning in our lives' (Driskill 2004, p. 52). In that way, activisms that centre Indigenous LGBTIQ+ lives lift the veil on heteropatriarchal settler colonialism and work towards decolonial practices of love and acceptance. Young Indigenous people on TikTok such as @melemaikalanimakalapua (Polynesian and Native Hawaiian) and @dineaesthetics (Diné) utilise the short-form video platform to teach and critically engage in Indigenous affairs. User @melemaikalanimakalapua has produced content that dispels myths and stereotypes about the history and cultures of the archipelago of Hawai'i. In several videos, they celebrate mahū identity by recognising the place of a third gender translated as 'the middle'. The comment section of inquiring minds are met with @melemaikalanimakalapua's staunch approach of acceptance and love towards mahū as an integral part of their culture. Diné user @dineaesthetics, Charlie Amáyá Scott, describes themselves as an avid user of social media. They say 'My hope is to always inspire joy and justice. I'm still learning ways to be accessible and compassionate alongside a community with inherited trauma and resilience' (Scott, n.d., para. 4). Scott discusses a range of topics including Two Spirit identity, settler colonialism, settler nativism and erotic sovereignties, for example, stating that 'I just want to remind the Indigenous LGBTIQ+ community that you come from legacies of resilience and resistance. Celebrate how far you've come, and how far you will go' (tiktok.com/@dineaesthetics). These platforms situate and validate Indigenous pluralities of gender and sexual identity as a reminder that all Indigenous peoples were sovereign in the past, are now and will be into the future.

Social media is employed as theoretical space for Indigenous LGBTIQ+ peoples across the globe to discursively produce and reclaim themselves. Marie Laing, who identifies as a queer Kanyen'kehá:ka person of mixed Haudenosaunee, and Irish/Scottish/South African settler ancestry, is a scholar and youth leader who works with urban Two Spirit youth populations. From their recent research, Laing (2021) found that urban Two Spirit identified Indigenous youths in Canada hold multiple and sometimes conflicting definitions of what it means to be Two Spirit. The term is used as a placeholder or umbrella term encompassing cultural epistemologies and ontologies of gender and sexuality. Like an urban landscape, social media hosts the complex diversities of urban Indigenous peoples who converge and interact. The digital lexicon is useful as Laing (2021, p. 52) theorises that culturally, gender and sexually diverse Indigenous community spaces are negotiated through hashtags that are described as a 'container that can hold multiple distinct truths'. They continue 'hashtags (which are not definitions) not only organize conversations, they help people find these conversations. Hashtags gather multiple different expressions and ideas; they can mobilize community and foster a sense of togetherness' (Laing 2021, p. 53). This metaphor resolves conflicting lines of dissent that definitions provoke while mitigating issues of difference and reflecting the meaningful relationships between diverse Indigenous peoples. Social media is positioned as a place where we may find ourselves through each other, through the relational ontologies shared between us, and across Indigenous communities locally, internationally, and globally.

Social media enables us to access representations of Indigenous communities invested in strategies of inclusion for LGBTIQ+ kin. Indigenous communities are not homogeneous in that all people contained within their boundaries share the same view of gender and sexual diversity. It is, however, very powerful to see governing bodies and community representatives undertake an allied position to Indigenous LGBTIQ+ concerns. Grand Council Treaty #3 is a community that exemplifies a move towards LGBTIQ+ inclusion. Grand Council Treaty #3 is the traditional government of the Anishinaabe nation that entered Treaty No. 3 in 1873. On their community website, they state that their overall goal is the protection, preservation and enhancement of Treaty and Aboriginal rights (Grand Council Treaty #3 2022). Anishinaabe queer identified writer Riley Yesno (2021, para. 7) explores the migrant flow back into community where there continue to be 'longstanding barriers [for Two Spirit peoples] reclaiming space in their home communities'. Grand Council Treaty #3 has revealed its inclusive approach to returning community members by installing LGBTIQ+ members into decision-making processes as well as cultural events, including a Two Spirit powwow and council. Promoted across Facebook and local and national digital news, these developments digitally prescribe the idea of 'coming in', as termed by Cree scholar Alex Wilson. Wilson describes 'coming in' as 'an act of returning, fully present in ourselves, to resume our place as a valued part of our families, cultures, communities, and lands, in connection with all our relations' (Wilson 2015, p. 3). Put into practice, and displayed online, coming in intervenes in queer displacement by reasserting acceptance and facilitating safety. This shift is invested in a future where Indigenous relationality rejects the exclusionary tactics of settler–colonial heteropatriarchy. While not an elixir, the strategies undertaken by Grand Council Treaty #3 provide hope.

The complex intersections of cultures and identities found in urban landscapes are articulated by Selasi (2014) who theorises multi-local identities that capture the shared experience of minority groups under the conditions of migration and colonialism. In the *TEDx* talk discussed previously, Selasi argues that we must 'replace the language of nationality with the language of locality [which] asks us to shift our focus to where life occurs' (Selasi 2014). Through Afropolitanism, Selasi argues that multi-locality privileges cultural identity over settler colonial claims to land through a shift in focus that does not dwell solely on challenges of settler–colonial occupation but emphasises subaltern identities in the processes of claiming space and place. Selasi builds a framework of locality through rituals, relationships, and restrictions. From these frameworks, we can come to recognise individual and collective relationships beyond the liminal spaces of migration and into life as it is built and continued. Indigenous LGBTIQ+ peoples' belonging, as explored through this chapter, is heavily invested in cultural continuity that prioritise relationships despite where our feet land. Reframing discussions around migrations to include the experience of Indigenous peoples, LGBTIQ+, and, in this chapter, Indigenous LGBTIQ+ peoples, addresses the multiplicity of Indigenous worldviews necessary in discourses of migration.

Conclusion

This chapter has explored migration through themes specific to Indigenous LGBTIQ+ peoples globally where heteropatriarchal settler colonialism continues to have a significant impact on Indigenous people's relationships to family, community and home. Settler colonialism broadly relates into the trajectory of Indigenous LGBTIQ+ lives through regimes of gender and sexual norms aimed to diminish and erase Indigenous societies. In the aftermath of first contact, Indigenous LGBTIQ+ peoples have faced waves of division fuelled by entrenched homophobia, transphobia, and heterosexualisation. From where we had secure, self-governed, and ancient sources of belonging, Indigenous societies must now overcome oppression, marginalisation, and violent erasure. The ongoing crisis of recognition for Indigenous LGBTIQ+ peoples continues to be ignored, denied and swept under the carpet. As shown in the many examples in this chapter, visibility of these issues has been achieved predominantly through the labour of Indigenous LGBTIQ+ people, which I have highlighted through HIV/AIDS activism and digital inclusion strategies on social media.

In this chapter, I focused on relationships between Indigenous peoples. However, these relations do not exist in a vacuum devoid of non-Indigenous people who occupy familial, intimate, and community spaces. What stands out in this chapter, through textural analysis, are themes of Indigenous relationalities that seek to resolve intracultural fractures between Indigenous peoples, which begin to reconstitute and heal Indigenous communities through mechanisms of safety and acceptance.

References

Browning, D. (n.d.). Small town black queer. *Small Town Queer*. https://museum.tweed.nsw.gov.au/small-town-queer/queer-history/black-queer

Buchanan, J. L. (2013). Decolonization and liminality: A reflective process for research as a cooperative and ethical practice. *Journal of Leadership, Accountability and Ethics*, 10(4), 73–79.

Carlson, B. (2013). The 'new frontier': Emergent Indigenous identities and social media. In Harris, M., Nakata, M., & Carlson, B. (Eds), *The Politics of Identity: Emerging Indigeneity*. Sydney and Guadalajara: University of Technology Sydney and University of Guadalajara Press, pp. 147–168.

Carlson, B. (2016). *Politics of Identity: Who counts as Aboriginal today?* Acton: Aboriginal Studies Press.

Carlson, B. (2020). Love and hate at the cultural interface: Indigenous Australians and dating apps. *Journal of Sociology*, 56(2), 133–150.

Carlson B. & Berglund, J. (2021). *Indigenous Peoples Rise Up: The Global Ascendency of Social Media Activism*. New Brunswick: Rutgers University Press.

Carlson, B. & Frazer, R. (2018). *Social media mob: being Indigenous online*. Sydney: Macquarie University. https://research-management.mq.edu.au/ws/portalfiles/portal/85013179/MQU_SocialMediaMob_report_Carlson_Frazer.pdf

Carlson, B., & Frazer, R. (2021). *Indigenous Digital Life: The Practice and Politics of Being Indigenous on Social Media*. Basingstoke: Palgrave Macmillan.

Clark, M. (2015). Are we queer? Reflections on 'peopling the empty mirror' twenty years on. In Hodge, D. (Ed.), *Colouring the Rainbow: Blak*

Queer and Trans Perspectives: Life Stories and Essays by Indigenous People of Australia. Cambridge: Wakefield Press, pp. 372–393.

Clarke, A. (2017). Young Aboriginal LGBTI people are killing themselves. We need to protect them. *IndigenousX*. https://indigenousx.com.au/allan-clarke-young-aboriginal-lgbti-people-are-killing-themselves-we-need-to-protect-them/

daKashay, J. F. (2008). From Kapus to Christianity: The disestablishment of the Hawaiian religion and chiefly appropriation of Calvinist Christianity. *The Western Historical Quarterly, 39*(1), 17–39.

Driskill, Q. L. (2004). Stolen from our bodies: Indigenous two-spirits/queers and the journey to a sovereign erotic. *Studies in American Indian Literatures, 16*(2), 50–64.

Driskill, Q. L. (2011). *Queer Indigenous Studies: Critical Interventions in Theory, Politics, and Literature*. Tempe: University of Arizona Press.

Farrell, A. (2016). Lipstick clapsticks: A yarn and a kiki with an Aboriginal drag queen. *AlterNative, 12*(5), 574–585.

Farrell, A. (2017). Archiving the Aboriginal rainbow: Building an Aboriginal LGBTIQ portal. *Australasian Journal of Information Systems, 21*, 1–14.

Farrell, A. (2020). Queer and Aboriginal in a regional setting: Identity and place. *Archer Magazine*. https://archermagazine.com.au/2020/06/queer-and-aboriginal-identity-and-place/

Farrell, A. (2021a). Feeling seen: Aboriginal and Torres Strait Islander LGBTIQ+ peoples (in)visibility, and social-media assemblages. *Genealogy, 5*(2), 1–11.

Farrell, A. (2021b). The rise of Black rainbow: Queering and Indigenizing digital media strategies, resistance, and change. In Carlson, B. & Berglund, J. *Indigenous People Rise Up: The Global Ascendency of Social Media Activism*. New Brunswick: Rutgers University Press, pp. 140–156.

Farrell, A. (2021c). 'It's just a preference': Indigenous LGBTIQ+ peoples and technologically facilitated violence on dating apps. In Powell, A., Flynn, A., & Suglura, L. (Eds), *Palgrave Handbook of Gendered Violence and Technology* (pp. 335–353). New York: Springer.

Fredericks, B. (2013). 'We don't leave our identities at the city limits': Aboriginal and Torres Strait Islander people living in urban localities. *Australian Aboriginal Studies, Canberra* (1), 4–16.

Gopinath, G. (2018). Diaspora, Indigeneity, queer critique. In G. Gopinath (Ed.), *Unruly Visions: The Aesthetic Practices of Queer Diaspora* (pp. 87–124). Durham, NC: Duke University Press.

Gorman-Murray, A. & Waitt, G. (2011). 'It's about time you came out': Sexualities, mobility and home. *Antipode, 43*(4), 1380–1403.

Gorrie, N. (2019). Rob, and queer family. In Law, B. (Ed.), *Growing up Queer in Australia* (pp. 21–24). Collingwood: Black Inc.

Goudie, S. (2015). My story, your story, our story: Recollections of being Aboriginal and queer in the 1980s and '90s, In D. Hodge (Ed.), *Colouring the Rainbow: Blak Queer and Trans Perspectives: Life Stories and Essays by Indigenous People of Australia*. Adelaide: Wakefield Press.

Grand Council Treaty #3 (2022). Home. *Grand Council Treaty #3*. http://gct3.ca/?fbclid=IwAR1bo3ONBF5VEf5a9mzG63VzTvenaHdFEq WDcXTYeMBfGFiWpsFuzoIWLbU

Gustafson, R. (2019). Heteropatriarchy and settler colonialism. *TedX Talks*. www.youtube.com/watch?v=-wRbfOmHgts

Hamer, D. & Wilson, J. (2014). *A Place in the Middle*. https://vimeo.com/99724455

Harris, R. (2015). 'We Exist. We're Not Just Some Fairytale in a Book': Migration Narratives of LGBTQ2S Aboriginal People in Toronto, Dissertation. https://tspace.library.utoronto.ca/bitstream/1807/70377/1/Harris_Rachel_201511_MA_thesis.pdf

Hill, B., Uink, B., Dodd, J., Bonson, D., Eades, A. & Bennett, S. (2021). *Breaking the Silence: Insights into the Lived Experiences of WA Aboriginal/LGBTIQ+ People, Community Summary Report 2021*. Kurongkurl Katitjin: Edith Cowan University.

Hobson, J. Wafer, J. & Walcott, P. (1993). Queers of the desert: E. J. Milera (1992–95). www.indigoz.com.au/qotd/milera.html

Laing, M. (2021). *Urban Indigenous Youth Reframing Two-Spirit*. New York: Routledge.

Lezard, P., Prefontaine, Z., Cederwall, D. M., Sparrow, C., Maracle, S., Beck, A. & McLeod, A. (2021). *MMIWG2SLGBTQQIA+ National Action Plan Final Report*. OFIFC. https://mmiwg2splus-nationalactionplan.ca/wp-content/uploads/2021/06/2SLGBTQQIA-Report-Final.pdf

Miranda, D. A. (2010). Extermination of the Joyas: Gendercide in Spanish California. *GLQ: A Journal of Lesbian and Gay Studies*, 16(1), 253–284.

Monaghan, O. (2015). Dual imperatives: decolonising the queer and queering the decolonial. In Hodge, D. (Ed.), *Colouring the Rainbow: Blak Queer and Trans Perspectives: Life Stories and Essays by Indigenous People of Australia* (pp. 195–207). Adelaide: Wakefield Press.

Morgensen, S. L. (2010). Settler homonationalism: Theorizing settler colonialism within queer modernities. *GLQ: A Journal of Lesbian and Gay Studies*, 16(1–2), 105–131.

Morgensen, S. L. (2011). *Spaces between Us Queer Settler Colonialism and Indigenous Decolonization*. Minneapolis: University of Minnesota Press.

Morgensen, S. L. (2012). Theorising gender, sexuality and settler colonialism: An introduction. *Settler Colonial Studies*, 2(2), 2–22.

Morgensen, S. L. (2015). Cutting to the roots of colonial masculinity. In Innes, A. & Anderson, K. (Eds), *Indigenous Men and Masculinities: Legacies, Identities, Regeneration* (pp. 38–61). Manitoba: University of Manitoba Press.

O'Sullivan, S. (2019). A lived experience of Aboriginal knowledges and perspectives: How cultural wisdom saved my life. In Higgs, J. (Ed.), *Practice Wisdom: Values and Interpretations* (pp. 107–112). Leiden: Brill Sense.

O'Sullivan, S. (2021). The colonial project of gender (and everything else). *Genealogy 5*: 67.

Pearson, L. (2016). #IndigenousDads – combating stereotypes and reclaiming the conversation. *IndigenousX*. https://indigenousx.com.au/indigenousdads-combating-stereotypes-and-reclaiming-the-conversation/

Picq, M. (2020). Decolonizing Indigenous sexualities: between erasure and resurgence. In Rahman, M., McEvoy, S. M., & Bosia, M. J. (Eds), *The Oxford Handbook of Global LGBT and Sexual Diversity Politics* (pp. 169–184). Oxford: Oxford University Press.

Rey, J. A. (2019). Dharug custodial leadership: Uncovering Country in the city. *WINHEC Journal (1)*, 56–66.

Riggs, D. W. & Toone, K. (2017). Indigenous Sistergirls' experiences of family and community. *Australian Social Work*, 70(2), 229–240.

Ristock, J., Zoccole, A., & Passante, L. (2010). *Aboriginal Two-Spirit and LGBTQ Migration, Mobility and Health Research Project: Winnipeg, Final Report*. www.2spirits.com/

Roy, J. (2015). The 'Dancing Queens': Negotiating Hijra Pehchān from India's streets onto the global stage. *Ethnomusicology Review*, 20. https://ethnomusicologyreview.ucla.edu/journal/volume/20/piece/872

Scott, C. A. (n.d.). Diné Aesthetics. https://dineaesthetics.com/about/

Selasi, T. (2014). 'Don't ask where I'm from, ask where I'm a local'. *TedX Talks*. www.youtube.com/watch?v=LYCKzpXEW6E

Simpson, L. B. (2017). *As We Have Always Done: Indigenous Freedom through Radical Resistance*. Minneapolis: University of Minnesota Press.

Urban Indian Health Institute. (2013). US Census marks increase in urban American Indians and Alaska natives. www.uihi.org/wp-content/uploads/2013/09/Broadcast_Census-Number_FINAL_v2.pdf

Waitt, G. & Gorman-Murray, A. (2011). 'It's about time you came out': Sexualities, mobility and home. *Antipode*, 43(4), 1380–1403.

Whitehead, J. (2018). *Jonny Appleseed: A Novel*. Vancouver: Arsenal Pulp Press.

Connecting back home   69

Whittaker, A. (2016). Queerness and Indigenous cultures: One world, many lives. *Archer Magazine*. https://archermagazine.com.au/2016/08/queerness-indigenous-cultures/

Wilson, A. (1996). How we find ourselves: Identity development and Two-Spirit people. *Harvard Educational Review*, 66(2), 303–317.

Wilson, A. (2015). Our coming in stories: Cree identity, body sovereignty and gender self-determination. *Journal of Global Indigeneity*, 1(1). https://ro.uow.edu.au/jgi/vol1/iss1/4/?fbclid=IwAR2eEHiCYobNXK7cgRY8ShkPja9V9iMr1SBeHgyp99iFSmJHq Oxq-XWvJao

Yescas Angeles Trujano, C. (2008). *Indigenous Routes: A Framework for Understanding Indigenous Migration.* Grand-Saconnex: International Organization for Migration.

Yesno, R. (2021). Life on the rez for 4 2SLGBT Indigenous people. *CBC News*. www.cbc.ca/news/indigenous/life-rez-2slgbt-indigenous-people-1.6152959?fbclid=IwAR2zWIinGLej2_6YK-I_xSj4kZE-9Sd0n3844 Bc44XSiPjZlpwY6l1jV-Lk

Young, K. (2011). From a Native trans daughter: Carcereal refusal, settler colonialism, re-routing the roots of an Indigenous abolitionist imaginary. In Stanley, E. A., & Smith, N. (Eds), *Captive Genders: Trans Embodiment and the Prison Industrial Complex* (pp. 83–96). Chico: AK Press.

Zanghellini, A. (2013). Sodomy laws and gender variance in Tahiti and Hawai'i. *Laws*, 2(2), 51–68.

5

Oceanic intimacies: Ngurra, Tūpuna and Wairua relationality

Lou Netana-Glover

Introduction

In this chapter I am using the term 'oceanic intimacies' which comprises combinations of individual and group interactions between and amongst Indigenous peoples from unique territories, both with each other (kin) and with Ngurra[1] (often referred to as Country, our homelands, waters, spaces and everything that encompasses). In short, 'intimacies' refers to our relationships or as we might refer to as relationality (see Tynan 2021). From these intimacies, new formations grow locally, across land masses and waterways, providing unique expressions of global Indigeneity at individual, familial and community levels.

Te Moana-nui-a-Kiwa (the Pacific Ocean) has always connected Aboriginal and Māori relatives with each other and with our greater Pacific whānau (family). Anglo invasion and subsequent settlement throughout Oceania has ostensibly brought with it greater Indigenous[2] mobilities that has created stronger inter-relating and intimacies between Aboriginal and Torres Strait Islander peoples, Māori and our relatives in other Pacific locations. Given the close proximity between this continent colonially referred to as Australia[3] and Aotearoa (New Zealand) it is likely that Aboriginal peoples and Māori have interacted, visited each other, traded goods before colonial capitalism increased ocean traffic to the extent it has today. The colonial record is lacking pre-colonial historical notation of Aboriginal and Māori intimacies and mobilities save Lauan historian Tracey Banivanua Mar's efforts to get it into the academic record before her untimely death (Mar 2015, p. 340), and Māori writer Jo Kamira's mention that 'Indigenous lore in

Australia tells of contact between the two' (Kamira 2010, p. 23). I too have heard of pre-colonial contact between Aboriginal people and Māori and many other peoples, through storytelling based on oral histories off the public record. Māori and Polynesian ancestral sea voyaging expertise, experience and waka (ocean going vessel) designs leave no doubt as to the possibility of pre-colonial oceanic intimacies between Aboriginal people and Māori (University of Waikato 2022).

Oceanic intimacies have flourished on the east coast of so-called Australia. Aboriginal-Māori families are not uncommon, as are creative collaborations across the arts and sport. The city of Sydney, on the lands of the Dharug and Gadigal people has hosted diverse populations and Māori diaspora for over 200 years (see Haua 2017, p. 16; Kamira 2010). Since the 1960s, Sydney has been a vibrant hub for Māori entertainers when the Māori Showband scene proliferated and was centred around Kings Cross (Kewene-Doig 2022, pp. 94–99). Sydney also provided a new home for many Indigenous peoples escaping oppressive policies dished out by the Aborigines Protection Board (see Curthoys 2011) and for LGBTQI+ peoples escaping homophobia fuelled by Christian missionaries that had also infiltrated Indigenous families and communities (see Carlson et al. 2022). It was a safe haven of sorts for many diasporic communities. Growing up, I had no idea of these diasporas or that my physical journey started from within one.

It is through my own story and the stories shared with me from others that I have become so interested in oceanic intimacies and the connection that Aboriginal people and Māori have established over time – for a long time. It is not just our relationships with each other, but also to place and our Indigenous spiritualities, our ways of being and knowing that intrigue me and are useful when applying theory to my own journey. My journey and relationships are the data in this chapter which merges theory and methodology as is typical of Indigenous 'research' or knowledge production methods where relationality *is* method and method *is* content because our positionality is not abstracted from our research (Graham 2014; Kwaymullina and Kwaymullina 2010, p. 197; Martin 2017; Wilson 2020). Other Indigenous scholars have mapped the terrain of Indigenist research (see Rigney 1999). Indigenous methodologists and theorists (for want of a better term) are upturning the inverted research method that the western academy has previously offered until Māori scholars like Linda Tuhiwai-Smith kicked open the floodgates for decolonial practice back in 1999 with her seminal text *Decolonizing Methodologies: Research and Indigenous Peoples*. Retrofitting Indigenist research methodological theories to my identity journey offers an opportunity to explicate a set of congruencies in global Indigeneity pertaining to the relationality between and agency of Ngurra (Country),[4] Tūpuna (Ancestors), Wairua (spirit) and people. Not that these things are separate.

The work of Palkyu scholars Ambelin and Blaze Kwaymullina has expanded my own understanding of life and given me rich scholarship to draw on since I started my undergraduate degree in 2014. The first article of theirs that I read, 'Learning to read the signs: law in an Indigenous reality' adeptly conveys the holistic nature of Aboriginal philosophy and law systems, and the relationality and aliveness of all existence, physical and non-physical (2010). When people have asked me what my academic work is about, I sometimes find myself timidly saying 'identity'. The inner dialogue I have experienced is similar to that eloquently argued by Māori scholar Alice Te Punga Somerville who stated, 'Identity' feels like the stuff of the individual, a navel-gazing luxury rather than the stuff of the collective, political, urgent' (2010, p. 37). If my audience seem lost at the mention of identity, I respond, 'identity as it relates to law, and Aboriginal and Māori connections'. I then segue to my personal identity journey story, which is a cracking yarn.

A cracking yarn

I was born on Dharug Ngurra to a settler couple in Sydney in 1969. The White Australia policy (see Jayasuriya et al. 2003) was firmly entrenched into the Australian psyche. My brown appearance placed me as 'other' in the white dominant cultural Australia. My familial enculturation was also as an 'Australian', and of course it was well established, in popular imagination and also through policy that Australians were white (Jayasuriya et al. 2003; Tranter and Donahue 2015; Ward 1958)! My parents were white, I was their child, it would be logical to assume that therefore I too was white. This conflicted with the racist remarks that were directed at me by other children at school, such as calling me a 'coon' or the friendlier 'charcoal'; and with the compliments from adults cooing at my cute and 'exotic looks' (see Figure 5.1). The mirror did not reflect whiteness either.

Then when I was in my early twenties, I learned of my father's Aboriginal ancestry from his non-Indigenous mother. I had rung Nan for answers as to why Aboriginal people had kept suggesting I was Aboriginal. When she told me about my grandfather's Aboriginality, it was both a shock to me and made sense at the same time. My Aboriginal friends at the time laughed that I did not know I was Blak.[5] After encouragement from my friends and building relationships with other Aboriginal people in the community

Figure 5.1 Photograph of Lou Glover on Worimi Country c. 1976

I identified with my newly uncovered identity as an Aboriginal person. This was an identity that more suited my appearance but at a deeper level of my 'spirit'. I also never felt 'white'. Identifying as Aboriginal was not a simplistic action, it is an identity that was carefully embraced and was contingent on being accepted by the community in which I lived and had been in a relationship with over my adult years. I reflected on this in a previous publication where I noted, 'I unlearned my unconscious settler conditioning to re-enculturate to Indigeneity and an Indigenous worldview' (Netana-Glover 2021, p. 4). I *re-enculturated*, I learned from the Aboriginal community. Like Country, local Indigenous people nurtured me, my sense of belonging, responsibility and obligation – relationships of care of each other and Country that are inherent in an Indigenous worldview.

Regardless of being welcomed, accepted and provided with kinship and care, I always held an uneasiness with my identity because only a few of us in my father's family identified as Aboriginal. It was also the case that knowledge of our pre-colonial kinship connections was scant. This is not uncommon however, as settler colonialism in all its violence also impacts records and including counting Aboriginal peoples with cattle and other possessions and not recording their names or tribal affiliations (see Carlson 2016). Overtime I began to feel a sense of belonging regardless of the complexities of colonial record keeping. On Walbunja-Yuin Country, sometime in the early 2010s, I finally began to feel comfortable with my displaced identity after being culturally adopted by some Walbunja-Yuin families.

In 2018, I met my Yuin/Biripi/Wiradjuri/Gomeroi partner. Bee is my soul mate who as a coincidence happens to be Walbunja-Yuin. When we met, Bee told me where she was from. I said, 'aw, you're people took me in, I'm one of them lost ones, I don't know my Country'.

We met randomly but found we were incredibly connected through community connections, Country and our work in the Indigenous film industry which I had since left but Bee was an emerging producer/director who would be called upon for acting as well. It was bizarre to both us that we had not met before, until viewed from a spiritual perspective. My partner is the daughter of Sandi, a close friend to many of my peers. Bee is younger than me and so would not necessarily be in my circle of friends. Sandi gave me her blessing for our relationship and shared that the family have always known that Bee would end up 'married-up' to an older dubay (woman) because as Sandi reflected, 'she has always been more mature than her generation'. Sandi went on to explain that Bee's spirit did not need to learn through personal relationship drama this lifetime as she has other things to do. Mamma Sandi's words have rung true. I cannot help but think that the old Yuin Ancestors brought us together when the time was right.

Then, while on Dharug Ngurra in 2019, three weeks before my fiftieth birthday, my maternal Aunty Janette told me that my dad is not my biological father. Dad and I later did a paternity test to investigate this claim. Dad had never previously questioned whether I was his offspring; he has darker skinned relations, as does Mum. It turned out that my dad and I are not biologically related. I felt a bit ill with this news because I love my dad and the thought of him being deceived for so long was deeply saddening. I wondered what it meant for me and my identity. Even though I had been accepted into the Aboriginal community and had grown more comfortable with that, I had always carried a level of trepidation of not being from an Aboriginal bloodline, so there was also a feeling of relief that I might uncover the real source of that fear. The truth has always been more important to me than any identity questions. I decided to take a DNA test to try and locate my biological father or other relations that could answer the question of who I am. In another twist in the story of my life, I eventually learned I am Māori.

Bee is from a big family and has ancestral connections to just about every part of the east of so-called Australia. We joke about her being related to most Aboriginal people we meet and Country we walk on. When my DNA test estimated me as 57.1 per cent Polynesian (problematic science aside), in a gesture of one-up-man-ship I cheekily pointed to the ocean and said to Bee, 'that! is *my* Country'. Within months I was able to locate close Māori relatives. Any sense of loss or disconnection to who I thought I was quickly became elation when I got to connect with my strong and loving whānau. I learned I am Ngāti Whātua-Ngā Puhi, Waikato-Tainui. The truth really did set me free. The sweet relief of knowing who I am. I became more grounded in my body, sure on my feet, stauncher in my blakness and lighter on my big Māori shoulders.

In February 2020, just before the world was forced into isolation and all travel was suspended due to COVID-19 I travelled to Aotearoa to meet my whānau. The lessons taught to me by my Aboriginal family such as reciprocity provided me with good grounding in shared values. For a newcomer to the whānau, I was adept at mapping generational relationships and connections to Country. I knew protocols of respect and could work out who to ask if I did not. Aotearoa was home – I knew and felt my place in the whānau instantly. For the first time, I saw myself reflected back through blood relations who looked like me. The familiarity was way beyond physical too. As I have previously written, the experience of meeting my whānau and being embraced *as* whānau was unbelievable and we 'felt and imagined the joy of our heavenly whānau seeing us reunited. Fifty years of separation dissolved. Our deep connections were instantly expressed' (Netana-Glover 2021).

Before taking that trip, I had learned that my biological father, Joe Nathan, had passed in Sydney the early 1970s. I would have been three years old at the time. I also learned that I have a younger sister and brother who, of course, also lost their father. Our father was very handsome, and I am told a beautiful singer and guitarist, a hard worker, a devoted son and a pool shark.[6] There was some disappointment in finally finding my whānau to only discover my father had passed away when I was so young. I have many more questions which now remain unanswered. There is always so much that is lost when we lose whānau.

Relationality as method, method as content

My identity story discussed above could be thought of as the big story in this chapter. The stories of intimacies and communications over place, time and dimension can be thought of as smaller stories within the big story that prove Indigenous theoretical and methodological understandings about relationality from established theory about 'Relationality' as method, method as content (see Graham 2014; Martin 2017; Wilson 2020). Applying the above theory to the research data provided by my story renders Indigenist Research Theory (Rigney 1999) and Māori ethical frameworks (Hudson et al. 2010) as results instead of methods intentionally applied. Hence proving relationality as method, method as theory. Further, these stories add to conceptualising 'global Indigeneity' as a sense, like the pan-Indigenous sense I felt when I was waiting to find out where my bloodlines were from or the Indigenous kinship relationships I have knowingly and unknowingly been connected to throughout my adult life.

The existence of these relationships and the events that have transpired lead me to believe that Ngurra (Country), tūpuna (Ancestors) and wairua (spirit) knew what my conscious brain did not. While some might see this as fanciful or even imagined, I believe Ancestors were with me all along. Aboriginal theorist Greg Lehmann (2006, p. 2) argues that western culture is 'the only culture in the world – perhaps the only culture that the world has ever known – that argues for the non-existence of any dimension or reality that the [physical] senses cannot perceive'. It is not a goal of this chapter to investigate the role that this anomaly plays in the domination processes of colonial capitalism. It is pertinent to point out that this exception to the rule happens to be held by the culture with the least amount of success at sustaining the myriad of life forms on the places over which it claims dominion on earth (Walker et al. 2021, p. 97). These points together render the ignoring and dismissing of enduring ancestral connection and non-physical entities as ridiculous.

This chapter also speaks of oceanic intimacies as conveyed through dreams, relationships, events and signs. 'Wairua' is a te reo (Māori language) word which has been translated to mean 'spirit' in English. Such terms, however, lose depth when translated into English. Wairua can be described in many ways including but limited to as 'a fundamental attribute that enables Māori to engage with their reality; an intuitive consciousness' (Valentine 2009, p. iii), and wairua that 'begins its existence when the eyes form in the foetus and is immortal' (Te Aka Māori dictionary). My wairua began this existence on Gadigal Country in 1968.

The inner pull to Sydney, Gadigal and Dharug Country

I was seventeen years of age when I fled to Sydney from Kempsey, the north coast rural town located on Dunghutti Country. This is where I had grown up. I thought it was a typical bright lights attraction, but Sydney also had an LGBTQI+ community through which I learned more about myself and formed a sisterly friendship with a woman named Shelley who also originated from Kempsey. Shelley is Yuin; however, did not know that at the time. Late 1980s and early 1990s Sydney unwittingly gave me significant connections to my birth whānau, extended whānau and adopted whānau that I did not know I had. Prior to this, back in the late 1960s, Sydney also attracted my father, Joe. Joe was in the original line-up of the band The Milford Sounds (Figure 5.2),[7]

Figure 5.2 The Milford Sounds. From left: Ray Tehira, Reihana Smith, Paul Smith, Joe Nathan. Taken in Sydney c. 1969
Source: Paul Smith personal collection

a band on the cusp of great success when Joe died unexpect-
edly after a car accident in 1972. The sadness of this great loss
still reverberates throughout our whānau and communities
associated to Joe.

In the late 1980s, the Māori diaspora was still very much situated
around the Eastern suburbs of Sydney, most notably Bondi. In
1987, I started working at Doyles Seafood restaurant in Watsons
Bay. Doyles was a world-famous fish and chip restaurant with a
large staff base and was considered a 'melting pot' of ethnicities and
cultures. The culturally diverse staff served international and local
celebrities, cashed up American and European tourists, European
royalty, working, middle class and upper-class Australians and
New Zealanders, blue collar and white-collar criminals, judges,
politicians and other usually unseen societal power brokers behind
the structures that govern our money systems.

The hot kitchen was headed up by a Japanese chef and had mostly
Portuguese staff. The cold larder was run and staffed by Māori, led
by Audrey, a tough-as-nails butch wahine Māori (Māori woman).
Audrey took me under her wing despite my negative answer to her
question asking, 'Are you Māori?' I found out thirty years later
that Audrey had organised protective eyes on me as the young thing
I was gallivanting around the vibrant streets of late 1980s Sydney's
Eastern Suburbs. I would learn later from my Uncle Taia that my
father Joe had walked the same streets and socialised or performed
in the same establishments as I frequented.

Waitressing at Doyles brought in lots of cash, connections and a
sociological education that no university could offer but the pressure
to choose an 'appropriate career' came from both my family and
from within me. My childhood career desires consisted of musician
or police officer. I had not practised my guitar and singing enough,
so I was not geared up for arduous task of making it in the music
industry. So police officer it was. I chose the Federal Police, partly
because I believed the physical requirements would be easier and
because it seemed more 'cloak and dagger' and my ego saw it as a
higher expression of status than the State police.

In 1990 I became an Australian Federal Police officer. After com-
pleting training on Ngunnawal Country, I was stationed at Eastern
Regional Headquarters on Gadigal Country in Sydney. I was
introduced to Jo and Craig, two detectives a few years ahead of

me in policing *and* Indigenous ways of being. Jo is wahine Māori (Ngā Puhi, Te Rarawa, Te Aupouri, Ngati Whakaue), and Craig, an Aboriginal man (Wodi Wodi). Jo was one of the first people I approached after I was told of my Aboriginal ancestry. I left my desk in the Major Crime Squad where I had just spoken to my (previously thought to be) paternal grandmother and she had told me of my Aboriginality through my father's Ancestors. Jo was fairly flippant at the time because she was in shock that I did not know I was Blak. For other brown people, it was verging on ridiculous that I could have ever perceived myself as white. Jo and Craig were like having a big siblings in 'The Job' (police nickname for the police forces). We drifted in and out of contact over the years after I left the police force in 1993. Interestingly now we are all connected as students in the Department of Indigenous Studies at Macquarie University. It is fascinating how our Ancestors bring people in and keep people in our lives when needed.

An identity story, so what?

This is the question I had to ask myself when starting this chapter. Seeking clarity for my approach, I went on my morning walk to the beach on Yuin Country where I offered karakia (prayer) and spoke to the Ancestors. I greeted the earth and sky, ocean and sun, and Yuin tangata whenua (people of the land we are on). I looked across the Pacific in the direction of my Ngā Puhi and Tainui whānau, I asked my tūpuna, the Old People for guidance on writing. The message I intuited as a response was 'write the waiata (song) of purpose. The waiata of purpose is the story of our connection'. I am not saying that this encapsulates the totality of our connections. It is what emerged for me in my relational methodology between Country, tūpuna and wairua.

My own waiata of purpose is what I have been singing from before I started my undergraduate degree in 2014. My passion and purpose is giving primacy to the rightful moral and lawful jurisdiction of place on place, that is, the law of the land, the law of the original sovereign people of the lands upon which we stand. This order of law is currently inverted and all life suffers because of that inversion (Glover 2017). Tanganekald, Meintangk-Bunganditj Law Academic Irene Watson (2000, p. 4) clarifies:

Today in the modern world, the will to live in a place of lawfulness is lost to the greater humanity. Evidence of this is found in the growing list of global crises, poverty, environmental disasters, famine, war, and violence. What the greater humanity have come to know as law is a complex maze of rules and regulations; the body of law is buried, barely breathing. Law came to us in a song, it was sung with the rising of the sun, law was sung in the walking of the mother earth, law inhered in all things, law is alive, it lives in all things.

For Indigenous people globally, our purpose is to sustain life and seek balance, to honour Earth law of Earth peoples – Indigenous law (Kwaymullina and Kwaymulllina 2010; Simpson 2017; Walker et al. 2021). I understand the Māori concept to be expressed as kaitiaki (guardianship) and that it is not as simplistic a concept as the English translation of the word allows (Kawharu 2000). Life sustaining knowledge through relationality is embedded in an Indigenous lawful paradigm as Turtle Island Nishnaabeg scholar, Leanne Betasamosake Simpson explicates 'existence is ultimately dependent upon intimate relationships of reciprocity, humility, honesty and respect with all elements of creation, including plants and animals' (2014, p. 9). Indigenous law is the original jurisdiction of every place, even by western colonisers' own law as expressed in the western maxim of law 'He who is earlier in time is stronger in law' (Duhaime Legal Dictionary; Fellmeth and Horwitz 2022).

The question is raised, how does my identity journey relate to or serve this purpose? I draw on my experience to approach this question from the level of the individual, where my journey and its blockbuster style reveal is an affirmation of the power of our tūpuna walking with us; and how that extends to family and community. I know many Aboriginal-Māori families who live the affirmation of the proper lawful order of place, strengthening each other culturally by living the values of honouring tangata whenua and supporting each other, their broader families and communities. Our oceanic intimacies exist both because of and fiercely independent of the presence of the colonial state.

During the first days I realised I had a whole new father and family somewhere in the world, and my life had been based largely on hidden truths. I was experiencing trauma symptoms where scenes from my whole life were flashing before me. I stuck close to Bee who offered endless support. We were in Sydney, and she got an acting job in Canberra so I joined her on the trip. While in Canberra, I took the opportunity to contact my old friend Jo Kamira. Unbeknown to me, Jo had just curated *Māori Markings: Tā Moko*, an exhibition of Māori face markings and tattoos for the National Gallery of Australia.[8] As luck would have it, I happened to be there for the opening day.

The exhibition opening was brimming with cultural richness. We were welcomed by local Nunnawal and Ngambri people and then sung into the exhibition by Māori. I was a little unsure on my feet, feeling between worlds in many ways. My years of practice in that state did not serve me on this particular day. Māori were coming up to me saying 'kia ora', and I was giving a shy nod in return. I was feeling both grounded by the mix of cultures and flighty as a bird about to take off at the same time. When we arrived in the exhibition the walls were filled with majestic Māori from over the centuries adorned with tā moko (tattoos) and traditional dress. They were looking down on me and I was wondering if I was related to any of them but not wanting to trespass energetically by assuming or questioning relatedness. My hair was standing on end. Jo showed me a carving, a self-portrait of her Ancestor Hongi Hika.[9] Jo told me the story of his time in Sydney. I thought it amazing how proud she must feel, doing this for her Ancestors, working with them, their energy, touching the wood that her Ancestor touched all of those years ago, feeling his mana (power/energy) in it. Of course, Māori there assumed I was Māori and kept greeting me accordingly. I was welling up with tears, especially when the waiata (singing) started. Eventually I was too overwhelmed and I made an early exit, not before talking to a few Māori, some of whom I now suspect I am related to.

In an Indigenous worldview where 'all "things" have agency and are interconnected through a system of relationality' (Martin 2017, p. 1392; Kwaymullina and Kwaymullina 2010, p. 196), it makes sense that I found myself at such an exhibition at such a profound time in my journey. It is also testament that following my intuitive consciousness, my wairua, I had the urge to accompany Bee on a job that happened to be on Ngunnawal Country (Canberra), that happened to be when an exhibition was on that would contain the largest collection of tūpuna images and artefacts that I was likely to see in one place in a lifetime. Images that tūpuna had sat and posed for and that reflected their wairua and mana. I did not know it but I met some of my Ancestors that day through those artefacts. Writing this, it is the first time I have realised that I met them at the start of this major part of my journey, before my whānau who are here in this realm with us now. The mana I was reading from Jo's Hongi Hika wood carving was the mana of my own relation. Jo and I were to later learn that we are Ngā Puhi cousins.

In my lost days, my faith mostly did not waver that I would eventually know who I am. I believed I would be a coastal person because of the large amount of cetacean 'signs' I have seen. Kwaymullina and Kwaymullina (2010, p. 206) argue that 'we must all learn how to read the signs, to listen to country' and that from an Aboriginal knowledge system, 'the world can only be known by acknowledging and respecting relationships, not by ignoring or denying them' (2010, p. 197). When I finally learned how the read the 'signs' a lot of my experiences began to make more sense to me. From dolphins swimming underneath my body board or appearing in dreams and cloud formations; to whales frequenting my home beach, I have always felt connected to the ocean. I did not speak that previously at fear of being viewed as some kind of 'wannabe' or 'new-age mystical hippy'. Now I reflect that if my biological father and grandparents and my tūpuna before them were trying to connect me to the truth from where they now are beyond this physical world, I cannot think of more methods than dreams, totemic animal visits, people, and feelings.

Kwaymullina and Kwaymullina (2010) assert the standing of dreams as a primary source in the Palyku world as they are an 'important part of the interface between human beings and the broader universe ... a means in which knowledge is communicated to human beings by the Ancestors' (2010, p. 207). I often pleaded with my Ancestors to get me more verifiable information about who my people are. I did not and could not always hear or act on some very clear messages, perhaps my conscious conditioning overrode the signals. One night in a dream, I was floating over a map of so-called Australia with New South Wales in view. The map started zooming into a place on the western side of mountain range just over halfway up the distance from south to north. I was then in that place at a camp and an old couple where there to greet me. The man was Māori and the woman was Aboriginal. We had some conversations which I diarised the following day. Unfortunately, I have misplaced that diary but I do recall that I could not make sense of the dream, it *felt* wonderful though. I wondered if the message was that a Māori man had married into my Aboriginal Ancestors. Mystery aside, I was excited to have a physical pinpoint to search around with my family tree information. My research revealed that I only had connections in that area on my mother's side. I did not investigate them deeply at the time. I now believe my Ancestors were trying to communicate the truth of my whakapapa (genealogy) to me when I had that dream. Perhaps that answer is obvious now – fifteen years later – but what of the woman? That is a matter from the dreamscape for future investigation. Aunty Janette also said that my maternal line has some unanswered ends that point towards Aboriginal ancestry. I chose to put that information to the side at the time as I was overcome with a sense of urgency to find out who my father is, who my family is, if I have siblings.

Reflecting on my relationships over time I can see further ways in which non-physical guidance reveals itself. My friend Shelley mentioned above is in a relationship with Niniwa. As it turns out I whakapapa (genealogy) to Niniwa through her Ngā Puhi linage. Shelley and Bee are related through their Yuin ancestry. As mentioned I am studying through the Department of Indigenous Studies at Macquarie University. My PhD supervisor is Aboriginal but her partner is Māori. I whakapapa to her partner who is Ngā Puhi as well. Additionally, I am also whakapapa to another very close Aboriginal sistagirl Paula's Māori administration team, Jurnan and Cheryl. I have known all of these people for decades. We have strong families and communities of Aboriginal and Māori solidarity, and I have only mentioned what I know without trying from the Ngā Puhi connections in some of my immediate relationships. Many of my Māori relatives who live on this continent express a strong sense of responsibility to tangata whenua.

Waikato

I am in the process of learning more about my connection to the Waikato. Sadly, I recently lost my Aunty Raukawa whom I had an instant deep connection with, not the least because of how much we look alike. Aunty was my cultural touchstone for our Tainui heritage. She has left that knowledge and wairua in good hands with my niece Terina. I will call on Terina in the near future. There is a story involving me and the Waikato before I knew that I am ancestrally connected to that place. Four months after learning that I did not know who my biological father was, I was attending the Native American and Indigenous Studies Association (NAISA) conference in Hamilton. I had hoped my DNA results would have been returned by then but they were not. The paper I presented was called 'Hidden generation and late identifiers: navigating positionality with integrity in spaces and places'. It was an opportunity for me to use my story and decisions I had made to demonstrate how I managed to keep in integrity despite the precariousness of my identity throughout my adult life. Between submitting the paper to NAISA and presenting it in Hamilton, the paternity question came up. This ended up enhancing the message in the paper which was about being 'upfront' about one's identity journey even if an arduous task, never claiming descent from a particular mob when you are not claimed by them and trusting your inner voice to investigate beneath cover stories.

The room was full and included Bee and over half a dozen of my 'blakademic'[10] family – friends with familial relationships. The paper was extremely well received and was followed by a late change to the program. Rachael Ka'ai-Mahuta presented on the Waitangi Tribunal rights of Māori living abroad who are now denied New Zealand Citizenship (2018). Even though I am old enough to not be affected by this government policy, the story of connection between places opened my awareness of the size of the Māori diaspora. Rachael also offered support in finding my whānau if my upcoming DNA test results revealed me to be Māori. Bee and I marvelled at the fortuitousness of the day. Everything went well for us in Hamilton and no wonder for I have since learned that my tūpuna, my kuia (grandmother) is from the Waikato. I was on my ancestral homelands, speaking from my heart, sharing my spirit. It is also sadly ironic that I was staying three kilometres away from my Aunty Raukawa's house, but we did not know that each other existed.

The 'stuff of the collective, political, urgent' (Te Punga Somerville 2010)

The political urgency of this research relates to the fact that for many Indigenous peoples, we are still fighting settler colonialism. Our lands are still occupied, our people and more-than-human kin are still enslaved to varying extents in systems of exploitation and oppression, and these conditions work against our fundamental values as Indigenous peoples – to affirm and play our role in creating life, in honouring all of our relations, in caring for Country.

When I travelled to Aotearoa in 2020, this was within six months of me finding my whānau and being invited to a family reunion for descendants of Patuawa and Rora Netana – my grandparents. My Aunty Hana accompanied me to Aotearoa for a profoundly wonderful trip meet our whānau. Within three weeks of my return, colonial governments locked down people and place because of the pandemic. I felt very lucky, and assisted by my tūpuna, that I got to make my trip. Fortunately, the Sydney Mardi Gras was able to take place before the shutdown as well. Bee is a drag performer. Her drag persona is 'BeeDazzled Shanks: the Prince of Redfern',[11] and she was one of the lead marchers in the First Nations float. A traditional welcome and smoking ceremony took place in the starting area where we were waiting to march (Figure 5.3). The emotionality in the air was positively high. Thousands of people partaking in this sacred ceremony and honouring Ancestors and Country brought a good feeling and blessing for the event. As that ceremony finished, emotions were turned up another notch as the 'Haka for Life' troupe led Māori in a powerful haka (Figure 5.4). They then moved to the side to form a guard of honour for the First Nations float of tangata whenua. Warriors honouring warriors.

Public events in so-called Australia, when performed respectfully, are opened with a formal Welcome to Country by tangata whenua or an Acknowledgement of Country respectfully by anyone

Figure 5.3 Smoking ceremony at Sydney Mardi Gras, 2020
Source: Photographer: Jo Kamira

else. These ceremonial practices work on physical and non-physical levels to set the stage and a respectful tone of the event – unless an acknowledgement is performed without spirit and integrity of such intention. Sometimes, when Māori are involved or are invited guests the acknowledging of place and people of place is followed by a haka. For example, the Australia New Zealand Army Corps (ANZAC) Services have increasingly had a smoking ceremony and corroboree followed by haka.[12] The lockdowns of 2020 also bought protest, where again, Aboriginal and Māori opened proceedings, in that order. Tangata whenua first, then Māori honouring that sovereignty by following with haka.

These ceremonies are an affirmation of the proper lawful order of place. Indigenous jurisdictions are the original jurisdictions of place – our local, original, natural jurisdictions that have proven the most successful model in history for managing ourselves and Country. These public ceremonial practices plant the seeds of the living law that Watson (2000) mentions above. They honour the physical and non-physical and when together, the song and dance of our cultures fills the atmosphere with the power of our tūpuna and our relationships to Country in the language of wairua. All who are

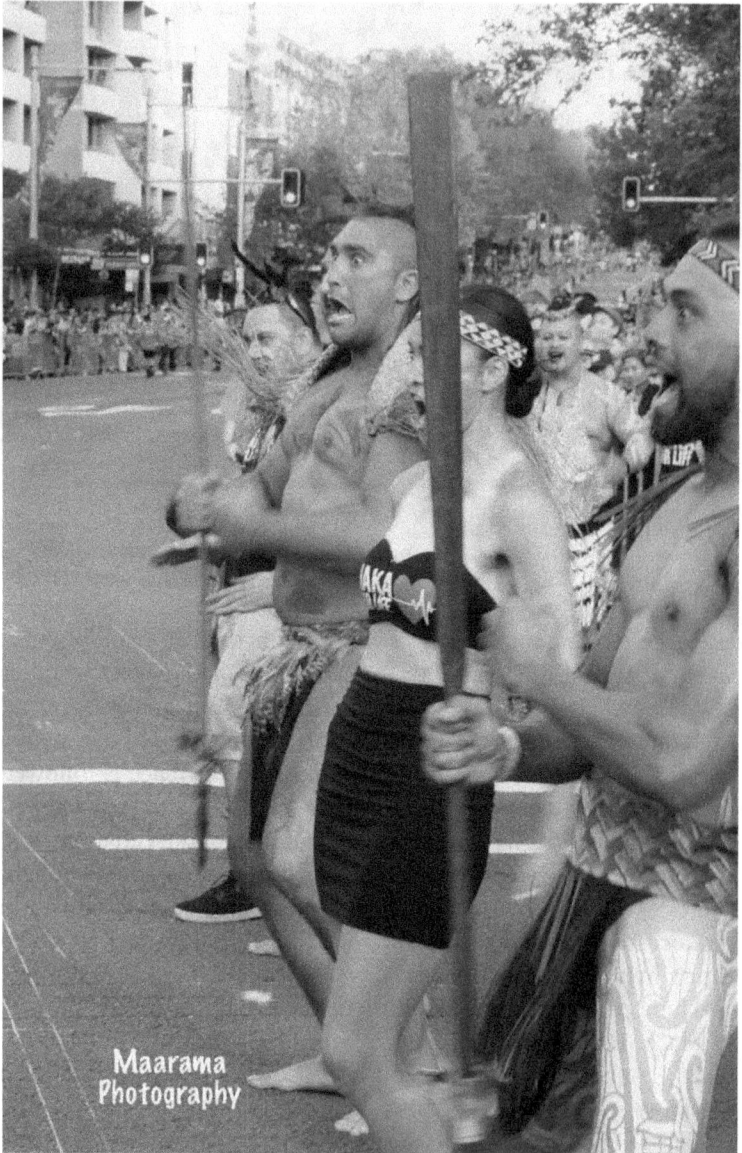

Figure 5.4 Māori performing haka for Aboriginal and Torres Strait
Islander Mardi Gras participants in 2020
Source: Photographer: Jo Kamira

present *feel* the powerful acknowledgement of our oceanic intimacies. Whether they are conscious of it or not, they are also *feeling*
law (see Watson 2000). Reinvigorating the proper law of the land
at a community level is an opportunity for diasporic Māori to prac-
tise their own culture as warriors for the Country from which they
glean a living. Whether performing haka or attending in solidarity,
our presences make a difference. Identity is certainly 'the stuff of
the collective, political, urgent' (Te Punga Somerville 2010). When
we stand in who we are in relationship to the tangata whenua, the
reciprocal recognition that occurs is 'a coded layering of intimate
interconnection and interdependence that creates a complicated
algorithmic network of presence, reciprocity, consent, and freedom'
(Simpson 2017, p. 185). This strengthens our Indigenous identities
which strengthens our oceanic intimacies, simply by expressing our
lawful mana tūpuna in giving thanks to our hosts.

Our oceanic intimacies are also expressed at familial and individual level within our Aboriginal–Māori families. Jo and Craig,
my supervisor Bronwyn and partner Mike have Aboriginal–Māori
children. If we were all in Aotearoa, I would say they were Māori–
Aboriginal children. There is a growing population of Aboriginal–
Māori, walking talking manifestations of oceanic intimacies who
carry the power of both cultures and thousands of Ancestors
within them.

Of course, as someone who has thought of myself as Aboriginal
for the last thirty years, my identity is still complicated and contextual. I am still culturally accepted as Aboriginal; I may still have
an Aboriginal bloodline so I may still fit the government definition of
Aboriginal. I know I am Māori, and my Aboriginal whānau see and
love me beyond definition, we are all Blak/Brown and dispossessed.
I am here on Yuin Country. My presence here brought Bee, and
later Sandi back to Yuin Country. We recently lost Mamma Sandi
to (colonially induced) cancer. She spent her final months with us.
Not only did Sandi receive visits from human kin but non-human
kin visited every day in the days leading up to her passing. Many
South Coast animal kin of totemic significance came to gentle Sandi
back to the Dreaming (Rose et al. 2003, p. 37).[13]

Sandi chose us to raise her nine-year-old youngest daughter.
Our girl had already lost her birth mamma to a colonially induced
health condition when she was four years old, she has now lost her

second mum. As much as I would love to return home to my blood whānau and Country in Aotearoa and immerse myself in the Māori world, I have obligations to Yuin Country that keep me/us here for now. I did work in the past in facilitating storytelling locally which gifted me much local knowledge. Ten years ago, one aunty chose me to hold onto some family and cultural history books of significance. Now these treasures are Bee's and serve as conduits for Bee's Yuin Country Ancestors to communicate to her, providing history and information to facilitate her sign reading and relationalities.

My journey has afforded me multi-linguality and strong code-switching abilities, or as Bee and Sandi would say, 'Lou speaks good white'. My experience with whitefella law word magic gives me a role in our family of dealing with, on paper or by phone, with the micro and macro aggressions constantly dished out against Aboriginal families by agents and institutions exercising their unearned power in settler colonial society. As I am Māori on Aboriginal land, I am proud to be a warrior for Country via my Aboriginal whānau, honouring their very strong bloodlines. It is natural reciprocity for the nourishment given to me all of my life. Maybe I am fulfilling a role or duty that I am unaware of on behalf of my tūpuna, maybe all of our oceanic intimacies are working for a greater significance than we are consciously aware of.

As someone whose childhood did not have an Indigenous world view reflected in my immediate surroundings, I contend that Country, tūpuna and wairua gave signs and made relationship connections in place which contributed to the epic nature of the narrative reveal in the story of my life. My life journey and choices have reflected my mana tūpuna (power through descent) even though I did not know who they were. The work of Indigenous scholars such as the Kwaymullinas have given me the strength and language to write from my mana tūpuna; just as my Aboriginal families gave me the belonging to live from it. I imagine that as I grow as a scholar and into my Māoridom through practising culture and spending more time with my whānau, Māori scholarship will feature more in my work. The confirmation of the great truth of who my magnificent father and whānau is opened my eyes to the oceanic intimacies throughout my life, my families and my communities in the physical and non-physical realms. The big story of this chapter is but a small story in the great story of our whānau, the greater Māori world, people of Te Moana-nui-a-Kiwa and our global Indigenous intimacies.

Notes

1 Ngurra refers to Country in the Dharug language.

2 A note on terminology – Indigenous refers to global original peoples, Ancestors and Country are also capitalised as proper nouns because they are referring to specific beings and places.

3 Like others in this collection, I make the point that this continent which was named 'Australia' by colonisers is actually home to hundreds of self-identifying nations of Aboriginal peoples.

4 In this chapter I use te reo Māori but also draw on Aboriginal languages when appropriate – terms such as Ngurra.

5 'Blak' spelt without the 'c' is an Indigenous spelling protocol that emerged from the 1990s and was first generated by Destiny Deacon. See www.sbs.com.au/nitv/article/2020/05/07/why-blak-not-black-artist-destiny-deacon-and-origins-word-1

6 Someone who is adept at winning money by playing snooker or pool.

7 There is a Milford Sounds clip on YouTube from a later line-up of artists filmed after Joe Nathan's passing.

8 See https://nga.gov.au/on-demand/ta-moko/

9 See https://teara.govt.nz/en/biographies/1h32/hongi-hika

10 'Blakademic' is a colloquial term used by Aboriginal people who are also academics.

11 See 'My Drag Story – BeeDazzled Shanks' https://youtu.be/hn57l8QiVsg

12 See 'Haka for Life' https://hakaforlife.org/anzac-day-haka-and-corroboree-abc-news-sydney/

13 Rose et al. (2003) convey some general understanding of inter-species relationships and is not an exact reference to the visitors I am referring to.

References

Carlson, B. (2016). *The Politics of Identity: Who Counts as Aboriginal Today?* Acton: Aboriginal Studies Press.

Carlson, B., Kennedy, T. & Farrell, A. (2022). Indigenous gender intersubjectivities: Political bodies. In Walter, M., Kukutai, T., Gonzales,

A., & Henry, R. (Eds). *The Oxford Handbook of Indigenous Sociology*. Oxford: Oxford University Press.

Curthoys, A. (2011). The NSW freedom rides. *Agora, 46*(1), 9–27.

Duhaime Legal Dictionary. (n.d.). Qui prior est tempore potoir est jure. www.duhaime.org/LegalDictionary/Q/QuiPriorEstTemporePotiorEst Jure.asp

Fellmeth, A. X. and Horwitz, M. (n.d.). *Guide to Latin in International Law (2 ed.)*. Oxford: Oxford University Press.

Glover, L. (2017). *Deep Time People: Resilience, Inundation and Fishing Rights on the South Coast*. Thesis, University of Wollongong.

Graham, M. (2014). Aboriginal notions of relationality and positionalism: A reply to Weber. *Global Discourse, 4*(1), 17–22.

Haka for Life. (n.d.). Anzac Day Haka and corroboree. https://hakaforlife. org/anzac-day-haka-and-corroboree-abc-news-sydney/

Haua, I. (2017). *The Little Whare In Waterloo: Thinking About Māori in Australia*. Master's thesis, Macquarie University.

Hudson, M., Milne, M., Reynolds, P., Russell, K., & Smith, B. (2010). *Te Ara Tika. Guidelines for Māori Research Ethics: A Framework for Researchers and Ethics Committee Members*. Auckland: Health Research Council of New Zealand.

Jayasuriya, L., Walker, D., & Gothard, J. (2003). *Legacies of White Australia: Race, Culture, and Nation*. Perth: UWA Press.

Ka'ai, T. M., & Higgins, R. (2004). Te ao Māori–Māori world-view. In Tania M. Ka'ai et al. (Eds), *Ki te Whaiao: An Introduction to Māori Culture and Society* (pp. 13–25). Harlow: Pearson Education.

Ka'ai-Mahuta, R. (2018). The right to return: Challenging existing understandings of 'citizenship' in Aotearoa/New Zealand. In Calla, P., & Stamatopoulou, E. (Eds), *Walking and Learning with Indigenous Peoples* (pp. 66–81). New York: Center for the Study of Ethnicity and Race and the Institute for the Study of Human Rights, Columbia University. https://academiccommons.columbia.edu/doi/10.7916/ D8W68347

Kamira, J. (2010). Maori in Sydney. *Sydney Journal, 3*(1), 23–34.

Kawharu, M. (2000). Kaitiakitanga: A Maori anthropological perspective of the Maori socio-environmental ethic of resource management. *The Journal of the Polynesian Society, 109*(4), 349–370.

Kewene-Doig, L. M. (2022). *He Kohinga Kōrero: A Selected Group of Māori Musicians and Performers' Experiences of the 1960s through the Māori Showband Movement*. Thesis, University of Otago. http://hdl. handle.net/10523/12860

Kwaymullina, A., & Kwaymullina, B. (2010). Learning to read the signs: Law in an Indigenous reality. *Journal of Australian Studies, 34*(2), 195–208.

Lehman, G. (2008). Two thousand generations of place-making. In Vanclay, F., Higgins, M., & Blackshaw, A. (Eds), *Making Sense of Place* (pp. 105–108). www.wellingtonpark.org.au/assets/wellingtonpark_welcometocountry06.pdf

Mar, T. B. (2015). Shadowing imperial networks: Indigenous mobility and Australia's Pacific past. *Australian Historical Studies, 46*(3), 340–355.

Martin, B. (2017). Methodology is content: Indigenous approaches to research and knowledge. *Educational Philosophy and Theory, 49*(14), 1392–1400.

Netana-Glover, L. (2021). Complexities of displaced Indigenous identities: A fifty year journey home, to two homes. *Genealogy, 5*(3), 62.

Rigney, L. I. (1999). Internationalization of an Indigenous anticolonial cultural critique of research methodologies: A guide to Indigenist research methodology and its principles. *Wicazo sa Review, 14*(2), 109–121.

Rose, D. B., James, D., & Watson, C. (2003). *Indigenous kinship with the natural world in New South Wales.* Parramatta: NSW National Parks and Wildlife Service.

Simpson, L. B. (2017). *As We Have Always Done: Indigenous Freedom through Radical Resistance.* Minneapolis: University of Minnesota Press.

Smith, L. T. (2021). *Decolonizing Methodologies: Research and Indigenous Peoples.* London: Bloomsbury Publishing.

Somerville, A. T. P. (2010). 'My poetry is a fire': Wineera and Sullivan writing fire from Hawai'i. In Hokowhitu, B., Andersen, C., & Kermoal, N. (Eds), *Indigenous Identity and Resistance: Exploring the Diversity of Knowledge* (pp. 37–54). Dunedin: Otago University Press.

Te Aka Dictionary online. (n.d.). Wairua. https://maoridictionary.co.nz/search?&keywords=wairua

Tranter, B., & Donoghue, J. (2015). National identity and important Australians. *Journal of Sociology, 51*(2), 236–251.

Tynan, L. (2021). What is relationality? Indigenous knowledges, practices and responsibilities with kin. *Cultural Geographies, 28*(4), 597–610.

Valentine, H. (2009). *Kia Ngāwari ki te Awatea: The Relationship between Wairua and Māori Well-being: A Psychological perspective.* Thesis, Massey University.

University of Waikato. (2022). Research into ancestral sea voyaging. www.waikato.ac.nz/news-opinion/media/2022/research-into-ancestral-sea-voyaging

Walker, D. P., Ataria, J. M., Hughey, K. F., Park, P. T., & Katene, J. P. (2021). Environmental and spatial planning with ngā Atua kaitiaki: A mātauranga Māori framework. *New Zealand Geographer*, 77(2), 90–100.

Ward, R. (1958). *The Australian Legend*. Oxford: Oxford University Press.

Watson, I. (2000). 'Kaldowinyeri Munaintya in the beginning'. *Flinders Journal of Law Reform*, 4, 4.

Wilson, S. (2020). *Research Is Ceremony: Indigenous Research Methods*. Nova Scotia: Fernwood Publishing.

6

'Whānau: an interconnected world': re-examining Māori and Pasifika connections

Innez Haua and Dion Enari

Anecdote one, from Innez: 'An Australian, New Zealand and Fijian passport'

Several years ago, on Bedigal Country (what we now know as an urban suburb of Sydney Australia), I was gathered with whānau (three of my sisters), drinking tea and discussing the renewal and application of my passport. I am a citizen of New Zealand and a long-term, nation-state recognised resident of Australia. During our conversation, a member of my whānau talked about the complicated issues and often unreasonable obstacles they faced as a Fijian passport holder when attempting to obtain Australian residency. At this point, my eight-year-old daughter interrupted the conversation and exclaimed 'that's me too mum, I have a Fijian passport'. This statement was received with many smiles and some giggles from her Aunties and I. Unlike me, my daughter was born in Sydney, Australia. She is one of four generations who have resided here (so far) and calls Australia home. She is a documented Australian passport holder – and yet like me, she is Māori. My daughter's claim and, more significantly, her claim's intent, assumes that she is Fijian except that my daughter is of Aotearoa (New Zealand) Māori descent. Through me (her mother), she will trace her whakapapa (genealogies and ancestry) to all of Te Tairāwhiti (the East Coast of the North Island of Aotearoa). Through her father's lines, she will trace her whakapapa to the iwi (Māori tribal Nations) of the Mātaatua Waka and to Taranaki Maunga. Additionally, she has Irish, Scottish and English ancestry. Being aware of this, her whānau were amused but mostly endeared with her claim of Fijian belonging, especially as all of her whānau gathered there with us, were iTaukei (Indigenous Fijian).

Introduction: whānau means family or does it?

There are points in the conversation above that we will explore throughout this chapter. We discuss the complications of Indigeneity, cultural belonging and colonial nation-states. We also examine instances of the above account, those which exemplify the workings of whakapapa (genealogy) and relationalities of Indigeneity and belonging, where time and place (and the histories of these places) shape complex identities and Indigenous networks. They speak of whakapapa and whānau. These are all tenets of Indigenous relationality, connection and sustained connection (Mead 2016; Smith 2012; Wilson 2008). 'Family' is the most commonly used English-language translation of the Māori word 'whānau'. However, this is a simplistic and limiting translation. As Indigenous peoples around the globe understand and live, Indigenous families are not constrained and simplified to blood relations or a western nuclear unit of mum, dad and 2.3 children. Indeed, whānau in this context means so much more. Tai Walker in Te Ara, the Encyclopedia of New Zealand, defines 'whānau' as:

> part of an interconnected world of tribe and sub-tribe, of the living and the dead. Although whānau members may live far apart or even overseas, their ties remain strong ... Whānau is often translated as 'family', but its meaning is more complex. It includes physical, emotional and spiritual dimensions and is based on whakapapa. Whānau can be multi-layered, flexible and dynamic. Whānau is based on a Māori and a tribal world view. It is through the whānau that values, histories and traditions from the ancestors are adapted for the contemporary world. (Walker 2011, paras 1–2)

In addition to the above, the verb whānau in the Māori Dictionary (2022, para. 1) is defined as 'to be born, give birth'. Therefore, the word whānau, in any context, bounds significant meaning around English concepts of birth, family and belonging, as well as time and place. Whānau then includes Innez's extended Fijian family. It is the most natural way to describe them together and their understandings of what and who they are to each other in their Indigenous Māori and iTaukei ways of knowing and being. Innez's sisters are iTaukei, and while they are not blood kin or in-laws, Innez's daughter has known and loved and been loved by them all her life. They have nurtured her, helped raise and support her, as Innez has their children – as nieces and nephews, cousins. There has never been any discussion nor need for agreement of roles and titles. There have only been aunties, uncles and cousins – all members of a Māori and iTaukei whānau filled with aroha/loloma (love and affection). These examples of kinship and whānau can be seen whenever Māori, iTaukei and other Pacific Island people gather.

On the other hand, Barnard's Encyclopedia Britannica definition of 'family' reads:

> a group of persons united by the ties of marriage, blood, or adoption, constituting a single household and interacting with each other in their respective social positions, usually those of spouses, parents, children, and siblings. The family group should be distinguished from a household ... It should also be differentiated from a kindred (which also concerns blood lines), because a kindred may be divided into several households. (Barnard 2004, para. 1)

Certainly, there are many non-Indigenous peoples who connect with others outside of the traditional western understanding of 'family'. There are many inspired quotations that declare the sentiment that 'family is not always about blood' but there are also affirmations, such as 'blood is thicker than water'. Connection to each other is an inherent human quality, and this chapter does not seek to diminish these connections, nor the ways that we connect with each other. We argue that it is, however, a distinction of Indigenous cultures. Connection is an innate aspect of Indigenous identity, ways of being and everyday realities; relationality to each other, to land and waters, to the beyond human, to ancestors and descendants. These are all critical elements of Indigenous existence. In many ways, this sets Indigenous peoples apart from those who are non-Indigenous. We can often see evidence of this in English definitions of Indigenous words and concepts. They often do not (or at least struggle to) correctly articulate an Indigenous way of being in the world and whānau is a great example of this. It is a concept of unity and network, that is embedded in Indigenous peoples and cultures across the globe (Mead 2016; Smith 2012; Wilson 2008).

It may be easy to question a young girl's perception of her cultural self-identity and understanding of being Māori outside of Aotearoa, especially when she readily claims to be a part of another. At the time, Innez's daughter, with an eight-year-old child's understanding (or thankfully, ignorance) of cultural-authenticity complexities, did not question her cultural identity. On the contrary, she is proud of her Māori whakapapa and identity. To her – and in her own words – being Māori 'just is'. There is no conflict in being Māori and expressing herself as being Fijian, or from elsewhere. Chatting with her revealed that she associated family with whānau. She applied the definition of whānau to family, and not vice versa. Her understanding is that people are not required to be blood-related or married to be 'family' or whānau. While she knew she probably did not have a Fijian passport, it made sense to her that the 'application process' for a Fijian passport would include her, as not only does she have Fijian whānau, she also 'belongs' to Fijian whānau. Therefore, part of her world is Fijian. If it is a matter of presenting evidence, then it made sense that naturally she could do so. There was never a depreciation of her Māori identity, but rather, as she explained later, her expression of Fijian belonging *was an extension of it*. There is much scholarship by Pacific academics in education, health, and anthropology that also speaks of the simultaneous cultural belonging people/s can have (see, for example, Anae 1998; Lemusuifeauaali'i & Enari 2021; Mila-Schaff 2010). For example, for a person from the Pacific, being Samoan and Māori at the same time does not mean the diminishing of one over the other. Instead, one can lay proud claim to all cultures with pride.

Some years have passed since these conversations were had with a young Australian-born Māori child. Revisiting these topics recently with her as a sixteen-year-old has revealed that not much has changed. What is evident, though, is that her connection to iTaukei and other peoples, cultures, and places in the Pacific, has magnified. Her three siblings (who are aged between twelve and seventeen and who were also raised on both Eora and Dharawal Country) similarly describe their relationships with their Pasifika whānau. Additionally, their relationships with their Pasifika friends, peers and peoples in general is all encompassing. They express a shared identity with Pasifika. There is a real sense of one – of unity and solidarity – and according to these young Australian-born Māori, Māori and Pasifika are the same. It might be that, at this point, you are asking 'so what is the issue?' Many of us will recognise that Māori and Pasifika share ancestry, place, histories, ontologies, epistemologies, linguistical similarities and even physical characteristics. Is this not an example of unity and solidarity? In this chapter we unpack some of these encounters, for, until recently and for various reasons that we will examine here, Aotearoa Māori are mostly categorised as Indigenous peoples, culture and lands, outside of the term Pasifika. Aotearoa is situated proudly within the Pacific. This can be explained in a New Zealand context, but here in Australia, why are Māori not Pasifika?

Māori and Pasifika in Australia

We use the experience of Innez's daughter to highlight one of the many ways in which Māori and Pasifika peoples consider themselves and each other in the contemporary setting and context of Australia. In an alternative perspective, there are Māori and Pasifika residents in Australia who view themselves as separate from each other. Essentially, their argument is that Māori are Indigenous to Aotearoa, ergo Indigenous to New Zealand and, by default, this distinction of identity should continue in Australia. As Māori and Samoan researchers who have been raised in Australia, we use our experiences as members of the Māori and Pasifika diasporic communities to explore our networks of Indigeneity and connection. This chapter seeks to illuminate new aspects of identity and their impact on Māori and Pasifika communities and their connection with each other in Australia. We consider the inclusion of Māori identities in the collective term of Pasifika and how this manifests in the Australian setting.

Before we embark on this discussion there are aspects of it that we must first clarify. Te reo Māori (Māori language) and Pasifika languages are used throughout this chapter. With the exception of iwi (tribal) names and proper nouns, a brief translation in English is provided in parentheses at the first use of a term from these languages, provided there is no explanation of the word and its meaning is immediately forthcoming. A glossary is provided at the end of the chapter; however, this is a point of reference and does not include a comprehensive definition of Māori and Pasifika concepts of these terms. Macrons over vowels are utilised where necessary to follow the contemporary convention of denoting a long vowel. However, these have not been inserted where original sources have not used them. 'Māori' is a term used by people who are Indigenous to the Cook Islands and to Aotearoa, and in this chapter 'Māori' will apply to Aotearoa unless otherwise stated. 'Pasifika' in this chapter refers to peoples from the Pacific Islands who have migrated to either New Zealand and/or Australia, and their subsequent generations. 'Pasifika' is the preferred term as it is a noun of self-determination that includes all peoples from the Pacific, excluding Australia and Māori but including the sub-categories of Micronesian, Melanesian and Polynesian (similar terms to describe Pasifika include Moana Pasifika, Pasefika, Oceania and Pasifiki) (Enari & Haua 2021). 'Aotearoa' refers to the sovereign lands of Māori that switches to 'New Zealand' when referring to Aotearoa in the colonial context. 'Oceania' is a regional term that is commonly used to include Australia in a collective with Pasifika and New Zealand.

Both Māori and Pasifika peoples are migrants to Australia. The authors recognise that any discussion about their connection with each other in Australia cannot proceed without acknowledging tangata whenua (the people of the land) – Aboriginal and Torres Strait Islander peoples and their sovereign unceded lands (now known as Australia). As migrants to Australia, Māori and Pasifika communities grow and prosper on Aboriginal and Torres Strait Islander lands and they benefit from the ongoing colonisation of these peoples and places.

There is much scholarship on Māori and Pasifika connection (and disconnection) and several academics have written comprehensively about the relationships between these cultures. (Samu 2006; Te Punga Somerville 2012; Wendt 1982). Often, this literature speaks of these connections and history from the context of New Zealand. We do not dispute that Aotearoa and New Zealand are often the main stage for exchange and connection for Māori and Pasifika peoples, sovereignty, and futures. However, we believe the narrative is remembered with either a combined Pacific history or a contemporary relationship of Māori and Pasifika within a New Zealand or Pacific context. There is much less written about the connections and networks of Māori and Pasifika in Australia. This chapter will present some of the ways Māori and Pasifika foster connections outside of New Zealand and Pacific home islands.

A history of Pacific whānau and migration

In spite of the contemporary tone set by the title of this edited collection, *Global Networks of Indigeneity: People, Sovereignty and Futures*, global networks of Indigeneity are not a modern concept. On the contrary, global networks of Indigenous peoples have existed for as long as there have been Indigenous cultures. In 2018, at the *Whales/Tohorā – Discover the giants of the Ocean exhibition* at the Australian Museum in Sydney, Māori Ahorangi Professor Sir Derek Lardelli presented on tohorā (whale) (Australian Museum 2018). Lardelli spoke of a shared common ancestor – tohorā, stating that tohorā is a universal ancestor to all Indigenous peoples around the globe, which one can often see revealed today through global traditional and contemporary cultural practices (in, for example, creative arts and music). According to Lardelli, Indigenous peoples across the globe are whānau. For millennia, prior to European contact, Indigenous peoples with distinct and diverse cultures and languages fostered networks with each other. Beyond ancestry, these networks were founded on love and intermarriage, building intricate networks of whānau and kinship, sharing foods, arts, traditions and knowledges. Oceans and waters would not limit such Indigenous connections and networks. For early Europeans, fear dictated their knowledges of global geography and especially oceans. However, the fear of crashing into the horizon just before one sailed off the edge of the world was an absurd notion for Indigenous peoples, who were utilising their scientific knowledges to navigate around the globe, mapping out journeys with their whānau towards Indigenous networks and known destinations of Indigenous futures (Natanielu 2020). Centuries of Pacific Ancestors have travelled by waka/va'a (sea vessel/canoe) around the vast Pacific Ocean to settle in various islands throughout.

The last of these great Pacific Ocean migrations was from Hawaiki to Aotearoa. Throughout the Pacific, the journeys of voyaging ancestors are remarkable when we consider the vast distances that were traversed. According to current empirical evidence, Māori ancestors began arriving in Aotearoa from Hawaiki in the fourteenth century (Walter & Reilly 2018). However, there are Māori narratives and histories that dispute this, claiming the migration began centuries earlier. While Hawaiki is an ancestral, physical and spiritual place for Māori, its explicit location is not known. Both Māori traditions and western scientific evidence estimate its existence as a zone in the eastern Pacific Ocean (Walter & Reilly 2018). The history surrounding the great migration to Aotearoa from Hawaiki and ancestral connections throughout the Pacific can be traced through oral tradition and whakapapa. Each iwi in Aotearoa have their own whakapapa – specific knowledges of their creation with Aotearoa which may, or may not include, a Hawaiki migration whakapapa. The migration whakapapa can look like rangatira Rongowhakaata Halbert's accounts of waka origins and journeys in his book *Horouta* (2012). Halbert writes that waka connections can be traced from Samoa to Tahiti, Fiji, Rarotonga, the Tuamotu Islands, Rotuma and Aotearoa – just to name a few (see also Williams 2021). For those Māori who are descendants of ancestors of Hawaiki, they can trace their whakapapa – their whānau – to various islands and cultures in the Pacific. Contemporary migration for Māori and Pasifika continues to be journeys of known destinations and Indigenous futures, albeit, in different vehicles and often requiring specialised skills that can navigate colonial nation-state immigration policies. Māori are tangata whenua of Aotearoa, New Zealand – the Indigenous peoples, people of the land. New Zealand is also the residence for the largest population of Pasifika peoples outside of their Pacific home islands.

Many Pacific Island people were able to migrate to New Zealand due to their colonial ties. For example, up until 1962 Samoa was under New Zealand administration and, as a result, many Samoans prior to 1962 were able to reside in New Zealand without issue. Mass migration from the Pacific nations to New Zealand commenced in earnest in the 1940s and has seen a continual wave of Pacific people arrive for educational and employment opportunities outside of village agriculture (Enari & Matapo 2021; Va'a 1995). There are approximately 381,642 Pacific people in New Zealand with 49 per cent being Samoan, 21 per cent Cook Island Maori and 20 per cent Tongan (Stats NZ 2019). Although migration continues from the Islands, there is also an ever-increasing New Zealand-born Pacific population with, for example, fifth-generation Tongans and sixth-generation Samoans.

Within New Zealand, there is a clear distinction between Māori and Pasifika – – the Indigenous and the migrant diaspora. According to the 2018 New Zealand census, European residents comprise up to 70.4 per cent of the population. Māori follow with 16.5 per cent, then Asian residents, which includes Chinese, Indian and Filipino ethnicities, at 15.1 per cent (Stats NZ 2019). The combined Pasifika community sits at 8.5 per cent of the New Zealand total population (Stats NZ 2019). In spite of the number and diversity of ethnic minority groups within New Zealand, a collective minority label is applied to 'Māori and Pasifika'. The label is loaded. Within this label, the ongoing colonial struggle for Māori creates tension with a 'colonial diaspora' of Pasifika. Here, we refer to a 'colonial diaspora' with the understanding that prior to the colonisation of Aotearoa, migration from the Pacific to Aotearoa would not have looked the same. If we think about migration throughout the Pacific in relation to our oral histories, Pasifika would look like Tuakana returning to Aotearoa – the older brothers, sisters and cousins (of Māori) – joining whānau. A reunion of whānau. Te Ātiawa and Taranaki scholar Alice Te Punga Somerville (2012) discusses Pasifika and Māori relationalities in depth, recounting the Tahitian navigator Tupaia and his reunion with Māori whānau in Aotearoa when he arrived with Cook in 1769. At present in New Zealand, there is a convergence label of lumping together an 'underclass' of brown people – Māori and Pasifika. Throughout media, public and government discourse, the term 'Māori and Pasifika' has been used to further perpetuate negative perceptions of these peoples as a coloured nuisance to western ideals. Many Eurocentric organisations have used the term 'Māori and Pasifika' to suggest this minority population is undeserving criminals, thugs and an angry minority group (Enari & Haua 2021).

A Pasifika Australia

Global Indigenous networks inevitably include Indigenous diasporic peoples. For Māori and Pasifika in Australia, according to the census of 2016, the diasporic population of Māori is 142,107, with Pacific Island groups counted collectively at 214,635 (ABS 2016). Australia shares the colonial regional name and identity of 'Oceania' with the islands of the Pacific and New Zealand. There is also shared colonial history within the region and both Australia and New Zealand have at some point governed, through various ways, several of the Pacific Island nations. The Cook Islands, Niue and Tokelau are currently 'states free in association' within the New Zealand 'realm'. From 1902 to 1975, Papua New Guinea was a territory of Australia. The geopolitical association and proximity of nations within Oceania saw Pasifika and Māori migrating to Australia from the 1960s in larger numbers (Ravulo 2015). Relaxed border control in Australia with New Zealand up until 2000 saw a great wave of migration from both Māori and New Zealand Pasifika to Australia. In the years prior, many were motivated to relocate by the economic opportunity and prosperity that Australia was believed to offer (Haua 2017).

The migration of Māori and Pasifika to Australia has been disparate and, up until the start of the twenty-first century, the reception of Māori in Australia has been privileged. By contrast, the experience of Pasifika migration has been discouraged by Australian governments and society (Enari & Haua 2021). Historically, Māori have received special status over other migrants as well as Aboriginal and Torres Strait Islander peoples, with policy granting residential status to Māori in 1903 (Haua 2017). Around the same time the *Pacific Island Labourers Act 1901* enabled deportation of nearly all Pacific Islanders from Australian shores (Hamer 2014). This was also in response to the increasing numbers of the Melanesian 'blackbirded' population in Queensland – Melanesian people who had been coercively brought to Australia for slave labour (see ASSIS.org.au 2012). The Act also restricted immigration of Pacific Islanders – anyone suspected of being Pacific Islander would be immediately deported. And as late as 1971, the Australian cabinet agreed that Pacific Islanders were too 'unsophisticated and unsuited' to settle freely in Australia (see Hamer 2014).

Similar mistreatment of Pasifika occurred in New Zealand during the 1970s and 1980s, with a government 'crackdown' on illegal overstayers by raiding the homes of Pasifika peoples. The 'dawn raids' (Anae 1997) was a blatant racist attack on Pasifika peoples in New Zealand for which Prime Minister Jacinda Ardern formally apologised to Pasifika communities in New Zealand in 2021 (Perry 2021). While policy has arguably eased around immigration for Pasifika in Australia, there remains an inherently racist superiority discourse and mindset around Australia and Pasifika. This is evident with the various examples of offensive, dismissive language and actions exhibited by former Australian leaders. In 2015, immigration minister Peter Dutton was overheard joking with the (then) prime minister Tony Abbott about climate change facing Pacific nations stating that 'time doesn't mean anything when you're, you know, about to have water lapping at your door' (Wahlquist 2015, para. 6). In 2019, deputy prime minister Michael McCormack stated that 'Pacific island nations affected by the climate crisis will continue to survive because many of their workers come here to pick our fruit' (Smee 2019). And again in 2019, prime minister Scott Morrison was insulting and alienating of Pacific leaders during that year's Pacific Islands Forum in Tuvalu (see Lyons 2019).

With this in mind, the situation with New Zealand-to-Australia migration has 'many trans-Tasman migrants regularly identify as "New Zealander"' (including both Māori and Pasifika), and 'many Māori, duplicating structural relations with Pacific migrants back in New Zealand, prefer to be counted or imagined separately from Pacific Islanders.' (Teaiwa 2016, p. 111). This preference, we suggest, can be attributed to colonial labels and narratives enforced on Indigenous identities from the nation-state (Enari & Haua 2021). We agree with fellow contributor to this book Lou Netana-Glover (2021) in their analysis of Indigenous identities:

> the complexity of Indigenous identities in the colonial era is context driven and subject to affect by infinite relational variables such as who has the power to control narrative, and other colonial interventions that occur when a displacement culture invades place-based cultures. With place as context for identity, continued imposition by colonial forces has given rise to complex identities, born of the disruption that has occurred with the attempted annihilation of Indigenous peoples. (Netana-Glover 2021, p. 6)

In the case of Māori and Pasifika in Australia, there are two main 'colonial narratives' (and subsequent interventions) and two 'place contexts' shaping Māori and Pasifika identities. These colonial narratives are the identities imposed by the nation-state imaginations of New Zealand and Australia. At best, simplifying the complexities of these identities, and at the most, neutralising its influence begins with decolonising the way we see and present ourselves. This can occur through the acknowledgement of whānau connection between Māori and Pasifika in Australia.

Anecdote two, from Innez: an Australian haka in New Zealand

In 2018, the very same daughter mentioned above competed in the Tag20 Nations Cup. Tag20 is a derivative of rugby football, very similar to what is known as Oz-tag in Australia and Rippa-rugby in New Zealand. The rules for Tag20 are very similar to Touch Rugby, however, instead of touching a player with the ball to complete a play, one must pull tags attached with velcro to a player's hips to complete a 'tag' and a 'play'. The Nations Cup was hosted by New Zealand and the tournament was held in Auckland. There were nine nations (all from Oceania) with over 300 players competing, including New Zealand-based teams representing Samoa, Niue, Fiji, Tahiti, Tokelau, Tonga, Aotearoa Māori, New Zealand and two trans-Tasman sides: Indigenous Australia and Australia (Te Karere 2018). My daughter was selected to play for Australia in the under-13s girls' team. The tournament was held over three days and was a largely successful spectacle of sporting ability and whanaungatanga (establishing relationships). There was much attention from Māori Television and Te Karere (News Program) was present throughout the tournament. Much of the interest was directed at the Australian teams as the majority of the competitors in each Australian team were of Māori and Pasifika descent. To be clear, the Australian contingent was not an indicative snapshot of girls, boys, women and men in Australia who participate in rugby-related sports. On the contrary, Tag20 was and remains a newly introduced sport and is not widely played in Australia. Of the four states that were combined (NSW, Victoria, Queensland and ACT) to create an Australian team, three of the organising state committees were Māori and Pasifika, which speaks to the scholarship around sports being a point of network for Indigenous peoples, particularly Māori and Pasifika (see, for example, Bergin 2002; Teaiwa 2016). Tag20, up to this point, was played through participant snowballing introduction. That is, new players were being recruited by existing (Māori and Pasifika) players and administration, which meant that new players were often whānau, resulting in a sport that has a predominantly Māori and Pasifika presence.

At the opening ceremony of the Nations tournament, the Australian contingent (primarily the youth and children) performed the haka (posture dance) of 'Ka mate'. My children had been playing this sport in Sydney for the previous two years. They are active children participating in a range of sports, however, Tag20 is their favoured sport. They enjoy the whānau and cultural aspects of the sport, something that I had witnessed (over those years) evolving into a fixed component of Tag20. Feelings of comradery and whānau have been identified as important elements that engage and support Māori and Pasifika athletes (Marsters et al. 2021). In Australia, Tag20 holds biannual state tournaments where competing teams represent their heritage. In a tournament in Melbourne the previous year, my children represented the Sydney Māori and competed against other teams such as Victorian Māori, Victorian Samoan, Sydney Niue, Sydney Fijian and many more. The tournaments are opportunities for cultural expression and whanaungatanga. They are enjoyed immensely by participants and spectators alike. As participants of these heritage tournaments in Australia, my children were taught haka and karakia (prayer, ritual chants) with the unique opportunity to compete with and against whānau. It did not seem unusual to me that cultural practices were a part of this sport until my daughter and her teammates performed the haka at the Nations Tournament in New Zealand.

Te Karere captured the Australian contingent performing their haka at the opening ceremony and over the following days interviewed a few players from the Australian teams (Te Karere 2018). It is important to note that while there may (or may not) have been Aboriginal and/or Torres Strait Islander players in the Australian team, the contingent representing Indigenous Australia did not perform the haka. I remember watching the coverage on television over the course of the three days, pondering: what does it mean that a national Australian team performs a haka in Aotearoa; to Aotearoa Māori; Aotearoa Pasifika and Indigenous Australia? Compounding this, despite the predominance of Māori and Pasifika involvement in the administration and competition of the sport, there were a number of Aboriginal and Torres Strait Islander competitors. What would it mean to have another culture represent your nation? Travelling to and from the event with the Australian contingent, and engaging with the teams prior to the event and after, there was no objection from either Māori or Pasifika for all participants to perform the haka. The haka from the Australian representatives was performed by nearly all of the players regardless of their heritage with passion and unity, reinforcing the whānau connection for all of Pasifika.

An interconnected world

The two anecdotes in this chapter thus far help us identify the issues that occur when we re-examine Māori and Pasifika connections in Australia. Additionally, highlighting aspects of historical narratives of these identities contextualised within the colonial projects of Australia and New Zealand can provide some insight when addressing the above questions.

Today, there are many Māori and Pasifika who are part of generations living in Australia. Māori and Pasifika are rooted in Australia. The speed of recognising and acknowledging the sameness or whānau with each other is exemplified in Māori and Pasifika Australian-born youth. The excess baggage of colonial narratives and labels that has accompanied many first-generation Māori and Pasifika migrants has been shed for those generations that have not been exposed to them. Indigenous peoples are, in many ways, explicitly a product of place and belonging and whānau. For Australian-born Māori, where and how else would they perform a haka with the passion that contributes to and encompasses all of their identities? For many, they are both Māori and Australian and the opportunity to express pride in both seems quite appropriate on a sports stage in New Zealand. One does not depart from being Māori if they have departed Aotearoa, New Zealand. In addition, the audience of Aotearoa Māori and Pasifika have the potential to completely understand what is being demonstrated in an Australian haka. Expression of cultural pride, solidarity and whānau (to name just a few) will be recognised in their performance, essentially validating their identity, which is invaluable when we consider what cultural authenticity issues can look like.

The situation with non-Māori or Pasifika peoples in Tag20 performing the haka also raises some questions. However, in New Zealand this does not appear to be an issue. There are many non-Māori performers in kapahaka (haka group) – there have been non-Māori leaders of the haka in the All Blacks, for which they have received much praise. The Tag20 haka performance, however, did raise the question: what does it mean for non-Māori to perform a haka when their only contact with Māori and Aotearoa is through Australia? In other words, what does it mean if a haka performer's only experience of Māori and Aotearoa is in, and through, Australia? This is certainly the case for a couple of Pasifika players of Tag20. They were born in Australia and the tournament in New Zealand was their first overseas trip. This is an interesting situation as it highlights issues around Indigeneity and what it means to be Indigenous. Can one be Indigenous outside of their lands? Additionally, can one teach Indigeneity outside of their Indigenous lands to someone who is not Indigenous? These questions can be addressed in several ways. However, in the case of Māori and Pasifika – bolstered by the experiences of Innez's daughter – we argue yes. With whānau, yes you can. To reiterate Tai Walker from the beginning of this chapter 'Whānau is based on a Māori and a tribal world view. It is through the whānau that values, histories and traditions from the ancestors are adapted for the contemporary world' (Walker 2011, para. 1).

Of course, we cannot have a conversation about Indigeneity and Indigenous connection and networks between Māori and Pasifika in Australia without recognising where we are standing. In fact, we cannot have any conversations about Indigeneity without acknowledging Aboriginal and Torres Strait Islander peoples and lands. Forging connections between cultures and peoples on Indigenous lands is one part but, in the case of Tag20 (as one example), what does it mean to have another Indigenous culture represent your nation-state with their distinct cultural expression? What does it mean for Aboriginal and Torres Strait Islander peoples that Māori and Pasifika perform haka for an Australian sporting team? By default, Māori and Pasifika as migrants to Australia are settlers that benefit from the Australian colonial project. Is this an example of Māori and Pasifika being complicit in the silencing of Aboriginal and Torres Strait Islander culture and voices? Or do we avoid being a part of the colonial project if we consider the knowledges of Ahorangi Prof Sir Lardelli when we can all lay claim to the same ancestor? Certainly there will be many instances of Indigenous solidarity and network between these cultures. However, exploring the interconnections (and disconnections) between diasporic Māori and Pasifika, and Aboriginal and Torres Strait Islander peoples and lands is unfortunately beyond the scope of this chapter. The cultural expressions of resettled Indigenous cultures on other Indigenous lands raises questions of complicated entanglements. Given the huge significance of these interactions, connections and entanglement with Indigeneity, sovereignties, histories and settler states, it is an area that both authors are keenly interested in. We also believe and encourage increased dialogue between our communities as global Indigenous whānau, while simultaneously acknowledging that Aboriginal and Torres Strait Islanders are tangata whenua, and Māori and Pasifika are manuhiri (visitors).

Looking out from the Pacific Ocean to global networks of Indigenous sovereignty, network and futures, the view is positive. In the past five years, there have been several events of Indigenous activism across the globe that has strengthened Indigenous solidarity and networks. There is a new understanding of decolonisation and sovereignty: the future is network- and social media-led by new generations. While it is a rather dull and obvious claim to promote 'new generations' as the key to better futures, protests such as Standing Rock, Mauna Kea and Ihumātao are instances where these elements have been successful. Each of these events actively used social media. As Carlson and Berglund (2021, p. 3) attest these 'technologies bridge distance, time and nation-states to mobilize Indigenous people to build coalitions across the globe to stand in solidarity with one another'. These acts of solidarity did not diminish specific cultural identities. On the contrary, it illuminated their cause, the uniqueness of their people and their lands. Simultaneously, these events both inadvertently and deliberately exhibited the peoples and cultures who supported them. The argument that a term such as 'Pasifika' homogenises cultures and diverse identities is not disputed by the authors. The fact is, quite simply, it does. However, one could also argue that the collective naming of minority migrant populations of both Māori and Pasifika (in both New Zealand and Australia) has fostered solidarity between sovereign Indigenous peoples, and it has garnered positive impact. Throughout New Zealand and Australia, you can see Māori performing Samoan Siva, Tongans singing Māori hymns and Niueans preaching in the Samoan language, not as strangers but as whānau, aiga (Samoan) and 'ohana (Hawaiian). The performance of a haka in a Tag20 tournament speaks directly to this.

Combining Māori with a Pasifika collective can be considered a threat to the ongoing struggle for sovereignty that Māori endure in New Zealand. However, we argue that the positions of Māori and Pasifika within the borders of Australia presents these sovereignties in a different light. Both peoples, as we have explained, are migrants on Aboriginal and Torres Strait Islander lands. As Pasifika scholar Katerina Teaiwa (2016, p. 125) states: 'Australia is a "new" and certainly less understood or researched diasporic space compared with the United States and New Zealand, and one that has deeply unresolved racial politics, but it is also a kind of open field for Islanders to transform and claim in their own ways.' Decolonising the ways that the world has previously viewed Māori and Pasifika can change in Australia. It can be a place where Māori and Pasifika can tailor their own sovereignties, a collective that informs Māori and Pasifika identity as connected; one which speaks to our history, our knowledges and presents a future of a united and diverse whānau. The example of a Māori/Fijian/Australian girl performing a haka with Pasifika teammates for an Australian national team in New Zealand is but a microcosm of Māori/Samoan/Pasifika relations in Australia. These examples speak to Indigenous networks, sovereign identities and futures and so much more. There is immense pride in being sovereign and distinctive, but this pride can be magnified by knowing that there are many of us like this in Australia, not just connected by place and waka but through whānau.

Glossary

Ahorangi	Māori: Professor
Aiga	Samoan: Family, kinship
Aotearoa	Māori: Pre-colonial New Zealand. Lit: the Land of the Long White Cloud.
Aroha	Māori: Affection, sympathy, charity, compassion, love, empathy
haka	Māori: Posture dance
hapū	Māori: Divisions of groups within iwi, determined by whakapapa.
Hawaiki	Māori: Ancient homeland
iTaukei	iTaukei: Indigenous Peoples of Fiji. Lit: owner (see Vunidilo 2020, p. 2)
iwi	Māori: Tribe
kapahaka	Māori: haka group, Māori culture performance group
karakia	Māori: to recite ritual chants, grace, prayers
kaumatua	Māori: Elder/Elders
kōrero	Māori: To tell, address, talk; story, narrative
Loloma	iTaukei: Love, affection
manuhiri	Maori: Visitor, guest
Māori	Māori: People Indigenous to Aotearoa (New Zealand); natural
Mātaatua waka	Māori: people descended from the crew of this waka (from Hawaiki). Whose territories are in Northland and the Bay of Plenty
ʻohana	Hawaiian: Family, kinship
rangatira	Māori: Chief, noble, master
tangata whenua	Māori: People of the land
taonga	Māori: Treasure; of precious value
Taranaki Maunga	Māori: Taranaki the Mountain Ancestor
Te Ao Māori	Māori: The Māori world
te reo Māori	Māori Language

Te Tāirāwhiti	Māori: East Coast of the North Island
tikanga	Māori: Laws, customs and traditions
tipuna/tupuna	Māori: Ancestor/s (tribal variance in dialect)
Tohorā	Māori: Whale
Tuakana	Maori: Elder brother/sister/cousin
Va'a	Samoan: Canoe (Also Tahiti)
Waka	Māori: Canoe, vehicle
whakapapa	Māori: Genealogy; lineage and descent.
whanaungatanga	Māori: Establishing relationships; fellowship
whānau	Māori: Family. Kinship
whenua	Māori: Land; placenta

References

Anae, M. (1997). Towards a NZ-born Samoan identity: some reflections on 'labels'. *Pacific Health Dialogue*, 4(2), 128–137.

Anae, M. (1998). *Fofoa-i-vao-ese: the Identity Journeys of New Zealand-born Samoans*. PhD thesis, University of Auckland.

ASSIS. (2012). About ASSIS. http://assis.org.au/

Australian Bureau of Statistics (2016). Census 2021. www.abs.gov.au/websitedbs/censushome.nsf/home/2016

Australian Museum. (2018). Whales – Tohorā. https://australian.museum/about/organisation/media-centre/whales-tohora-discover-the-giants-of-the-ocean/

Barnard, A. (2004). Family. In: *Encyclopedia Britannica*. www.britannica.com/topic/family-kinship

Bergin, P. (2002). Maori sport and cultural identity in Australia. *The Australian Journal of Anthropology*, 13, 257–269.

Carlson, B., & Berglund, J. (2021). Introduction. In Carlson, B. & Berglund, J. (Eds), *Indigenous Peoples Rise Up: The Global Ascendency of Social Media Activism* (pp. 1–13). New Brunswick: Rutgers University Press.

Enari, D., & Haua, I. (2021). A Māori and Pasifika label: An old history. *New Context', Genealogy* 5(3): 70.

Enari, D., & Matapo, J. (2021). Negotiating the relational vā in the university: A transnational Pasifika standpoint during the COVID-19 pandemic. *Journal of Global Indigeneity*, 5(1), 1–19.

Halbert, R. (2012). *Horouta: The History of the Horouta Canoe, Gisborne and East Coast*, 2nd ed. Auckland: Libro International.

Hamer, P. (2014). Unsophisticated and unsuited: Australian barriers to Pacific Islander immigration from New Zealand. *Political Science, 66*, 93–118.

Haua, I. (2017). *The Little Whare In Waterloo: Thinking About Māori in Australia*. Master's thesis, Macquarie University.

Lemusuifeauaali'i, E., & Enari, D. (2021). DUA TANI:(Re) evolving identities of Pacific Islanders. *Te Kaharoa, 17*(1), 1–24.

Lyons, K. (2019). Former Tuvalu PM says he was "stunned" by Scott Morrison's behaviour at Pacific Islands Forum. *Guardian*. www.theguardian.com/australia-news/2019/oct/23/former-tuvalu-pm-says-he-was-stunned-by-scott-morrisons-behaviour-at-pacific-islands-forum

Māori Dictionary. (2022). Whanau. *Māori Dictionary*. https://maoridictionary.co.nz/search?idiom=&phrase=&proverb=&loan=&histLoan Words=&keywords=whanau

Marsters, C. P. E., Tiatia-Seath, J. and Uperesa, L. (2021). Young Pacific male athletes' attitudes toward mental health help-seeking in Aotearoa New Zealand. *Asia Pacific Journal of Public Health, 33*, 789–791.

Mead, S. M. (2016). *Tikanga Māori, Living by Māori Values*, 2nd ed. Wellington: Huia Publishers.

Mila-Schaaf, K. (2010). *Polycultural Capital and the Pasifika Second Generation: Negotiating Identities in Diasporic Spaces: A Thesis Submitted in Partial Fulfilment of the Requirements for the Degree of Doctor of Philosophy in Sociology at Massey University, Albany, New Zealand*. Doctoral dissertation, Massey University.

Natanielu, S. (2020). *Tautau: An Exploration of the Journey through Pain and Adversity*. Doctoral dissertation, Auckland University of Technology.

Netana-Glover, L. (2021). Complexities of displaced Indigenous identities: A fifty year journey home, to two homes. *Genealogy, 5*(3), 62.

Perry, N. (2021). Jacinda Ardern apologises for New Zealand's "dawn raids" on Pacific people. *Sydney Morning Herald*. www.smh.com.au/world/oceania/jacinda-ardern-apologises-for-new-zealand-s-dawn-raids-on-pacific-people-20210801-p58evo.html

Pryke, J. (2014). Pacific Islanders in Australia: Where are the Melanesians? DEVPOLICY Blog, 28 August. www.devpolicy.org/pacific-islanders-in-australia-where-are-the-melanesians-20140828

Ravulo, J. (2015). Pacific communities in Australia. Western Sydney University. https://ro.uow.edu.au/cgi/viewcontent.cgi?article=4901& context=sspapers

Samu, T. W. (2006). The 'Pasifika Umbrella' and quality teaching: Understanding and responding to the diverse realities within. *Waikato Journal of Education, 12,* 129–140.

Smee, B. (2019). Pacific islands will survive climate crisis because they 'pick our fruit', Australia's deputy PM says. *Guardian.* www.theguardian.com/australia-news/2019/aug/16/pacific-islands-will-survive-climate-crisis-because-they-can-pick-our-fruit-australias-deputy-pm-says

Smith, L. T. (2012). *Decolonising Methodologies,* 2nd ed. Dunedin: Otago University Press.

Stats NZ. (2019). New Zealand's population reflects growing diversity. www.stats.govt.nz/news/new-zealands-population-reflects-growing-diversity

Te Karere. (2018). Māori carving up for NZ and Australia at Tag20 competition. Te Karere. www.youtube.com/watch?v=WhLhKJO8I78

Te Punga Somerville, A. (2012). *Once Were Pacific.* Minneapolis: University of Minnesota Press.

Teaiawa, K. (2016). Niu Mana, Sport, Media And The Australian Diaspora. In Tomlinson, M., & Tengan, T. (Eds), *New Mana: Transformations of a Classic Concept in Pacific Languages and Cultures* (pp. 107–126). Canberra: ANU Press.

Va'a, L. F. (1995). *Fa'a-Samoa: Continuities and Change: A Study of Samoan Migrants in Australia.* Canberra: ANU Press.

Vunidilo, T. (2020). Indigenous iTaukei Worldview. *Te Taumata toi-a-iwi.* www.tetaumatatoiaiwi.org.nz/wp-content/uploads/2020/07/Indigenous-iTaukei-Worldview_by-Dr-Tarisi-Vunidilo.pdf

Wahlquist, C. (2015). Peter Dutton apologises for 'water lapping at your door' jibe. *Guardian.* www.theguardian.com/australia-news/2015/sep/13/peter-dutton-apologies-for-water-lapping-at-your-door-jibe

Walker, T. (2011). Whānau – Māori and family. *Te Ara – the Encyclopedia of New Zealand.* www.TeAra.govt.nz/en/whanau-maori-and-family/print

Walter, R. & Reilly, M. (2018). Ngā hekenga waka: Migration and early settlement. *Te Kōparapara: An Introduction to the Māori World.* Auckland: Auckland University Press, 65–85.

Wendt, A. (1982). Towards a new Oceania. In G. Amirthanayagam (Ed.), *Writers in East-West Encounter: New Cultural Bearings* (pp. 202–215). London: Palgrave Macmillan.

Williams, M. (2021). *Polynesia, 900–1600.* Nieuwe Prinsengracht: Amsterdam University Press.

Wilson, S. (2008). *Research Is Ceremony.* Nova Scotia: Fernwood Publishing.

7

Erasure, resilience, continuity: narratives of Sámi migration and contemporary culture in the USA

Ellen Marie Jensen and Tim Frandy

Introduction

During the period following the American Civil War to 1920, amid the 2.1 million Nordic people who migrated to the United States, smaller numbers of Sámi immigrants also crossed the Atlantic in pursuit of more opportunities. Despite the obscurity of the Sámi in migration scholarship, a widely circulated figure – of unknown origin – is that there are 30,000 to 60,000 descendants of Sámi migrants living in the contemporary United States and Canada. While not inconsequential, this number pales in comparison to the estimated 13 million people with Nordic ancestry living in the United States and Canada today. The story that emerges from Sámi migration is one of erasure alongside both continuity and recovery. Although some in the Sámi diaspora have acute awareness of their ancestry, the overwhelming majority of descendants are still unaware of their own heritage, which was frequently buried to spare them the pain associated with the low social status of Sámi people. Nonetheless, in the last three decades, an increasing number of North Americans are uncovering and embracing their diasporic–Indigenous heritage (cf. DuBois 2019) – a piece of themselves they often know with certainty was missing. Some of these people have formed semi-formal organisations, loose-knit local communities and online communities where they engage with each other and their Sámi friends and relatives from Sápmi (the Sámi homeland region). Many have also been called to work with other Indigenous people, to be allies and advocates, and to engage in political activism in solidarity with Indigenous peoples in the Americas and across the globe. Being both Indigenous and displaced from ancestral lands creates discord with most popular land-based conceptions of Indigeneity that exist in the Western world. The Sámi people who left Sápmi – whose emigration was largely driven by the economic, political, and social circumstances that emerge from Nordic settler colonialism – exist between the complex and sometimes overlapping spaces of Indigenous and immigrant, colonised and coloniser. The shortage of 'available narratives' to explain these nuances of migrant identity has been challenging to the community's sense of self, as Sámi migrants and their descendants attempt to define and represent themselves to homeland Sámi and non-Sámi alike. Mark Watson, among others, has pushed forward the idea of 'diasporic Indigeneity', which explores the continuities, ruptures, and reconnections that occur as an ongoing and dynamic process of identity-formation (Fox Tree 2015, pp. 1–14; Jensen 2019; Uzawa 2020; Watson 2010, pp. 268–84). Within diasporic Sámi communities specifically, Jensen has argued that 'diasporic Indigeneity in historical and contemporary Sámi America is a dialogic of 'consciousness' and 'condition'; that is, Sámi Americans express a consciousness of Sámi belonging flowing from a homeland called Sápmi, while living in a permanent diasporic condition' (Jensen 2019, p. 62). Frandy, however, locates diasporic Indigeneity within frameworks of learned ontologies and epistemologies of performative expressive culture, 'Because few Sámi Americans were given Sámi identity from birth, performative identity and expressive culture is deeply intertwined with the mechanisms of cultural revitalization and reclamation' (Frandy 2015), in turn causing sometimes racist critiques about a lack of continuity and authenticity in Indigenous communities. In short, being Sámi while displaced from Sápmi (and many of the corpus of accepted identity markers that have come to define Sámi identity) is no simple matter. It involves maintaining relationships to land and people, past and present, suturing the wounds of discontinuity brought about by settler colonialism, reclaiming tradition and identity, and building and maintaining new transnational and trans-Indigenous communities that thrive in our contemporary world.

Emerging from these ideas, we focus on the historical contexts of Sámi identity formation, Sámi migration to North America and the experiences of Sámi Americans from the Upper Midwest – focusing on two representative case studies of Sámi American descendants from the Forest Sámi tracts of Finland. As researchers, public humanists, and members of the Sámi and Sámi American communities (with more than three cumulative decades of active collaboration within them), we have deemed these two particular case studies as representative examples of many Sámi Americans' experiences that illustrate the complexities and struggles of identity formation today. We feel the case of Forest Sámi descendants is especially illuminating because of the high degree of politicisation of Forest Sámi identity in Finland today, because of the weakened kinship networks in these regions due to out-migration, and because they complicate place-based notions of Indigeneity. That is to say, we wish to present two case studies of Forest Sámi descendants whose experiences negotiating Sámi identity reflect the complexities of borderland and diasporic Indigeneity that are the reality for many diasporic Sámi today.

Colonisation in the Sámi homeland

The Sámi people are the only Indigenous people in Western Europe and the European Union and are recognised as an Indigenous people in all four of the nation-states where they live. They have been active in the United Nations Permanent Forum on Indigenous Issues and are also recognised as an Indigenous people by other Indigenous peoples globally. Until recent times, the Sámi had a subsistence-based economy, with varying degrees of nomadism and settlement depending on the specific economic subsistence strategies and resources they made use of in an area, such as reindeer, grouse, fish, berries, plants and edible pine bark flour. The Sámi people's traditional organisational unit was called a siida (in the North Sámi language), which roughly translates to a constellation of families or extended kin who lived, hunted, gathered, herded reindeer and fished together. In the sixteenth and seventeenth centuries, the extended Sámi siiddat (siida in singular) network extended over large tracts of Fenno-Scandinavia and Kola Russia.

The siida had an integrated relationship to the pre-Christian way of life, which was polytheistic and animistic. The changing pressures of colonisation, however, exerted great strain on many traditional lifeways over the past many centuries (outlined briefly below). For Sámi people, like many Indigenous peoples, the nature of compulsory exogenous drivers of change through the process of colonisation has come to both define and separate Sámi identity today in important ways from other Nordic identities.

The process of colonisation in Sápmi is extraordinarily complex, spanning back through the Middle Ages to the northward settlements of Scandinavians along the coasts in the Viking Age, and enduring today in the neocolonial policy of the Nordic states. In South Sámi communities, missionisation began (largely unsuccessfully) as early as the twelfth century. Built around 1308, the first Church in Romsa/Tromsø was called 'Ecclesia Sanctae Mariae de Trums iuxta paganos' (Rasmussen 2020, p. 270) or Church of Saint Maria of Tromsø in the Vicinity of the Heathens. Russian Orthodox monasteries reached Beahcáma (Petsamo) in the Kola peninsula in the mid-sixteenth century. Sweden-Finland had more than a dozen churches in Sápmi before 1700, and church-building on the Norwegian side began more intensively after 1700. In the interior, churches were often placed near winter camps, and Sámi people were expected to make periodic appearances to conduct official state and church business, including tax-paying, court, marriage and baptisms. In the village of Aanaar (Inari), for instance, Sámi people were required to attend church three times a winter and once in the summer (Inarin Seurakunta, n.d.). Beginning in the 1500s, the Sámi endured intense and often violent pressure to both abandon the siida-system of governance and to adopt Christianity, including sorcery-trials where Sámi spiritual leaders – noaiddit (noaidi in singular) – were burned at the stake, their sacred drums confiscated, and other forms of spiritual expression were violently suppressed (Hagen 2015, pp. 51–90). These religious pressures transformed into other assimilation policies that drove language loss, land loss, cultural knowledge loss, and economic disruption, peaking around the turn of the twentieth century (Lehtola 2004, p. 44).

In the 1800s, missionaries as well as other church and crown authorities imposed 'Lapp Taxes' as part of a colonial process to compel the Sámi to become Christian and give up their ways of life. In the mid-1800s, a powerful Lutheran revival movement, spearheaded by a Sámi-Swedish pastor, Lars Levi Laestadius (1800–1861), had taken hold in much of the North and Lule Sámi communities of Tornedalen (Kristiansen 2015, pp. 96–135). Named for its founder, Laestadianism quickly took hold in large areas of Northern Finland and coastal areas of Northern Norway. Both Sámi and Finnish Laestadians eventually brought the movement with them to the United States and Canada, where seven Laestadian (Apostolic Lutheran) sects operate across broadly intersecting Finnish and Sámi communities in North America. Despite adherence to Christianity, pre-Christian ways of life find expression in local Sámi and diasporic Sámi beliefs and cultural practices, especially in folk medicine, art, and oral tradition (Solbakk 2015, pp. 138–159), and in more recent religious revitalisation efforts.

In addition to the pressure to Christianise, was pressure to abandon traditional grazing lands and fishing waters. Settler encroachment took place at different times in different parts of Sápmi as well. Coastal territories like Ubmi (Umeå) in Sweden, which were used for seasonal reindeer herding Sámi until the early 1900s, had Swedish settlers as early as the fourteenth century. By the sixteenth century, heavy multi-state taxation in the border-regions caused increased demands for furs, which, in turn, is believed to have driven a major economic shift from small-scale intensive reindeer herding to the larger extensive herding practices that have come to characterise Sámi identity for centuries (Kvist 1992, pp. 64–65). Still, Sámi lands were historically recognised as under the authority of Sámi people, with laws like the Lapp Codicil of 1751, which point to the recognised sovereignty of Sámi peoples. However, with the rise of western European nation-states and threat of war between them, and with the rise of extractive industries coupled with improved transportation networks, the Nordic states invested in securing their northern borders. This project involved the manufacture of a homogeneous nation-state, wherein people shared a common ethnicity, language, religion, history and economy. In the late nineteenth and early twentieth century, Swedish eugenics and ethno-racial classification were also crucial elements of furthering the consolidation of the identity of Nordic nation-state (Keskinen 2019, pp. 163–181; Mattson 2014, p. 350). To justify the erasure of Sámi language, lands and lifeways, they were considered inferior relics of a bygone age, and it became the benevolent mission of the colonial state to 'modernise' them. The Norwegian state annexed the province of Finnmark in 1863 (Lehtola 2004, p. 44; Pedersen 2010, pp. 167–182) and mining operations brought large influxes of settlers and workers into Sámi areas. In addition to Norwegian settlers, many of the workers were recruited from Northern Finland and Tornedalen, including ethnic Finns, Sámi, and culturally hybrid people. Many of the Finnmark recruits were later recruited to work in mining operations in the United States, including in the Upper Peninsula of Michigan and in Northern Minnesota on the 'Iron Range'.

On the Finnish side, Finns actively worked to promote agriculture in Lapland through settlement and education programs. In the village of Aanaar (Inari), for example, Sámi families were farming as early as 1810, following the establishment of some Finnish farms in the area in the mid-1700s. And agriculture further developed in the region in the 1830s, after potato cultivation was promoted by a government initiative led by the Oulu Household Association of Ostrobothnia (DuBois 1995, p. 65; Kent 2014, pp. 29 and 237). Aanaar Sámi educator Matti Morottaja suggests that a community's upholding of the traditional values of humility, peacefulness, and deference ultimately worked against the best interests of the community (Lehtola 2004, p. 64). However, some of these changes are perhaps best understood as not assimilation but as strategic adaptations to ensure cultural survival, which have helped preserve Aanaar language, economic fixtures (fishing, reindeer-work, farming) and a distinct cultural identity from other Sámi communities (Frandy 2019, p. 32).

To the south, in Forest Sámi tracts of southern Lapland, similar processes were happening nearly a century beforehand, with a relatively sparse historical record detailing these cultural shifts. The Kemi Sámi language is believed to have disappeared sometime in the mid-nineteenth century. In 1829, Jacob Fellner wrote a short Kemi Sámi vocabulary based on his time in Salla. But by the time of A. V. Koskimies' fieldwork in Anár in 1886, the residents of Anár periodically made reference to the old Kemi Sámi language, and sometimes used Kemi Sámi phrases in storytelling as they voiced Kemi Sámi people. Still, despite the loss of the language, certain elements of Sámi identity endured, including subsistence practices, worldview, customary practices, oral tradition, and more.

As noted by folklorist Barre Toelken, all traditions and cultures are subject to the tensions that exist between conservative and dynamic elements (Toelken 1996, p. 39–40). Community members selectively conserve and change different aspects of their own culture – a process that is negotiated with other community members in embedded systems of social hierarchy and power – in relation to their immediate political, economic, and social needs, creating the appearance of divergence or drift between cultural groups. Because living within a culture is an ever-changing process, claims of identity are fundamentally rooted in the metacultural process of heritage production (Kirschenblatt-Gimblett 2004), as groups wrestle with each other over authority to claim which ethnic markers are fundamental to identity maintenance, and which ones are open to adaptation. This is to say that while Forest Sámi identity was grossly disrupted by colonisation – or at least disrupted in different ways than among reindeer-herding North Sámi – it was not simply made extinct. Rather, aspects of Sámi identity endured in ways that were befitting to the new sociopolitical contexts in which Forest Sámi (or Forest Sámi descendants) found themselves.

Divided over what would become four nations, divided by religion, divided by languages, divided by a large geographical area host to diverse environments, not all Sámi people shared in the same experience. Sámi people who lived in the interior – who were semi-nomadic and owned larger reindeer herds – had a greater degree of economic independence and less oversight from a colonial society than their relatives and kin living in close contact with settlers. Because of this, reindeer-herding mountain Sámi were in a better position to protect their language, their economic stability and a cultural distinctiveness based around extensive reindeer-herding that was better recognised by settlers. These elements of 'distinctiveness' have come to serve as the cornerstones for defining Sámi identity over the past three centuries. Although fishing, hunting, and foraging have always been as culturally significant as reindeer-herding in parts of Sápmi, they were not elevated to the same status as reindeer-herding because neighbouring Nordic peoples also were heavily involved in these subsistence activities (DuBois 2007).

Sámi who lived in colonial borderlands (like Forest or Coastal Sámi) in close contact with settlers had a different experience than the mountain Sámi in the interior. Coastal Sámi were enmeshed in interethnic fishing villages along the Norwegian coast where they often shared in the Laestadian faith with their Kven neighbours, and like Norwegian settlers, had been raising sheep since the Viking age. Many Sámi in the forested southern tracts of Sápmi adopted settler lifestyles, turning to a mixed economy of hunting, fishing, and gathering alongside small-scale agriculture. Forest Sámi lived in areas more conducive for agricultural development, and less suitable for large-scale reindeer herding. With the influx of settlers, their economies were stretched thin and destabilised through the increase in farmsteads (and disruption of reindeer migration routes) and through the rapid decline of the wild reindeer herds in the late 1700s and early 1800s. They necessarily spoke multiple languages, which led to earlier language loss. Their mixed economies differed only in degrees from settler mixed economies (combining fishing, small-scale agriculture, reindeer-herding, hunting, foraging, and later wage-labour in logging or mining), and they had better access to emerging transportation networks that better enabled out-migration when times turned hard. Though fully Sámi, they possessed fewer recognised identity-markers, allowing for Sámi to pass as Nordic more easily during times when being openly Sámi was being a target for ridicule, harassment, and even violence.

Because of the sparse written record, there has been substantial debate over the history of settlement in the Forest Sámi regions of Finland. Broad consensus acknowledges that Kemi Sámi people formerly inhabited the territories around Kuusamo, that Kainuu Sámi lived around Suomussalmi, and that Sámi populations formerly extended as far south as Lappeenranta. However, what exactly happened to these Sámi peoples remains in question: were these Sámi communities displaced, or did they intermarry with settlers? If they were displaced, where did they end up? These questions have generated intense and heated debate in Finland (Aikio and Åhren 2014, pp. 123–43; Joona & Joona 2011, pp. 351–88; Joona 2012, pp. 698–702; Junka-Aikio 2016, pp. 205–33; Laakso 2016, pp. 1–6; Sarivaara 2010, pp. 51–69, Sarivaara 2012). As 'non-status Sámi' have attempted to actively claim or reclaim Sámi identity, some Sámi have opposed their efforts, attacking their genealogical credibility, the veracity of church records, and the problems of claiming an identity rooted in supposedly 'extinct' Sámi groups. Non-status Sámi further contend that definitions of Indigenous identity linked exclusively to language, to blood quantum, or shibboleths such as reindeer-herding are colonial tools designed specifically to undermine and eliminate Indigenous people. While this debate is complex and speaks to the many important and unresolved issues of quantifying an amorphous notion such as identity in a highly mobile and increasingly diasporic world, suffice to say that there are a great number of individuals who legitimately claim Forest Sámi heritage and identity today, both in Finland and in the Sámi descendant community of North America, and it is important to recognise their lived experience as a valid and meaningful aspect of Indigeneity today. The point of our work is not to examine, undermine, or elevate the veracity of any claims on either 'side' of this highly polarised, unfinished, and painful debate, but rather to look at how Indigenous diasporic identity works as a process more than a birthright.

Cross-Atlantic Sámi migrants

Sámi migration largely coincided with the great waves of migration from Fenno-Scandinavia, roughly between 1860 and 1920 but, as illustrated above, the historical circumstances of settler colonialism leading some Sámi people to migrate to North America may have differed from their Nordic neighbours.

The first Sámi migrants documented through genealogical and oral history records came around the time of the American Civil War (1861–1865), with migration continuing until the early 1900s. Importantly, documenting Sámi migration in official immigration records and US-based census records has been challenging for a number of reasons, the foremost being that ethnicity was almost always aligned with the nation from which a new arrival had emigrated (Jensen 2005; 2019). In other words, with a few notable exceptions, the Sámi were almost always recorded as Norwegians, Swedes, or Finns on ship manifests and US census records in migrant and settler communities, thus obscuring their cultural belonging, language, or complex ties to various communities in Norway, Sweden and Finland. Another reason for scant evidence of Sámi migration was the aforementioned colonial assimilation policies. At the time the Sámi migrated, they had already been under intense pressure to assimilate. Many of the Sámi who came to America had already experienced forced language shift, and most of them had shed highly visible forms of dress, perhaps with the exception of reindeer leather shoes, jewellery, scarves, or other less identifiable clothing or material culture (Jensen 2019; Lehtola 2004, p. 44). Importantly, many Sámi who emigrated appear to have been from borderland communities, where assimilation pressures were likely greater, or at least more constant. We have, through decades of active participation in the Sámi descendant community, noted that although many different Sámi groups emigrated to North America, there tends to be proportionally fewer Mountain Sámi and a greater abundance of Sámi who emigrated from borderland communities. Although Alaskan Sámi have roots centred in the North Sámi epicentres of Guovdageaidnu and Kárášjohka, the overwhelming majority of Sámi migrants to the lower forty-eight states were from the North Sámi coastal populations, followed by Forest Sámi from Finland and then South Sámi from both the Norwegian and Swedish sides. Other groups represent much smaller numbers but include Anár (Inari), East (Skolt), Julev (Lule) and inland North Sámi peoples from around Gárasavvon (Karasuando). Although North American Sámi come from diverse parts of Sápmi, they have come to recognise a kinship with each other through their shared heritage and experiences as Indigenous settlers in the 'New World'.

Sámi people settled all over the North American continent, and their settlement patterns tend to mirror other Nordic settlements, with identifiable concentrations of descendants in the Upper Midwest (Michigan, Wisconsin, Minnesota, North Dakota), the Pacific Northwest (Oregon and Washington), and Alaska on the North Slope. Generally, people speak of two different experiences for the Alaskan Sámi who were brought to create a reindeer-herding industry in Alaska, and the hidden migration of Sámi to the lower forty-eight states. In the lower forty-eight states, two areas of settlement that stand out as the earliest destinations with documented concentrations of Sámi migrants are the Keweenaw Peninsula of Upper Michigan, with the town of Hancock as a regional epicentre, and the settlement of East Lake Lillian on the prairies of western Minnesota. In Canada, Sámi descendant communities exist near Toronto, Thunder Bay, Calgary and Vancouver Island. Many communities have witnessed visible development of Sámi American cultural revitalisation and consciousness which finds expression in events, social gatherings, publications, and festivals. In part, the Sámi American awakening, which began in the late 1980s, emerged from the revaluation of ethnic identity in the United States (which began in the 1960s), alongside improved access to genealogical and communication tools available through emerging digital technologies. Within a few short years, families whose pasts were buried because they were considered shameful began finding each other, connecting to each other, celebrating what survived, and participating in cultural recovery efforts. These developments parallel those of both other immigrant groups and those of Native American communities, with whom many Sámi Americans felt kinship. Today, several regional organisations exist, and a North American siidastallan (gathering) occurs every other year in rotating locations, as determined by rotating organisational leadership.

Due to their experiences of forced assimilation and discrimination in their home communities, it is understandable that first-generation Sámi migrants sought to blend in with both local Fenno-Scandinavian communities, as well as into mainstream Anglo-American society. Such desire to pass as Nordic has resulted in the community referring to the migration as 'hidden migration' (cf. DuBois 2019, p. 56). In North America at this time, the pressures to eliminate 'old world' ethnicities were intense, and a rigid ethnic hierarchy was crucial in defining one's social station and access to employment. Swedes and Norwegians held higher status than Finns, and Sámi people held the lowest status of Nordic immigrants. In part, these hierarchies manifested in the spurious Mongolian migration theory of Finnish and Sámi people (Kivisto & Leinonen 2011). We've encountered many families who had shameful whispers of 'Laplander' heritage, terms such as 'black Finn' or 'black Norwegian' that were used to describe the perceived racial characteristics of Sámi immigrants, and individuals whose elders repeated the tenet: 'Just because you're a black Finn, doesn't mean that you're not a Finn.' Pressure to assimilate to Anglo-American cultural norms was fairly universal for migrant groups in the mid-twentieth century, but in the case of Sámi migrants, there were parallel pressures to assimilate into several sets of majority cultural norms.

Few Sámi migrants from the first generation spoke openly about their Sámi identity with their descendants. We can assume this silencing of cultural descent was due to the intense colonial pressures Sámi people had been under to assimilate into majority Scandinavian and Finnish cultures, as well as the pressure to assimilate into Anglo-American culture. When first- and second-generation migrants have been confronted about their possible Sámi background by their descendants, the younger generations have often been met with a number of literal silences as well as figurative silencing strategies aimed at avoiding the topic of Sámi identity (Kurtti 1998; Wagner-Harkonen 2010, p. 10). Still, other first- and second-generation migrants shared with their descendants that their silences were due to traumatic experiences in their home countries, as well as to the exigencies of migration that prioritised survival over concerns over ethnic identity. Many descendants have also heard the term 'shame' in hushed tones in their families with reference to their Sámi heritage. That is, older generations were made to feel ashamed about their background and therefore resorted to silence to protect their descendants from what they had experienced as a burden. While silence and 'shame' have oftentimes been written about as the norm in Sámi American communities, there were certainly others who taught their descendants about their ancestry without hesitation. It is also critically important to point out that cultural continuity was manifested within Sámi migrant families through oral tradition, the Laestadian faith, and other folkways, even if Sámi identity was not spoken of outright (Xavier 2011).

In the lower forty-eight: East Lake Lillian township and the Keweenaw Peninsula

The community of East Lake Lillian Township was founded in 1864 by the Reverend Johannes Bomstad from Balsfjord, Troms Province, Norway. Bomstad was not an ordained minister but was nonetheless referred to as 'reverend' as the religious leader for a group of Norwegian State Church dissenters (Sundin 2013). Like many other religious dissenter groups in Europe, they migrated to the USA in search of 'religious freedom'. They founded the Tromsø Lutheran Free Church in East Lake Lillian, and while the congregation bore features of the Laestadian congregations, it had no direct theological connection to them (Sundin 2013). Like the Finnish and Sámi migrants destined for the Keweenaw Peninsula, the Balsfjord group arrived through Thunder Bay and made their way through the Great Lakes to Chicago and from there they travelled on to western Minnesota. The group arrived in October 1864, when winter was fast approaching (Sundin 2013). Unlike their Swedish counterparts who had also staked a claim and settled in the area, the Balsfjord community had limited economic resources to buy building materials and plywood. They made it through their first harsh winter by building Sámi-style turf huts, adapting their traditional knowledge to their new environment. Later, these structures would come to be called 'dugouts' by the descendants of both the Sámi and Kven settlers and Swedish settlers alike (Nelson 2001, p. 199).

In both local family lore and recorded history, it is well-known that Reverend Bomstad 'beat the Swedes' to stake the claim at Lake Lillian by a few hours, making him the official founder of the township (Sundin 2013). Over time, and with some prosperity, Bomstad travelled back to Balsfjord, Ullsfjord and Tromsø to conduct missions and recruited more dissenters to join the East Lake Lillian settler colony. Even after his death, many others followed. Swedish settlers were also from a group of dissenters from the Swedish Church who had migrated to America in the 1840s and first settled in Illinois. From the very foundation of the township, the Swedish community and Sámi/Kven community lived apart. The animosity between the two communities persisted for several generations. After the first road was built, it was referred to as the 'Mason-Dixon Line', a reference to the famous line dividing the Union and confederate states during the American Civil War. The Swedes stayed on their side, and the Sámi and Kven on their side. Local oral history maintains that the Swedish settlers looked down on the Kven and Sámi community, reportedly referring to them as 'sub-humans' who lived in 'dugouts' (Nelson 2001). While in the contemporary setting, most of this is spoken of in tongue-in-cheek among descendants of 'both sides', the discrimination the Sámi and Kven community experienced at the hands of the more well-to-do Swedes, and from the majority culture that had suppressed them back home, could go far in explaining why Sámi and Kven identity was suppressed in later generations. But alongside the suppression of Sámi and Kven heritage were expressions of cultural continuity, especially in oral tradition, folk medicine, beliefs, and extended kinship.

The first recorded Finnish and Sámi migrants to arrive on the Keweenaw Peninsula in Upper Michigan were from the northern Finnish provinces of Lappi (Lapland Province) and Oulu and the northern Swedish province of Norrbotten. Importantly, Upper Michigan is also one region of the United States where one finds a substantial concentration of Forest Sámi descendants, many of whom are aware of their Sámi heritage. The Great Finnish Famine of 1866–1868 resulted in Finnish and Sámi migration to the coastal fisheries of Finnmark and Troms in Norway, and many of them were later recruited to work in mining industries in the USA. Other Sámi and Finnish recruits had experience working in the mining industry in Northern Sweden (Niemi 1996, pp. 127–156). European mining companies had prospected for copper in the Keweenaw Peninsula of Upper Michigan, and a Norwegian businessman was hired to recruit experienced miners to work in the newly established copper mines. Soon there was a large-scale industrial recruitment effort underway in the northernmost provinces of Norway, Sweden and Finland (Kurtti 1998). Like the East Lake Lillian settlers, the first settlers to the Keweenaw arrived through Thunder Bay, Ontario, in 1864 and, by 1873, there were at least 1,000 settlers from the northernmost provinces of Finland and Sweden. Reminiscent of the landscape and culture 'back home' the new migrants referred to the Keweenaw Peninsula as *Amerikan Lappi*. As a matter of course, many of these migrants also brought the Laestadian movement to the area where they founded one of the first Laestadian congregations in North America. To this day, sermons are often given in Finnish with English translation and strong cross-Atlantic ties remain between the American Apostolic/Laestadian congregations from the Upper Midwest and Swedish and Finnish Laestadian congregations in the homelands (Wagner-Harkonen 2010, p. 10).[1]

There are also many descendants in the Keweenaw from Tornedalen with strong ties to Laestadianism. Many descendants of settlers claim pan-Scandinavian and Finnish heritage, where Sámi is also a feature of their hybrid cultural mosaic. Common adages in the area are: 'I don't really know where Finnish ends and Sámi begins' and 'I don't really know where Laestadianism ends and Sámi culture begins'. If looking for 'evidence' of Sámi heritage or ties to Sápmi on the Keweenaw, one need only open a local phone directory or visit a local cemetery to find surnames which are found among Sámi people in contemporary Sápmi or are indicative of Sámi belonging, including Rimpi, Keskitalo, Blind, Grape, Kemi, Hetta, Puolju (Buljo), Suompio (Somby), Muotka, Lappalainen, Laplander. Some descendants of migrants to the Keweenaw grew up with explicit knowledge of Sámi heritage, while others have discovered their Sámi heritage after conducting extensive genealogical studies.

Many – likely a majority of – Sámi descendants on the Keweenaw Peninsula have heritage from areas in Northern Finland that are currently not considered part of contemporary Sápmi. While there is a limited number of descendants from the Sámi domicile area, most Keweenaw descendants (as well as most Sámi Americans with roots from Finland) have ancestry in the municipalities of Muonio, Kittilä, Salla, Kolari, and Savukoski in Lapland, as well as surrounding Kuusamo on the Lapland provincial border. Many of these descendants (particularly from Tornedalen) also have ties to Laestadianism, either as practicing Laestadians themselves, or as descendants of practicing Laestadians. Oftentimes, it is their quest to better understand their faith that leads them to uncover their Sámi heritage. Finally, the people of the Keweenaw express a deep sense of belonging to both Finnish and Sámi culture in their festivals, events, genealogy workshops, and social gatherings.

Narratives of Forest Sámi diaspora

Although the many discontinuities present in many Sámi American experiences tend to obscure the continuities, the organised North American Sámi community – now more than three decades old – has created a network that both validates existing continuities and repairs ones that are broken. One Elder of the Sámi American community, whom we will call Donald, experienced these continuities directly, and has helped inspire other Sámi Americans to accept the resiliency of many Sámi cultural traditions.

At the time his oral history was recorded, Donald was well over eighty years old. He shared that his grandparents migrated from Finland to the small town in the Upper Midwest in 1893. By 1900, they had established a farmstead. He has lived in the small Finnish American town his whole life. In this region, there is a strong link between Laestadianism and the retention of the Finnish language over three generations. Most people his age have Finnish as their mother tongue and use it daily. He reflected, 'Even though I was born in America, I didn't speak a word of English until I started school. Just about everybody spoke Finnish here, even the telephone operators. We are all Finnish around here, and many of us are part Sámi too.'

He always knew that his father's family were not like other Finns. His mother's family and his father's paternal family were different. 'People could look down on us in the old days, you know. We were so dark and small.' But it was not until the 1980s that he heard the word 'Sámi' used at a local historical centre where they were holding a meeting with other Sámi descendants in the area. 'People here always said Lappalaisia when I was growing up. My dad told me that he came from Lappalaisia people. Most people didn't admit that they were Sámi or Lappalaisia, but there are many people here with Sámi roots, you know from the North.' He remembers that his father knew at least one Sámi phrase, but he doesn't remember it and he doesn't remember his grandfather ever talking about his roots. He did remember that his grandfather had made a cradle-board, calling it a *komsa*. He also remembered a local woman who used the word *duorte* for her spinning wheel.

There was a man named Piera, he was a Maraenen, he worked in the mines. There were some other people from Karesuando, from up there in Swedish Lapland. There were Raattamaas, and they claimed to be healers or some sort of shamans. They used to split the cow's tail. I am not sure what that was about, but it was some sort of ritual.

There were also women who did cupping, bloodletting, and massages. 'I have only visited Finland one time. It was in 1956. I went to my grandfather's place where my great uncle was still living and working as a reindeer herder in one of the southernmost districts, but it was still in the north,' he said, while pointing at an old faded black-and white photograph on the wall. In the photograph, his great-uncle is wearing a reindeer fur coat and standing with a reindeer.

When I got there, the place, it was far away from the main road. I had to walk 18 kilometers. One of my cousins met me there. He yelled across the lake for a woman to row over and pick us up. I was related to everyone there, and all of them looked like us. They were dark, short people. They did not live like other Finns, you know. They lived in a remote place, close to the Russian border. It was more primitive. They told a lot of stories about the war. My great uncle had a reindeer mark and had somewhere between 200 and 300 reindeer before the war. But after the war when they came back, they could only find thirty-eight reindeer with his mark.

Donald has been instrumental in opening a local historical society with a small museum. At the museum, he pointed to photographs of various Finnish immigrants on the wall, identifying all the people he suspected had Sámi roots; this he did within earshot of guests and other local people, in open defiance of former norms that dictated secrecy and shame regarding Sámi heritage. The small museum was packed with material culture, some from the earliest days of settlement, and some that had been brought over from Finland, including reindeer-fur boots and freshwater fishing nets and gear. Although Donald's family was relatively open in discussing their roots, most Sámi descendants spoke little of their heritage, which was considered shameful.

For many younger Sámi Americans, the silence and rediscovery – often inspired by elders like Donald – surrounding Sámi heritage has come to define their experience as Sámi descendants. With Indigenous identity far less stigmatised and with greater accessibility to information about Sámi people via the Internet, many Sámi descendants have unearthed their Indigenous heritage in a variety of ways. We have heard countless stories of Sámi descendants finding pictures of ancestors in gákti or even finding ancestral gákti stashed away in attics or basements, of elders giving yoik-songs to infants, and the like. Others discover their identity by reconnecting with relatives abroad, by confessions from elder relatives. 'I didn't grow up knowing I was Sámi,' explains one man whom we will call Michael, whose family is from Michigan's Upper Peninsula.

> We were black Finn. But as I became interested in my own roots, and started messing around with genealogy, it turns out my family wasn't actually from where I was told we were from. We were from Oulu, I was told. Well, this was sort of true. The province at the time extended up towards Kuusamo. And I was able to find my relatives around Posio and Yli-Kitka. Genealogy is messy, right? You can't always tell whose child was illegitimate, which of the people sharing

names in the village are your direct ancestors, or what other sordid secrets are hidden from the church records. But you're going back, and then you see that you've got an Aikio in your family tree. Or, you see a death notice for your great grandfather, who's just identified with a traditional Sámi name. I mean, it raises some red flags. So, how do you make meaning of it? What does this information mean to me today? While this didn't really change who I was, it did explain a few things, and help me understand who I was a little better.

Michael speaks of the disruption in his family, in part because the Sámi lines were mixed with Finnish ones from southern Ostrobothnia, the centre of later Finnish migration to the United States, and in part because his family was more concerned with where they were as opposed to where they had been. Like many families with northern roots, his family spoke Finnish in the United States and participated more in Finnish customs than Sámi ones. Still, he feels the identity was not completely lost.

In the woods, my family always acted differently: with a respect and reverence, with a humility and with quietude. I know some Finnish-identifying people have that too, and lots of them are from the same region as my family. But for me it's always felt more in line with the values of my Sámi friends. Make of that what you will.

Being in North America complicates identity substantially. Michael explains that since he grew up in the deep woods, that his connections aren't just to the abstract notion of bloodlines and heritage, rooted in distant Sámi homeland. Rather, his identity is more a product of his lived everyday culture, and the way he situates and conducts himself in the world. Lacking reindeer and salmon, the intensity of relationship to whitetail deer hunting and walleye (two foods critical to local Anishinaabe people) took their place. 'My relationships to the woods and waters are here. It's not about just reindeer. It's about how we have these mutually dependent relationships with the environment around us. We have a responsibility to take care of the deer and berries and fish, and they take care of us.'

Like many Sámi American families, Michael mentions feeling a disconnect with other settler families, who held values and beliefs that seemed quite alien to him, which ultimately led to a long bout of depression as a teenager and young adult. 'We would be told these things in school, that as white settlers we believed in humans being above nature. "What?" I thought. I'd give my own life for the health of our forests and waters. I'm part of this nature. I belong to it, not the other way around.'

When asked about the recent political tensions over Forest Sámi identity, Michael explains:

> It's difficult to be part of an unrecognised community. My family has spent years being excluded from all sides. We're not Sámi enough to be Sámi today. Before we weren't Finnish enough to be real Finns. And my grandparent immigrants weren't welcome to be called Americans. Racial biologists said in the early 1900s we were too Mongolian to be white, and now we're too white to be Indigenous. It's as if people only want to put us into these categories so that they can use our bodies, our stories, and experiences to advance their own agendas and view of the world. If people can gain social or political or economic capital by calling us Indigenous or Finnish or whatever, then they will invariably do so. It's exhausting. Do I get a say in any of this?

He continues:

> I'm sorry my existence is an inconvenience for your worldview. But am I supposed to lie about my ancestry? In the afterlife, am I supposed to tell my great-great grandfather that his culture didn't matter to me because it's been five generations instead of three since we had our language? I get it. I well understand my life is different from a reindeer herder in a big family from Guovdageaidnu. I understand the whole Cherokee princess thing, where community outsiders claim to have a drop of Native blood, often spuriously, to oppose Indigenous interests or sovereignty. But my family's trauma, their experience on the frontlines of colonisation, should count for something: a little inclusion, a little empathy, a little compassion. This history is Sámi history too. And we need better definitions of Indigeneity that meet those kinds of global realities of Indigenous people in the twenty-first century.

To rekindle connections, Michael has lived in Sápmi, studied Sámi languages, and been active in the Sámi American community to help cultivate Sámi identity and culture within diasporic communities. For Michael, his connection to Sámi culture is not an inheritance, so much as a continual and creative struggle to maintain his beliefs, customary practices and identity in a world that seeks to erase it from multiple sides. Connecting with other Forest Sámi descendants has been important for him. 'It's strange meeting someone whose worldview and beliefs you actually share,' says Michael, 'It's like coming home.' This community does not simply lie in an imagined past and what it formerly meant, but rather exists at the creative and generative intersection of what Sámi diasporic identity can mean for himself, for his community, and for the future generations. 'I want my children to have a stronger sense of cultural belonging than I ever knew,' he concludes.

Sámi futures from Sámi roots

Although Nordic nationalist histories of migration have obscured the distinct migration narratives of Sámi Americans, the tacit knowledge and re-emergence of Sámi descendant identity in North America helps demonstrate that identity works as a creative process of relationship building and maintenance in diasporic communities. Indeed, we stress that all culture, all tradition, all history is a product of the present and a creative re-invention of the past to serve varying social, cultural, political, or personal needs. All too commonly, Indigeneity has been confined to exist as a relic of antiquity, where traditional culture, knowledge, and worldview are regard as idealised states of the past that can only be deteriorated from. Contrary to this popular trope, Sámi Americans have shown how heritage-making, community-building, and epistemological and ontological shift can be a creative process of personal and social liberation that counters the discourses of shame that have historically pervaded Sámi migration narratives. As Sámi Americans rekindle connections to their ancestral communities, struggle to learn the language and culture, re-learn their hidden histories, participate in revitalised traditions, and learn better to see the world with Sámi eyes, they participate in the ebbs and flows of learning and unlearning, evaluating and reevaluating their own family histories in historical context. Although their ancestors may have chosen to abandon these identities under extreme duress for what they understood to be the wellbeing of their children, many Sámi Americans have decided to reclaim and re-assert this identity as valid and meaningful, both on an individual and community level.

Note

1 See also https://medium.com/our-arctic-nation/week-8-michigan-d9c590fe8a22

References

Aikio, A. & Åhrén, M. (2014). A reply to calls for an extension of the definition of Sámi in Finland. *Arctic Review on Law and Politics* 5(1), 123–143.

DuBois, T. A. (1995). Insider and outsider: An Inari Saami case. *Scandinavian Studies* 67(1), 63–76.

DuBois, T. A. (2007). *Fishing as Subsistence and Symbol in Sámi Culture*. Conference Paper. *Annual Meeting of the American Folklore Society*. Quebec, pp. 17–20.

DuBois, T. A. (2019). *Recalling – Reconstituting – Migration: Sámi Americans and the Immigrant Experience*. In Leinonen, J., & Kostiainen, A. (Eds), *Translational Finnish Mobilities: Proceedings of FinnForum XI* (pp. 49–68). Turku: Migration Institute of Finland.

Fox Tree, E. (2015). Diasporic Indigeneity: Indigenizing Indigenous immigrants and nativizing native nations. *Special Issue 2015: Ni sombras ni proscritos: Indigenous Presence in US Latina/o Community*, 1–14.

Frandy, T. (2015). Why they hid their drums in the mountains: Cultural reclamation within the North American Sámi Siida. Conference Paper. Delivered at the Society for the Advancement of Scandinavian Study's Annual Conference, Columbus.

Frandy, T. (2019). Introduction. In Frandy, T. (Ed. and Trans.), *August Koskimies and Toivo Itkonen, Inari Sámi Folklore: Stories from Aanaar* (pp. xxiii–xxxv). Madison: University of Wisconsin Press.

Hagen, R. B. (2015). *The Sámi as Sorcerers in Norwegian History. What We Believe In: Sámi Religious Beliefs from 1593 to the Present*. Ed. Ellen Marie Jensen. Karasjok: Čálliidlágádus, 51–90.

Jensen, E. M. (2005). *'We Stopped Forgetting': Diaspora Consciousness in the Narratives of Five Sami Americans*. Tromsø: Department of Social Science, University of Tromsø.

Jensen, E. M. (2019). *Diasporic Indigeneity and Storytelling Across Media: A Case Study of Narratives of Early Twentieth Century Sámi Immigrant Women*. Dissertation, UiT, The Arctic University of Norway. https://munin.uit.no/handle/10037/15353

Johnson, R. (1975). *A Samic View of Norwegian American Ethnicity. Norwegian Influence on the Upper Midwest*. Proceedings of and International Conference. Duluth: University of Minnesota, 121–124.

Joona, T. (2012). The political recognition and ratification of ILO Convention No. 169 in Finland, with some comparison to Sweden and Norway. *Nordic Journal of Human Rights 23*(3), 306–321.

Joona, T. (2013). Statuksettomat Saamelaiset Paikantumisia Saamelaisuuden Rajoilla (Non-status Sámi locations within Sámi borderlands). *The Yearbook of Polar Law Online 5*(1), 698–702.

Joona, T. & Joona, J. (2011). The historical basis of Saami land rights in Finland and the application of ILO Convention No. 169. *The Yearbook of Polar Law Online 3*(1), 351–388.

Junka-Aikio, L. (2016). Can the Sámi speak now? *Cultural Studies 30*(2), 205–233.

Kent, N. (2014). *The Sámi Peoples of the North: A Social and Cultural History*. London: Hurst.

Keskinen, S. (2019). Intra-Nordic differences, colonial/racial histories, and national narratives: Rewriting Finnish history. *Scandinavian Studies 91*(1–2), 163–181.

Kirschenblatt-Gimblett, B. (2004). Intangible heritage as metacultural production. *Museum International 56*, 52–65.

Kivisto, P. & Leinonen, J. (2011). Representing race: Ongoing uncertainties about Finnish-American racial identity. *Journal of American Ethnic History 31*(1), 11–33.

Kristiansen, R. E (2015). Laestadianism. In Jensen, E. M. (Ed.). *What We Believe In: Sámi Religious Beliefs from 1593 to the Present* (pp. 96–135). Karasjok: Čálliidlágádus.

Kurtti, J. (1998). *Finnish or Sámi? Finnish Settlement in Michigan's Copper County*. Árran: Publication of the Sámi Siida of North America.

Kvist, R. (1992). Swedish Saami Policy, 1550–1990. In Åkerman, S., and Granatstein, J. (Eds), *Welfare States in Trouble* (pp. 66–77). Umeå: Swedish Science Press.

Laakso, A. M. (2016). Critical review: Antti Aikio and Mattias Åhrén (2014). A reply to calls for an extension of the definition of Sámi in Finland. *Arctic Review on Law and Politics 7*(1), 10–17585.

Lehtola, V.-P. (2004). *The Sámi People: Traditions in Transition*. Trans. Ludger Müller. Fairbanks: University of Alaska Press.

Mattson, G. (2014). Nation-state science: Lappology and Sweden's ethnoracial purity. *Comparative Studies in Society and History 56*(2), 320–350.

Minde, H. (2003). Assimilation of the Sami: Implementation and consequences. *Acta Borealia 20*(2), 121–146.

Nelson, M. (2001). *Feudal Fire: A Case Study of a Northern Norwegian Immigrant Community in Minnesota*. MA thesis, University of Minnesota.

Niemi, E. (1996). Emigration from northern Norway: A frontier phenomenon? Some perspectives and hypotheses. In Gulliksen, O. T., Mauk, D. C., & Tolfsby, D. (Eds), *Norwegian American Essays* (pp. 127–156). Oslo: The Norwegian-American Historical Society.

Pedersen, S. (2010 [2002]). Norwegian nationalism and Saami areas as noman's land: Steinar Pedersen. In Karppi, K., & Eriksson, J. (Eds), *Conflict and Cooperation in the North* (pp. 167–182). Umeå: Kulturgräns norr.

Rasmussen, S. (2020). Post-reformation religious practices among the Sámi. In Høgetveit Berg, S., et al. (Eds), *The Protracted Reformation in the North* (pp. 265–287). Berlin: De Gruyter.

Sarivaara, E. K. (2010). Máttuid Giela Gáhtten: Stáhtusmeahttun Sápmelaččaid Sámegiela Eláskahttin Suoma Bealde Sámis (Saving the language of our ancestors: Language revitalization of 'non-status'). *Sami on the Finnish Side of Sápmi*, 51–69.

Sarivaara, E. K. (2012). *Statuksettomat Saamelaiset: Paikantumisia Saamelaisuuden Rajoilla* (Vol. 2/2012). Guovdageaidnu: Sámi Allaskuvla.

Solbakk, A. (2015). Nature Heals Guvhlláruššan: An Introduction to the Tradition of t Sámi Folk Medicine. In Jensen, E. M. (Ed.), *What We Believe In: Sámi Religious Beliefs from 1593 to the Present* (pp. 11–47). Karasjok: Čáliidlágádus.

Sundin, R. (2013). *The Salt of the Earth: The Lake Lillian Colonists: Who They Really Were Part I*. Árran: Publication of the Sámi Siida of North America.

Toelken, B. (1996). *The Dynamics of Folklore*. Logan: Utah State University Press.

Uzawa, K. (2020). *Crafting Our Future Together: Urban Diasporic Indigeneity from an Ainu Perspective in Japan*. UiT Norges Arktiske Universitet Institutt for Samfunnsvitenskap. Dissertation.

Wagner-Harkonen, J. (2010). Honoring our Sami ancestors. *Finnish American Reporter, 12*.

Watson, M. K. (2010). Diasporic Indigeneity: Place and the articulation of Ainu identity in Tokyo, Japan. *Environment and Planning A 42*(2), 268–284.

Wisuri, M. (1998). Cromwell Sami settlement. http://home.earthlink.net/~arran2/archive/crom.htm

Xavier, J. E. (2011). *Interview*. Ellen Marie Jensen.

8

Weaving Indigenous relationalities for the Anthropocene: activating ground-up networks across Ngurras (Countries)

Jo Anne Rey

Introduction

Floods, fires, famines and pestilences (with the COVID-19 pandemic as the latest example): these are the conditions playing out across the globe within the Anthropocene – where human-centricity, driven by patriarchal hierarchies, has dominated and decimated ecological networks for at least 2000 years (Plumwood 1993). More recently, across more than 200 years, on the continent today known as 'Australia', this domination has clubbed the delicate balances of Nature more rapidly and stridently through the enacted narratives of 'progress' to the point where human beings have forced planetary systemic imbalances, destroying lives, cultures, and ecosystems globally (Plumwood 1991). These approaches have focused on sucking from, rather than nurturing for, regeneration and sustainable futures. Systemic existential threats are now not only affecting other-than-humans but also ourselves. This human-centric thuggery ignores the place of relationality and human reliance on the systems of other-than-humans (Intergovernmental Panel on Climate Change (IPCC) 2021; Pugliese 2020).

It could be argued that human agency is functioning now as a kind of human-centric vortex, which disrupts and sucks winds, waters, landscapes and regional climatic zones, hastening extinctions. As reported in relation to recent megafires in south-eastern Australia:

> There is emerging evidence from ecosystems worldwide that catastrophic events such as extreme drought and large bushfires can push terrestrial ecosystems past tipping points that result in abrupt

ecosystem change ... During the spring and summer of 2019–2020 south-eastern Australia experienced a severe bushfire season (the 'Black Summer') during which millions of hectares of natural vegetation along the eastern coast, much of which had already been exposed to prolonged drought and record high temperatures, were burnt. The area burned was almost an order of magnitude larger than other major global fires of the past decade. Given the magnitude of this event we now need to identify and prioritise conservation and recovery actions across the fire-affected areas ... Some 200 major fires burnt through 10.4 million hectares (Mha; ca. 25.7 million acres) of land in south-eastern Australia until extinguished or brought under control in mid-February 2020.

Our findings show that the megafires extensively burnt a broad range of vegetation communities, including 72–83% of rainforests, eucalypt forests and woodlands, and shrublands and heathlands within individual subcontinental-scale bioregions. (Godfree et al. 2021, p. 2)

Additionally, according to the Australian Conservation Foundation (ACF), Australia's cities and towns are in an 'extinction crisis' (ACF 2020, p. 1). Their report focuses on the often-overlooked biodiversities within towns and cities in the context of broader environmental extinction narratives. As Ives and colleagues (2016, cited in ACF 2020, p. 7) show, '25% of all nationally listed threatened plants and 46% of nationally listed threatened animals can be found in Australia's 99 cities and towns'. These cities and towns have arisen since British invasion in 1788, a mere 232 years in comparison to more than 65,000 years of Indigenous sustainable relational sovereignty on this continent. On Dharug Ngurra (Country), also known as most of the Sydney Basin, which is now Australia's largest urbanised area, these factors come together and are expressed in a persistent determination by governmental agencies to respond to human-centric needs at the expense of other-than-humans. As such, governance persists as a patriarchal, hierarchical, and colonising paradigm that enacts destructive agency over other-than-humans, rather than acknowledging any relationality and agency underpinning Indigenous ways of knowing being and doing (Rey 2019; Watson 2015). Such an approach to governance poses questions about the place of ethical sovereignty rather than bureaucratic sovereignty. 'Sovereignty' is defined here as ultimate authority. Why should sovereignty continue to be enacted through unsustainable practices? Why should sovereignty be considered worthy or appropriate when that sovereignty creates extinctions of bio-diversities upon which human sustainability relies?

This chapter contests the premise that colonising bureaucratic governance can equate to 'ethical sovereignty' when the system neglects the Indigenous (human-other-than human) sovereignty of natural systems on planet Earth. Recent work focusing on localised activism highlights successful efforts to decompose hundreds of years of Anthropocentric benefit, at the expense of local, regional, and global sovereignties (Larsen & Johnson 2017; Ngurra et al. 2019; Rey 2021b). However, the fundamental argument raised, relevant to Dharug Ngurra/Sydney, in particular, and more broadly, settler-colonised areas in 'Australia' and by extension globally rests first in the ill-legality (my term, a form of legality making others ill) of the current colonial legatee sovereignty, and secondly in the noxious top-down governance structures that colonising bureaucratic systems have developed and imposed. Given the current global challenges that climate-change is producing, with repercussions that are a direct consequence of the European mentalities that drove conquest and colonisation from 1492 to 1914, across more than 80 per cent of the entire world, this chapter contributes examples of localised activism to foster alliances with other colonised peoples to challenge and demand ethical sovereignty for globally sustainable futures.

The ill-legality of colonisation derives from the false premise that British law enacted through colonisation should be countenanced and continued even though there is/are no treaty/treaties. As Indigenous scholar Moreton-Robinson (2007) shows, this falsity is further fostered through international law. As such, from an ethical perspective, sustainable natural law, or as Coorong peoples' Elder and Professor Irene Watson (2015, p. 1) calls it, Indigenous 'raw law', offers an alternative that benefits all interconnected sentience. This authority is evidenced through 65,000 years of sustainable practice as precedent, maintained through Ngurra-centric, rather than human-centric practices. Therefore, given that it is the cities and towns where such ill-legal bureaucratic sovereignty is causing extinction crises, it is within those cities and towns that activating grounded, localised Ngurra-centric raw law is most required.

Accordingly, using three New South Wales (NSW) bureaucratic examples: Local Aboriginal Land Councils (LALCs), the
Aboriginal Heritage Information Management System (AHIMS)
and state-based education, I will evidence how the system effectively extinguishes traditional custodians' rights to their own voice,
knowledges and educational practices on Dharug Ngurra, when
they are supposedly established for the benefit of Aboriginal communities. Ethical and ecological sovereignties are then discussed
as the basis for an alternative and sustainable future framing for
Dharug Ngurra. Finally, by drawing from current educational
pedagogy and research (Rey 2021b) into three Dharug Ngurra
sites: Yallomundee (Shaw's Creek Aboriginal site), The Blacktown
Native Institution site (BNI, Plumpton) and Brown's Waterhole
(Lane Cove National Park), consideration of re-emerging relational
sovereignty and the agency of interconnectedness as the essence of
Indigenous sovereign practice is presented as a foundation for sustainable futures and ethical sovereignty.

False sovereignty: inscribing unethical and unsustainable possession of Ngurra

The foundation of enacted 'sovereignty' by the existing ill-legal
system on this continent today is white patriarchal violence, ignorance, and has, as Colin Tatz (2017) described, 'genocidal intent'.
While internationally it is term for the 'supreme authority' of a
state (Moreton-Robinson 2007, p. 35), in the case of an 'Australia'
without a treaty, the notion of 'supreme authority' is open to inter-
pretation as to whose or what authority is supreme. This arose with
colonisation on Dharug and Dharawal people's Ngurra with the
British arrival in 1788. Rather than 'supreme authority', it is a sovereignty embedded in unethical practices towards and against the
Indigenous peoples of the Australia today across two centuries and
implemented through biopolitical destructions (Pugliese 2020). As
Special Rapporteur of the UN Study on Treaties, Miguel Martinez
found, there was an 'ethical dilemma' within the 'Indigenous problematic' (Watson 2015, p. 146).

At the centre of the settler–colonialist agenda is the appe-
tite for possession (Moreton-Robinson 2015). The Indigenous

custodians, and their critical collective sustainable care for Ngurra were removed, either through massacres or dispersal, and became part and parcel of the focus of Indigenous genocide and associated Indigenous ecocide (Reynolds 1987; Tatz 2017; Watson 2015). Removing the resistant Indigene (human and other-than-human) when necessary is integral to the colonising agenda of possession (Moreton-Robinson 2015; Pugliese 2020). As Kyle Powys Whyte, of the Potawatomi people, explains:

> Settlers can only make a homeland by creating social institutions that physically carve their origin, religious and cultural narratives, social ways of life and political and economic systems (e.g., property) into the waters, soils, air and other environmental dimensions of territory or landscape. That is, settler ecologies have to be inscribed into Indigenous ecologies. (Whyte 2016, cited in Pugliese 2020, p. 84)

These possession-inscriptions were carved into human bodies, landscapes, languages, and other-than-humans. As such, colonial sovereignty has been unethically enforced by the British replacing original supreme authority through Indigenous law by ill-legally inscribing their own authority on Dharug Ngurra. As apologies from former Labor prime ministers Paul Keating (1992), known as the 'Redfern Speech', and Kevin Rudd (2008), known as the 'Stolen Generations Apology' prove, if there hadn't been unethical and violent practices enacted, there wouldn't have been a need for apologies.

Until the ill-legality of the existing 'Australian' sovereignty-without-treaty question is settled, the coloniser's vulnerability continues to be exposed, and its *raison d'être* to take over, possess and consume the Indigene (human and other-than-human) remains. As Watson (2015, p. 155), strongly argues:

> The Australian state is unable to point to any evidence of any First Nations having renounced sovereignty … The question remains: by what lawful authority did imperial Britain assume sovereignty over First Nations territories? By what means, other than by force of arms, could First Nations have been deprived of their sovereignty?

What also continues to remain unsettled is by what 'supreme authority' does the settler–coloniser have the ethical right to consume the Indigene (both human and other-than-human)? As Karskens (2010) notes, it was the early vulnerabilities creating myopic self-interest of the colonising British agenda that perpetrated consumption of the Indigene for the purpose of possession. It was the later vulnerabilities and myopic self-interest of the convicts and settlers that established the narratives to become colonial settlers (Karskens 2020). In the process, consumption of the Indigene (human and other-than-human) was enacted.

According to Moreton-Robinson (2007, p. 4) 'the possessive logic of patriarchal white sovereignty operates to ensure its continued investments in itself'. This sovereignty is articulated through the privileging of the democratic process 'where citizenship rights are the means through which Indigenous rights should be contained and exercised' (Moreton-Robinson 2007, p. 6). Such is the universalising and self-perpetuating logic that characterises the continuing colonising mentalities and agendas into the twenty-first century.

It is a myopic narrative that funnels relationality through a fabricated hierarchical prism. As Moreton-Robinson (2007, p. 6) further notes, neo-liberalism holds that the narratives of Indigenous peoples' suffering arise from 'dysfunctional cultural traditions and social pathology'. Neo-liberalism continues the myopic viewpoint that cannot allow for any other perspective, because if another system and or perspective is given credence, then that throws into doubt the righteousness of colonising mentalities and agendas that sustain it. It becomes vulnerable and unsustainable.

One example involves the famous case brought by Eddie Mabo, who held ownership of Mer (Murray Island), in the group of islands located in the Torres Strait, north of Australia. On 3 June 1992 the decision by the High Court of Australia recognised for the first time the traditional rights of the Meriam people to their land, and as such held that native title existed for all Indigenous people of the continent called 'Australia'. However, as Falk and Martin (2007) discuss, even former Chief Justice of Australia, Justice Brennan recognised the vulnerability and unsustainability of the colonising practices of the last 234 years, when he proposed 'that recognising Indigenous sovereignty would fracture the skeleton of the law' (Moreton-Robinson 2007, p. 7). Thus, within the judiciary, there is an incentive to deny the reality of pre-existing (and continuing) Indigenous law because that would be too great a threat to the status-quo.

Nevertheless, without engaging with Indigenous raw law there can be no sustainable justice only unsustainable possession, and what Pugliese (2020) calls 'necropolitical agendas'. The 'possessor' mentality itself becomes possessed: a system I call the 'possessed-possessor', as eventually it consumes everything upon which it relies. Linking settler–colonialist agendas for possession and bio-necropolitical outcomes clarifies what we are seeing playing out in urbanised settings today. Both transgress Indigenous ways of knowing, being, and doing and ultimately consume the consumer rather than the Indigene as natural systems, previously equanimous upon which humans rely, become increasingly unbalanced.

To clarify, raw law is founded on relational respect and reciprocity. Indigenous sustainable sovereignty is underpinned and practised through a logical and nurturing web of interconnective and interactive relationships. Those relationships enact respect and reciprocity through connection, caring and belonging to presences, places, and people within and across Ngurra (Rey 2019). The applied logic of raw law demonstrates that without active connection to Ngurra, there cannot be caring and a sense of belonging (through care and connection) cannot be grown. Without caring for Ngurra, Ngurra cannot sustain community. Caring for Ngurra (presences, places and people) strengthens community. Strong communities raise strong families. Strong families raise strong individuals – strong in connection, caring and belonging. Thus, the sustainable cycle of continuing human health and wellbeing is embedded within Ngurra, and the inter-woven natural systems of Indigenous law. Through more than 65,000 years of continuing First Nations' applied logic, it becomes the definition of sustainable practice. The web of sustainable logic and interconnectivity sustains First Nations health and wellbeing (Burgess et al. 2009).

On Dharug Ngurra, unfortunately, as in many towns and cities, human-centricity and the hunger to possess results in colonising and noxious sovereignty inscribing itself into landscapes through disconnections, uncaring and reinforced by a lack of a sense of belonging. Without caring for Ngurra, conditions are fostered that, when combined with climate changing weather patterns, result in catastrophic consequences such as the mega-fires experienced in what has been referred to as the 'Black Summer' of 2019–2020

(ACF 2020). In Sydney, as polluted creeks pollute the rivers, as development for ever-more housing eats the natural landscapes that support ecological balances, as coastal foreshores are ripped away in ever-more violent storms that damage and topple houses with them, and as historically predictable floods wash away housing developments that ignored the knowledges that have fostered the rivers forever, clearly, following neo-liberal agendas for human-centric development cannot be legitimate as they are unsustainable.

At the time of writing, the UN's Intergovernmental Panel on Climate Change (IPCC) 2021 scientific report on the state of climate change affecting the planet has just been published. It clearly articulates and reinforces previous reports expressing the dire consequences that will unfold if governments do not change course. Across this continent, the current recalcitrant government continues to be deaf to the call for dramatic change and blind to the damage the last 234 years of 'possession politics' (my term) has done to this continent. Human futures are now at risk because of the possessed-possessor policies that refuse respectful, reciprocal relationship with the Indigene (human and other-than-human). Instead, false sovereignty is spun through a web of hierarchical, patriarchal systems of power. For the purposes of this work, three examples are provided to illustrate how the possessed-possessor works through bureaucratic systems to enact false relationships with the Indigene in Dharug Ngurra.

False relationships and fabricated authorities: a noxious web on Dharug Ngurra

Having outlined the way false sovereignty has historically been inscribed across Ngurra, and how that process has unethically had noxious impacts not only on Indigenous peoples but also broader human and other-than-human ecologies for the purpose of possession, this section focuses on the way that false sovereignty is currently spun across Dharug Ngurra. Three examples of state bureaucracy are provided. Supposedly established for the benefit of Indigenous peoples (as homogeneous 'other'), instead they are consuming Ngurra and the traditional custodians and follow the consumptive practices of the possessed-possessor, setting a 'divide and conquer' process in place. They are: local Aboriginal land councils (ALCs), the Aboriginal Heritage Information Management System (AHIMS) and state education.

Aboriginal Land Councils

Aboriginal Land Councils in NSW began as a state-wide non-statutory initiative by various individual Aboriginal activists forming a coalition to fight for land rights at the Black Theatre in Redfern, on Dharug Ngurra, in 1977. Their intentions and aspirations embraced raw law:

They called for community ownership of land on the basis of traditional ownership rights, cultural heritage, and social and economic needs; and emphasised the aspirations of local communities to have direct control over the land they occupied. In addition, most of the claims called for compensation for loss of land, loss of livelihood, and damage to 'our Dreamtime, to our culture and society, to our tribes … and to all the individual men, women and children who have suffered and died' (NSW Aboriginal Land Council 2021, paras 13–14).

This extract evidences the coalition sought relationships requesting respect for traditional ways and reciprocity through compensation. However, it quickly becomes clear that the initiatives being proposed and claims for return of land did not include Dharug Ngurra and custodians, beyond the immediate local La Perouse and Gadigal Ngurrungra (clan area). Those activating the coalition in the main came from other Indigenous Countries across what is now known as NSW: Wiradjuri, Birripai, Gomeroi, Dunghatti, Yuin and Dharawal areas (NSW Aboriginal Land Council 2021). The greater part of Dharug Ngurra was unrepresented. Already the state narratives of *terra nullius* and an education system that taught a white colonising and celebratory curriculum, which implied Dharug Ngurra as not having any 'real Aborigines' left was having an effect. As I experienced as a child, and Moore (2017) notes, 'Textbooks published in the White Australia era [1950s and 1960s] openly taught a celebratory version of history in which Aborigines were either absent or derided.' This administrative 'whitewalling' impacted the way Aboriginal people from other Ngurras positioned the agenda and were functioning not according to raw law and privileging the right for custodial voice on Country, but instead negotiating on behalf of masses of Indigene across NSW, as the homogeneous 'other'. As such, they worked according to the system laid out by and for the colonising possessed-possessor, albeit with good intent. Arguably, they became consumed within the process. At that point, homogenisation and the practice of universalising Indigenous peoples into one 'Aboriginal' other was accepted and employed for strategic purposes by the group.

As a result, the state could legitimise systems of mass administration and power, and in the process employ Aboriginal peoples from all over NSW to enforce this mass 'possession' and another colonisation–consumption on Dharug Ngurra became legitimised. As the NSW Aboriginal Land Council website (2021, para. 22) states, 1978 saw the creation of a:

> Select Committee … assisted in its work by an Aboriginal Task Force established to maintain close contact with Aboriginal communities during the course of the inquiry through liaison, facilitating field trips, and community meetings. It released its first report in August 1980 which dealt with land rights and the protection of sacred and significant sites.

Further the findings of the Select Committee, which formed the basis for recommendations to establish a land rights system and an Aboriginal Heritage Commission in NSW that would protect and maintain sites was envisaged, to gradually take over the roles of the National Parks and Wildlife Service in relation to such sites (NSW Aboriginal Land Council (NSWALC 2021). While on the surface these changes are seen to be moving away from an assimilationist model, in fact, as Moreton-Robinson (2007) and Watson (2015) both acknowledge, the patriarchal white sovereignty that underpins settler-colonising mentalities and creates a possessed-possessor form of unethical sovereignty has disavowed Indigenous sovereignty by co-opting and assimilating Indigenous assistance into itself.

By 1983, within five years of the establishment of the non-statutory NSWALC, the system of bureaucratic Land Councils was established under the *NSW Land Rights Act*. At the same time, as Aboriginal activist and scholar Gary Foley (2020, p. 191) notes, 'By 1983 the Traditional Custodians of the Sydney clans were grossly outnumbered by those who had come to Sydney since the Second World War.'

The problematics of current state bureaucratic Local Aboriginal Land Councils (LALCs) on Dharug Ngurra reside in the foundational framing, which basically separates the state from any connectivity with the way LALCs engage with the traditional custodians of Dharug Country. As Foley (2020, p. 190) shows, what looks innocent enough actually fails to recognise that the system relies on Aboriginal people to deal with each other without prejudicial or personal malice and to conform to raw law. Within the wording of Clause 53 of the *Aboriginal Land Rights Act 1983* resides the possessed-possessor: 'The members of the Local Aboriginal Land Council for a Local Aboriginal Land Council area are the adult Aboriginal persons who are listed on the Local Aboriginal Land Council membership roll for that area' (NSW Government 1983, clause 53).

In other words, LALCs get to pick and choose who is listed, while the state walks away. This has resulted in Dharug traditional custodians being blocked from joining either the Metropolitan LALC (covering Eastern Sydney) or the Deerubbin LALC (covering Western Sydney). Between them, they have consumed Dharug custodians' rightful voice according to Indigenous law and divided control and decision-making between them. This blockage occurred when those who had come from other places and those working and co-opted into the colonising system became the voices that the NSW state government heard. While they live on Dharug Ngurra, they do not belong Indigenously to Dharug Ngurra because only traditional custodians have the family stories of continuous connecting and caring for Ngurra across millennia (Rey 2021a; 2021b). In the meantime, unethical sovereignty is extended through the control of Dharug knowledges by the state bureaucracies controlling the Aboriginal Heritage Information Management System (AHIMS).

Aboriginal Heritage Information Management System (AHIMS)

Any reading of the AHIMS Fact Sheet of May 2020 cannot fail to note that the system is framed through the colonising and ill-legalistic voice of the NSW state government's *National Parks and Wildlife Act 1974* and its Indigenous bureaucratic branch, the NSW Aboriginal Land Council. It is clear therefore that state

bureaucracies (both Indigenous and non-Indigenous) are controlling access to Aboriginal knowledges held physically within Ngurra
through this system. The ill-legalistic messaging is the dominant
voice. In response to the question 'What is AHIMS?' we are told:

> The National Parks and Wildlife Act 1974 (NPW Act) is the main law
> administering Aboriginal culture and heritage in New South Wales.
> Section 90Q of the NPW Act requires the Department of Premier
> and Cabinet (DPC) (formerly the responsibility of the NSW Office of
> Environment and Heritage), to keep a register of all information and
> records regarding Aboriginal objects, sites and places registered to
> DPC. (NSWALC 2011, p. 1)

Only after this is it explained to the reader that AHIMS is a database 'of recorded Aboriginal sites across NSW, and an archive
of related documentation and reports' and that it contains 'over
93,000 recorded sites and over 13,500 archaeological and cultural
heritage assessment reports' (NSWALC 2011, p. 1). While it notes
that it does not hold all knowledges on Aboriginal sites but only
those recorded for the database, it clearly states that only LALCs
can update information. Thus, their possessive control over the
access and relationships Dharug and other Aboriginal communities
can have with the site and its contents is clear.

In answer to the question 'What is AHIMS used for?' it states:

> AHIMS is intended to be used by Aboriginal people, organisations,
> academics for research purposes, authorities and local governments
> for planning purposes. Developers wishing to undertake groundwork
> are also encouraged to search AHIMS as part of DPC's Diligence
> Code of Practice for the Protection of Aboriginal Objects in NSW,
> and any other related Industry Code, before undertaking their
> proposed activity. (NSWALC 2011, p. 1)

Here we see a clear framing of the purpose for the use of and
access to the information in the database, and the colonisation of
the NSWALC as it carries out business. While it purports to be
acting for the protection of Aboriginal objects, the main emphasis is
clearly for companies, organisations and bureaucratic institutions.
Again, similar to the *NSW Land Rights Act, Clause 53*, as exposed
by Foley (2020, p. 190) above, while it looks innocent enough, by
saying it gives access to 'Aboriginal people', it neglects to say until
the very bottom of the sheet on the second page that:

The DPC [Department of the Premier and Cabinet] decides what information about a registered site is to be given out as a result of an Extensive Search and what information is to be kept confidential. A fee of $50 [currently $60 at time of writing] is currently charged for an 'Extensive Search' request, with additional costs for GIS or express services. These fees are able to be waived for Aboriginal organisations and Local Aboriginal Land Councils. (NSWALC 2011, p. 2)

Thus, ordinary Dharug and other Aboriginal community individuals accessing any useful information beyond what is provided in a free 'Basic Search' (that is, 'Yes' there is an Aboriginal site located in proximity to the search location or 'No' there is no Aboriginal site located in proximity to the search location) have to pay the sum of $60.00 per search and 40 cents per page of information. Such costs are certainly prohibitive to most individuals, setting up an access barrier to knowledges of Aboriginal people's own Ancestral places and the knowledges held within them.

As such, the information on the system is functionally only available to those Indigenous, or non-Indigenous people working for corporations, organisations such as universities, and government bureaucracies – a system for the 'possessor', activated by the 'possessor's' agents. By encouraging use by land developers, purportedly for protection purposes, supporting urban development has grossly impacted Dharug Ngurra and other-than-humans. Such support, by association, profits the marketisation of Ngurra, the carving up of Ngurra to capitalise on the possession of Ngurra at the expense of, and consumption of, other-than-human ecologies. Clearly, within the Aboriginal Land Council bureaucracy the Indigene has been and is being consumed by the colonising possessed–possessor.

State education

Western education has always privileged the written form as an elitist domain within religious and academic realms. As Van Toorn's (2006) book title notes, 'Writing never arrives naked': there is always a political agenda. In colonising 'Australia', from almost the earliest outset, educating the 'natives' became a consumptive and possessing technique, undertaken by Governor Lachlan Macquarie and his Christian missionaries Reverends William Shelley and William Walker, with the establishment of the Parramatta Native Institution, in 1814, and later the Blacktown Native Institution in 1822 under Macquarie's successor Governor Brisbane (Brook & Kohen 1991; Norman-Hill 2019). Together they form the earliest examples of what later became known as 'The Stolen Generations'. With the aim of 'civilisation', the state dismantled the existing educational practices that were engaged as raw law forever (Watson 2015). The process took the little children away, broke their relations with families and cultural practices, destroyed their relationship with Dharug and other Indigenous languages, and replaced it with English speaking, writing and reading (Rey 2021a).

Since those times, the Anglophone cultural domination of the educational landscape has been enacted through language, place naming and the perpetration of possession of land, space, place and people, by the colonising possessed-possessor cannibalising the human Indigene and the other-than-humans integral to Ngurra's continuity, health and wellbeing (Moreton-Robinson 2015; Pugliese 2020).

From these three examples, we clearly see the noxious web of the possessed-possessor continuing to consume the Indigene on Dharug Ngurra. So, what are the possibilities for the resumption of raw law and ethical sovereignty? It is argued that ethical sovereignty resides within a web of relationality, respect and reciprocity for Ngurra, within which sustainable futures can be rewoven.

Ethical sovereignty as a web of relationality

As has been shown, the mindset of settler colonialism privileges its own existence above all others (human and other-than-human). It is imperative, therefore, that we recognise that this is not the only way sovereignty can be exercised. After all, for more than 65,000 years an alternative has been enacted. Proliferating the false notion that Dharug Ngurra's natural systems are dead, including Ngurra's Aboriginal custodians, means as an Indigenous place, it can be ignored, custodial ways can be denied, and cultural connections, caring and belonging do not matter. Instead, bringing these approaches forward into the daylight of considered, thoughtful relevance for the future is well overdue.

Given the impacts and imbalances from a changing climate, survival is no longer simply an Indigenous matter but one for global consideration (IPCC 2021). Moving towards relationality with other-than-humans (Watson 2015) offers an important alternative. However, the question arises: how do we bring back into general living practice such a relationality? It is argued here that if colonising mentalities are driving mass-extinctions of other-than-humans upon which humans rely, then change must be activated from the ground up. Across this continent, as shown, it is in the cities and towns that the greatest extinctions are occurring (ACF 2020). As such, it must be in the cities and towns that the collective well-being is initiated for sustainable futures and equanimity drawing on localised relationships, responsibilities and reciprocities.

One approach that is being undertaken in this manner in Sydney is recognition and activation of the 'Dharug Web of Interrelatedness' through teaching and post-doctoral research (Rey 2021a; 2021b). Following Rey's (2019) doctoral research, Dharug-led pedagogy was provided to undergraduate students at Macquarie University to show how relationality is at the heart of Dharug and, more broadly, Indigenous cultural practice. In the process, students are opened to their own experience of Ngurra by taking out-on-Country visits, framed through respectful relational protocols of engagement. Students learn to recognise how Ngurra can influence and transform us, and how together we co-become as Ngurra (Bawaka et al. 2016; Bawaka Country et al. 2015). Fostering relationship with place, through Indigenous protocols, is shown to open the human to our place *within, not above* the web of agency that Ngurra enacts.

The following examples of two student responses to their experiential learning show how this pedagogical approach is being undertaken, and their greater consciousness opens them to a deeper connection to places, their presences, and the ways we rely on Ngurra for our wellbeing and equanimity. In doing so, the possessed-possessor systems underpinning bureaucratic consumptions of the Indigene (human and other than human) are being disrupted.

Delivering Indigenous 'doing-learning': relationship
as decolonising praxis

The Indigenous Studies Department's undergraduate unit ABST1020, Dharug Country: Presences, Places and People at Macquarie University, on Wallumattagal Ngurrungra has now been delivered for two years and enrolment numbers have grown exponentially. Some comments from students (2020) supply evidence of the impact and transformation of engaging with custodial pedagogy. Student AD writes:

> Throughout this unit, we have been privileged to hear from Elders about their stories, experiences, and connections to country. Through their commentaries, we have gained a better knowledge of how life is different for them, and they are a clear example of how we can care for Country in Sydney. The readings we were given throughout this unit has provided a deeper understanding of the concepts we were introduced to. Through our experiential learning by visiting significant sites, we have been able to learn by doing. I found this invaluable for the connection it provided me to the stories and knowledges we have been taught. We should all be inspired to take responsibility for our actions, Country needs us, and we need Country.

As first-year university students coming from diverse cultural and experiential backgrounds, they are not told *what* to think, or what is the 'right answer' that will get them through. Rather they are shown *how* to engage through a Dharug (and more broadly, Indigenous) cultural lens. They meet this alternative approach through the community Elders' narratives, the Dharug lecturer and Dharug tutors' own narrative journeys and, of course, through Ngurra. From their out-on-Country experiences, research, readings, and viewings, they are asked to reflect on their connections, their sense of caring and belonging to/with/as other-than-humans. Student KO tells us:

> Taking the time to stop and immerse oneself in Country by connecting through the other than human facets that make up Country allows for an awakening to the intricacies and diversity of a place. Country as a city is immensely diverse and often hard to see as Country ... Creating relationship with place by way of education and revelations of depth and diversity of that place, breaks the mould of the colonial monoculture ... and allows for the actor to find their meaningful place within Country.

Over time, students recognise their changing responses as they move through the thematic conceptual phases and emphasis of the unit: Ngurra, Presences, Places and People. In the two final fortnightly themes, students are asked to engage in broader critical social reflection, concerning the provocation of 'Why Bother?' and deeper thinking about 'Sustainable Futures?'. By taking the time in one semester to show students an alternative educational approach, fostering futures that challenge the 'business as usual' pedagogical class-room approach, the possessed-possessor mentalities and social discourses that objectify, separate, and hierarchically position humans over the other-than-humans on which they depend are arrested. As such, it is an ethical form of enacting relational sovereignty in-place, through fostering relational education that restores raw law by positioning Ngurra at the centre through respect and reciprocity and does so within Ngurra-as-city.

Having outlined an example of educational praxis that arrests colonising mentalities, the next example of decolonising process involves relational research as ethical praxis.

Education research as decolonising and ethical praxis

Western higher education institutions simultaneously enact and sustain the possessed-possessor colonising mentalities, while having an obligation to support self-examination through rigorous enquiry as part of their research functionality and social ethic. While schooling embeds narratives that result in consumptive possession, higher education institutions are drawn into their own place of relationship and web of interconnectivity when they recognise and admit the ill-legality of the existing claims to sovereignty by the 'Australian' system of governance. To date, being forced to acknowledge that ill-legality has been avoided despite introduction of the practices of custodial 'Welcomes' and 'Acknowledgements'. However, such practices open opportunities for reflective engagement with colonising legacies, narratives and practices. To accept and engage with the ethic of Indigenous raw law forces not only a challenging self-reflection but a shift in the relationship with physical and metaphysical places as Ngurra. Ethical relationality requires reciprocity, something that has not been forthcoming in the continuing 'colony' of Sydney. The current (2020) post-doctoral Macquarie University

Fellowship for Indigenous Research (MUFIR) being undertaken by the author presents that dilemma as it tackles the legacies of 'His-storying' on Dharug Ngurra and particularly on Wallumattagal Ngurrungra, where the university resides.

The project engages three Dharug Aboriginal sites: Yallomundee on the western edge of Sydney Basin, beside the Dyarrubin/ Hawkesbury River; Blacktown Native Institution (BNI), in the Cumberland Plains heartland of the Sydney Basin; and Brown's Waterhole in Lane Cove National Park (LCNP), bordering Sydney Harbour. The latter is also a neighbour of the Wallumattagal Campus of the university. While connections to the BNI and Brown's Waterhole have been blocked due to COVID-19 restrictions during 2021, engagement with Yallomundee has been possible. This engagement involved final year Bachelor of Screen, Professional and Community Engagement (PACE) students who engaged in their own out-on-Country 'doing-learning', with the purpose of filming their own development of a relationship with Ngurra through the same Indigenous protocols as offered to the ABST1020 students. As the site was only introduced to them the day after a flooded Dyarrubin River and Shaw's Creek stopped being inundated with rain, both limitations and unique opportunities arose. The flooding of both river and creek meant large parts of the site were not available for walking on. However, the flood brought out large numbers of insects (moths, butterflies, and spiders, predominantly), the clarity of sound was enhanced from resident birds, particular the bell-minors, as nearby traffic was stopped, and visually as a water-washed light and sky offered a particular beauty that the student filming captured. It was as if the river in its power was awakening vulnerability across all ecological relatives to enhance life-giving and life-changing activations. Seeing our Dyarrubin river in the torment of flood produced a consciousness of vulnerability for us that ordinary conditions do not evoke. As such, relational oppor-tunities were particularised by the existential timing and circum-stance of the conditions.

These conditions provoked in the researcher a resonance with Judith Butler's work on vulnerability and the ethics of cohabitation. As Butler (2012, p. 141) notes, 'ethical obligation not only depends upon our vulnerability to the claims of others but establishes us as creatures who are fundamentally defined by that ethical relation'.

Likewise, if a higher education institution in Dharug Ngurra is a community with an identity, then it is ethically obliged to address and activate its obligations to respond to its colonising legacies, care for Ngurra, and cultivate equitable voice and responsive reciprocity with custodians and other-than-humans. Such responsiveness goes beyond the fence and at least to the neighbouring river of its immediate locale.

From this activation of Dharug Ngurra at Yallomundee, students provide and receive such a relational reciprocity. Through their film production, they establish a transformative experience as they learn both about Ngurra and her custodians. Recognising the agency of Ngurra through the flooded river awoke their own creativity through the film. As one student, RW, reflected:

> The best way I can describe the feeling of being at the site was that it brought a sense of calm and comfort over me. I have anxiety and am almost constantly plagued by a subtle feeling of fear. As soon as we drove out of the site, I remember noticing anxiousness creeping back into me and had only realised at that moment that I had not felt a drop of anxiety during our time at Yellomundee … It was a pleasure to have been a part of this experience. For me, it was transformative in the way that I view and appreciate the world around me and has made me more aware of these presences too.

Together connecting and co-becoming was enacted.

Conclusion

In an era of catastrophic climate-changing Anthropocentric extinctions, recognising both the hindrances and opportunities for change is critical. By contextualising important Indigenous scholarship on ill-legal sovereignty and the continuing necro-biopolitical agency of settler colonialism, this chapter has sought to expose the hindrances and opportunities in relation to Dharug Ngurra. Using three state bureaucracies as examples of ill-legal 'sovereignty', it is shown how the systems both claim to support the Indigene, while functionally possessing and consuming it, enacting the possessed-possessor mentalities, by controlling, undermining, and preventing cultural practices that have sustained both communities and Country/Ngurra for millennia. It then shows, through current undergraduate Indigenous experiential pedagogy and post-doctoral research, how relationality sits at the heart of Indigenous law, and offers a basis for sustainability and ethical sovereignty. In so doing, opportunities to activate change for the benefit of all sentience can be enhanced, even in cities, by regenerating practices that position humans within a web of interconnectivity. It is shown that localised relationality is fostered collectively through connecting, caring, and belonging to presences, places and people.

It is argued that institutional and bureaucratic engagement with their grounded localities, and caring for Ngurra, brings the activism that is required to arrest the dangerous spiral of extinctions that denial of relationship fosters. Arresting narratives and practices that privilege the possessed-possessor requires therefore systems that flatten the hierarchies, centre the collective, enhance equanimity through reciprocity rather than competition, and strengthen localised relationality.

As has been shown, relational education and fostering relational research that strengthens human and other-than-human equanimity opens us to ways of connecting, caring, and belonging by bringing Ngurra into an influential role in our lives. The practice of collective caring for Ngurra has underpinned sustainable wellbeing for multi-millennia and fostered strong communities, strong families, and strong individuals. By networking from the local to the global, underpinned by grounded, collective Indigenous Ngurra-centric relationalities and initiatives, ethical sustainable sovereignties can be activated and re-imposed across urban landscapes to protect and nurture Ngurra from possessed-possessor extinctions. Such an approach offers ways forward in the face of cataclysmic climate-changing challenges for the benefit of all sentient beings.

References

Australian Conservation Foundation (ACF). (2020). *The extinction crisis in Australia's cities and towns: How weak environment laws have let urban sprawl destroy the habitat of Australia's threatened species.* www. acf.org.au/reports?page=3

Bawaka Burarrwanga, L., Ganambarr, R., Ganambarr-Stubbs, M., Ganambarr, B., Maymuru, D., & Sweeney, J. (2016). Co-becoming time/s time/s-as-telling-as-time/s. In Thorpe, J., Rutherford, S., &

Sandberg, L. A. (Eds), *Methodological Challenges in Nature-Culture and Environmental History Research* (pp. 106–108). London: Routledge.

Bawaka Country, Wright, S, Suchet-Pearson, S., Lloyd, K., Burarrwanga, L., Ganambarr R., & Ganambarr-Stubbs, M. (2015). Co-becoming Bawaka: Towards a Relational Understanding of Place/Space. *Progress in Human Geography*. http://phg.sagepub.com/content/early/2015/06/30/0309132515589437.abstract

Beresford, Q. (2021). *Wounded Country: The Murray-Darling Basin a Contested History*. Sydney: New South Wales University Press.

Brook, J., & Kohen, J. (1991). *The Parramatta Native Institution and the Black Town: a history*. Kensington: New South Wales University Press.

Burgess, C. P., Johnston, F. H., Berry, H. L., McDonnell, J., Yibarbuk, D., Gunabarra, C. … Bailie, R. S. (2009). Healthy country, healthy people: The relationship between Indigenous health status and 'caring for country'. *Medical Journal of Australia*, 190(10), 567–572.

Butler, J. (2012). Precarious life, vulnerability, and the ethics of cohabitation. *The Journal of Speculative Philosophy*, 26(2), 134–151.

Falk, P. & Martin, G. (2007). Misconstruing Indigenous sovereignty: Maintaining the fabric of Australian law. In Moreton-Robinson, A. (Ed.), *Sovereign Subjects: Indigenous Sovereignty Matters* (pp. 33–46). London: Allen & Unwin.

Foley, D. L. G. (2020). *What the Colonists Never Knew: A History of Aboriginal Sydney*. Canberra: National Museum of Australia Press.

Godfree, R. C., Knerr, N., Encinas-Viso, F., Albrecht, D., Bush, D., Christine Cargill, D. … Broadhurst, L. M. (2021). Implications of the 2019–2020 megafires for the biogeography and conservation of Australian vegetation. *Nature Communications*, 12(1), 1023–1023.

Intergovernmental Panel on Climate Change (IPCC). (2021). Sixth assessment report. www.ipcc.ch/assessment-report/ar6/

Ives, C. D., Lentini, P. E., Threlfall, C. G., Ikin, K., Shanahan, D. F., Garrard, G. E. … Kendal, D. (2016). Cities are hotspots for threatened species. *Global Ecology and Biogeography*, 25(1), 117–126.

Karskens, G. (2010). *The Colony: A History of Early Sydney*. London: Allen & Unwin.

Karskens, G. (2020). *People of the River: Lost Worlds of Early Australia*. London: Allen & Unwin.

Keating, P. (1992). Redfern speech. https://antar.org.au/sites/default/files/paul_keating_speech_transcript.pdf

Larsen, S. C., & Johnson, J. T. (2017). *Being Together in Place: Indigenous Coexistence in a More Than Human World*. Minneapolis: University of Minnesota Press.

Martinez, M. A. (1999). *Study on Treaties: Agreements and other Constructive Arrangements between States and Indigenous Populations.* Geneva: United Nations.

Moore, R. (2017). History textbooks still imply that Australians are white. *School News Australia*, 11 July. www.school-news.com.au/news/history-textbooks-still-imply-that-australians-are-white/

Moreton-Robinson, A. (2007). *Sovereign Subjects: Indigenous Sovereignty Matters.* London: Allen & Unwin.

Moreton-Robinson, A. (2015). *The White Possessive: Property, Power, and Indigenous Sovereignty.* Minneapolis: University of Minnesota Press.

Ngurra, D., Dadd, L., Glass, P., Scott, R., Graham, M., Judge, S. ... Suchet-Pearson, S. (2019). Yanama budyari gumada: Reframing the urban to care as Darug Country in western Sydney. *Australian Geographer*, 50(3), 279–293.

Norman-Hill, R. (2019). Australia's residential schools. In Minton, S. J. (Ed.), *Residential Schools and Indigenous Peoples: From Genocide via Education to the Possibilities for Processes of Truth, Restitution, Reconciliation, and Reclamation* (pp. 66–94). Abingdon: Routledge.

NSW Aboriginal Land Council. (2011). Factsheet Aboriginal Culture and Heritage: Aboriginal Heritage Information Management System. https://alc.org.au/wp-content/uploads/2020/01/110701-ahims-fact-sheet.pdf

NSW Aboriginal Land Council. (2021). Our history. https://alc.org.au/our-history/

NSW Government. (1983). Aboriginal Land Rights Act 1983 No 42. https://legislation.nsw.gov.au/view/html/inforce/current/act-1983-042#sec.53

Plumwood, V. (1991). Nature, self, and gender: feminism, environmental philosophy, and the critique of rationalism. *Hypatia*, 6 (1), 3–27.

Plumwood, V. (1993). *Feminism and the Mastery of Nature.* London: Routledge.

Pugliese, J. (2020). *Biopolitics of the More-Than-Human: Forensic Ecologies of Violence.* Durham, NC: Duke University Press.

Rey, J. A. (2019). *Country Tracking Voices: Dharug Women's Perspectives on Presences, Places and Practices.* Doctorate thesis, Macquarie University. http://hdl.handle.net/1959.14/1269323

Rey, J. A. (2021a). Changing places: Weaving city learnings into country futures. In Lopez Lopez, L., & Coella, G. (Eds), *Indigenous Futures and Learnings Taking Place* (pp. 10–36). Melbourne: Routledge.

Rey, J. A. (2021b). Indigenous identity as country: The 'ing' within connecting, caring, and belonging. *Genealogy*, 5(2), 48.

Reynolds, H. (1987). *Frontier.* London: Allen & Unwin.

Rudd, K. (2008). Stolen generations apology. www.aph.gov.au/Visit_
Parliament/Whats_On/Exhibitions/Custom_Media/Apology_to_
Australias_Indigenous_Peoples

Tatz, C. (2017). *Australia's Unthinkable Genocide*. Bloomington: Xlibris.

van Toorn, P. (2006). *Writing Never Arrives Naked: Early Aboriginal Cultures of Writing in Australia*. Canberra: Aboriginal Studies Press.

Watson, I. (2015). *Aboriginal Peoples, Colonialism and International Law: Raw Law*. Abingdon: Routledge.

9

Social media and global networks of Indigeneity

Bronwyn Carlson

Introduction

Social media has provided Indigenous[1] peoples with a variety of platforms where we can connect on a global scale. While access remains a significant issue for many Indigenous people, it is also true that Indigenous people are keen users of the internet and especially for accessing social media (Carlson & Berglund 2021; Carlson & Frazer 2021; Lindgren & Cocq 2017; Virtanen 2015; Wilson et al. 2017). For example, even in the most 'remote' areas of this continent now referred to as Australia,[2] mobile technologies are becoming increasingly commonplace as more and more Aboriginal and Torres Strait Islander people access apps such as Facebook, Twitter, TikTok, Instagram and the like (Carlson & Frazer 2018; Rice et al. 2016). This is also true for many Indigenous peoples across the globe (Carlson & Berglund 2021; Lindgren & Cocq 2017; Virtanen 2015; Wilson et al. 2017). Virtanen (2015, p. 351) notes that in Brazilian Amazonia even small towns now have access to high speed internet providing the means for Indigenous peoples to be online and they argue that social media platforms have opened 'new forms of affinity and alterity' for Indigenous peoples. In a relatively short period of time, social media technologies have become a central part of our everyday lives.

My interest in Indigenous peoples' use of social media began back in 2010 when participants in my doctoral research spoke about how they used social media and particularly Facebook to express their identities (Carlson 2013; Lumby 2010). My research focused on the politics of identity as it relates to Indigenous peoples (see Carlson 2016). I was then interested in how people were navigating online spaces as Indigenous people (Carlson 2013; Lumby 2010). This was exciting as the topic was new and I had not considered the issues of identity or community in digital settings. Back then, people spoke about life in two different domains – online and offline, offline being considered in the real world or in real life (Carlson & Frazer 2021). These days this is not the case – being online is an everyday part of life for many Indigenous peoples.

This chapter draws from my research to examine social media's possibilities for dissent and action, locally and globally. I consider social media users as encultured subjects whose use of sites can afford significant support for identity and collective action. In addition, the chapter approaches the use of 'fun' on social media as a means of resistance. Finally, and importantly, I will discuss the concept of 'imagining otherwise' where we, Indigenous social media users, can contemplate a reality that shaped by online activism and executed offline through movements that continue to augment our history, our existence and our future aspirations.

Cultured subjects

Indigenous peoples access social media apps as cultured subjects. In general the concept of anonymity is not one that describes being Indigenous online. For example, many Indigenous people are situated within complex kinship systems, which work to shape the ways in which people may socialise with one another (see Virtanen 2015), and there are often protocols regarding the distribution and expression of cultural knowledges. This can include, for example, the sharing of images, and the customs of dealing with death and dying – what Aboriginal and Torres Strait Islander people call Sorry Business (Carlson & Frazer 2015). DuBois and Cocq (2019) comment on Sámi use of digital technology and note that Sámi use technologies like social media, in specifically Sámi ways, to promote and maintain their cultural practices and keep connected. Lee (2022) similarly, notes that Māori use social media platforms to 'reflect their cultural aspirations and Indigenous ways of being (Lee 2022, p. 879). While this is not to suggest that Indigenous peoples are not capable of creating anonymous accounts, I am suggesting that Indigenous people generally do not. Being Indigenous is about being connected and belonging and not being unambiguous about who we are when on social media. It is often a source of pride. This sense of connectedness was captured by Twitter user @BundjalungBud in an article on Blackfulla Twitter:

> Blackfullas have always found ways to get together with a magnetic force that has strengthened throughout time. We share, we care and we lair, together! So, it's no surprise that through one of the biggest social media platforms there is that we'd find each other – or more truthfully, be drawn to each other – to form a strong online community. (@BundjalungBud 2022, n.p.)

Indigenous people understand that we do not stop being Indigenous because we are online. For us the internet is not a disembodied place where you are no longer connected to human and more-than-human relations. The internet for us is a real place that is right here and is composed of communities of people with real lives that are connected through our responsibility and relationships, including our relationships to Country/homelands (Carlson 2021a). In an early study of Inuit identities online, Christensen (2003) found that Inuit 'are generally embedding offline life into cyberspace' and that 'the internet is not necessarily a space to hide in, nor is it a space that mysteriously filters away the cultural identity of people'. Similarly, Pascua Yaqui/Chicana scholar Marisa Elena Duarte speaks to the 'place-based nature of the Internet' in her 2017 book *Network Sovereignty* stating that for non-Indigenous people the internet is imagined as something that is 'out there' whereas for Indigenous people we understand it as 'right here'. It is a place: we go there and interact as we would go to a mall, a park, or a concert. Just like our social relations exist on the internet, settler colonialism exists also. I have previously described settler colonialism as being 'like a hungry beast that seeks our land and in doing so seeks our erasure' (Carlson 2021a, p. 60). Settler colonialism is experienced daily by Indigenous people online.

Indigenous people around the globe are also still very much impacted by colonisation and the complex, violent and ongoing history of material, cultural and physical dispossession that it entails (Wolfe 2006). Participants in my own research have variously noted the effects of settler violence online on their health and safety (Carlson & Frazer 2018). Participants in my study have also note the affordances of social media to keep connected and to build networks of Indigenous allies to learn from and to provide support for issues that are familiar to all Indigenous peoples.

From the local to the global

Digital technologies such as social media enable the symbolic vanishing of physical borders allowing users to maintain relationships across vast distances and time zones, thereby increasing social and political connectivity (Carlson 2013). Social media users transcend time and space to produce and connect to communities of practice (Wilson et al. 2017). In this way, Indigenous peoples have been able to be part of a global network of peoples who often share similar histories of colonisation, dispossession, and other forms of violence. Wilson and colleagues (2018, p. 1) suggest that Indigenous peoples are 'reterritorializing social media' noting that, 'social media is transforming the way Indigenous peoples interact and connect with each other at a local, regional, national and global level'. Indigenous peoples are harnessing social media to resist colonialism and to imagine different futures for ourselves. Social media can provide a sound basis for imagination; as disembodied subjects (invisible to other users), we have opportunities to imagine, to think and to conceive of possibilities without the interruption of any reactions betrayed by facial embodiment. We can then choose to share, circulate our ideas and thoughts, agree and disagree, make plans, activate our imagined futures.

Activism is one of the ways Indigenous peoples are connecting with each other from the local to the global and increasingly using social media as a powerful organising tool. Political campaigns are often established at the local level where momentum is built then shared across social media platforms building global solidarity and support. Some scholars have questioned whether social media has the capacity for 'giving voice' to Indigenous peoples that will bring about substantive change to policies or practices (Dreher et al. 2016). Others have questioned whether social media driven activism is just 'slacktivism' and is meaningless and ineffective for bringing about real change (Morozov 2009). However, many scholars have also highlighted the importance of social media for

Indigenous peoples and particularly for political activism (Carlson & Frazer 2021; Carlson & Berglund 2021). As Carlson and Frazer (2021, p. 169) articulate:

> Indigenous people globally have less access to political power, in the forms of voter power, capital, proximity to politicians, and representation in politics. Instead, political power, for Indigenous peoples, comes from their relational connections to one another, their irrefutable moral claim to sovereignty, and their immense creativity in political strategy.

The uptake of digital technologies is often framed as antithetical to Indigenous peoples and cultures (Belton 2010). Generally, when it comes to technology, Indigenous people are only ever included when it comes to discussions about the digital divide. Carlson and Frazer (2021, p. 3) argue: 'This apparent "divide" is not only in relation to technology; it also points to the idea that [Indigenous] people are considered somehow technologically "deficient" and incapable of engaging in the digital world.'

These ideas according to Arias (2019, p. x) describe a 'compulsion to perceive Indigenous peoples as located outside of technology's purview aligned with the stereotype that has its origins in many colonial narratives which seek to position Indigenous people as 'backward' and 'primitive'. However, it is very clear that digital technologies, including social media have strengthened the 'counter-power' of Indigenous politics (Castells 2013). One significant affordance we have in enacting our 'counter-power', is our ability to distribute news and information outside of the 'whitestream media' (Johnston 2011). The media is dominated by settlers and operates to sustain settler power that reproduces negative and stereotypical images of Indigenous peoples and communities. The other important factor inherent in digital technologies is the global reach. Local issues are often reported on by local media. Local Indigenous issues rarely come to the notice of local media let alone national or international broadcast. Social media, by its very design, immediately opens up the viewership to the world.

Campaigns such as the #IdleNoMore movement originating in Canada (Wilson & Zheng 2021), the #SOSBlakAustralia campaign on this continent (Carlson & Frazer 2016) and the #NoDAPL protest centred on Standing Rock in the United States (Deschine

Parkhurst 2021) have all harnessed social media drawing global support and attention to situations that would have otherwise remained specific to a local area. This would also mean they would rarely attract media attention or the scrutiny of the world. No longer can atrocities and violence against Indigenous people remain unknown. This does not necessarily mean that it won't happen as the #NoDAPL protectors can attest but it does mean there will be a record. As Parkhurst (2021, p. 38) writes:

> One moment that garnered attention of international media was the confrontation between militarized police and Water Protectors that happened in the middle of the night on November 20, 2016. This incident has been known as the Battle of Backwater Bridge (aka Backwater Sunday), as Water Protectors were met with an extreme display of militarized police violence. This incidence was livestreamed through multiple Facebook accounts of individuals, citizen journalists, Indigenous organizations, and the independent media organization *Unicorn Riot* … Live video streams of the incident showed militarized police using water cannons and firehoses and deploying rubber and plastic bullets on Water Protectors in subfreezing temperatures.

Both the #IdleNoMore and #SOSBlakAustralia movements like many others, began as online local resistance movements that examined oppressive practices by governments. Both these sites grew into social media global movements. In 2012 the Canadian government proposed a series of bills to amend or repeal existing legislation. These bills aimed to remove environmental protections for nearly all of Canada's freshwater bodies and reduced requirements for environmental assessments associated with the permit process for activities such as pipeline development. They were a direct attack on Indigenous treaty-based rights (Wilson & Zheng 2021). In response, four women based in Saskatchewan began to organise community teach-ins and rallies to share information about the impacts of the proposed legislation within the broader community. This according to Cree scholar Alex Wilson and colleague Corals Zheng (2021, p. 14) was the start of Idle No More (INM), an organisation they describe as 'a movement to affirm Indigenous sovereignty and to protect lands and waters'. The movement according to John (2015, p. 38) 'spread … like a fire on the prairie' and has become a massive action-based organisation that has moved from online spaces to on the streets protests. Social media has provided a space according to Wilson and Zheng, 'where all Indigenous people were invited to speak and be heard' as opposed to media selecting who they deemed as leaders (2021, p. 18).

In 2014, Western Australian Premier Colin Barnett announced the closure of 150 of the state's 274 remote Aboriginal communities, displacing up to 12,000 people (Carlson & Frazer 2016). Members of the Bieundurry family in Wangkatjungka and a small group of other Kimberley women across the state were strategising a response to the impending threat of community closure. In support of their community, Sam Cook, a Nyikina woman, activated the Facebook page titled 'Stop the Forced Closures of Aboriginal Communities'. They hoped by sunrise the page might garner 1,000 likes. But due to the impact of social media, the word spread faster than they had either anticipated or hoped. This was the beginning of the global movement. Over the next five days every state and territory had mobilised in response to the social media post to do so. This resulted in at least thirty rallies and up to 30,000 people marching in the streets – from geographically remote locations to regional towns and major cities.

A virtual protest also raged online, with international celebrity endorsements coming from the likes of Bianca Jagger, Hugh Jackman and Russell Crowe among others. Well-known artists and athletes stood solid in their support with major statements made at their various events and public platforms. In less than thirty days, '#SOSBlakAustralia, Stop the Forced Closures of Aboriginal Communities' created a global social media movement. On 10 April, the cities of Naarm (Melbourne) and Warrane (Sydney) shut down to hold rallies, sit-ins and cultural celebrations, showing how strong the Aboriginal continuum is in contemporary times. The following day, 11 April, the whitestream *Herald Sun*, which had largely ignored the efforts, ran a headline concerning the protests in Naarm, 'Selfish Rabble Shut City'. Rather than be agitated by this, the community fought back online, initiating #SelfishRabble on Twitter. In less than one hour, it had trended to number one on the Australian Twitter feed. Posts included images of politicians for example, with comments such as 'This is what the real #SelfishRabble look like' and others targeting the whitestream media posting that the media is the real #SelfishRabble.

Both examples make clear that social media is capable of effecting a mass galvanisation, politicisation, and animation of geographically diverse bodies. These social media platforms offer opportunities to creatively subvert the official discourse of government, which so often works to both contain and suppress the voices of Indigenous people. More importantly, perhaps the sites afford possibilities for Indigenous peoples to powerfully assert their presence through exercising their right to protest against government policy. In other words, we become 'visible' through activities that arise from imagining other possibilities. Both cases also highlight the inherent racism of whitestream media. Barker (2015, p. 50) argues that the media in Canada, for example, has always been 'silent on issues of concern to Indigenous peoples, only engaging with Indigenous peoples and communities when they can be portrayed as threatening to the interests of corporations or framed as destabilising Settler Canadian society'. Across the continent colonially referred to as Australia, the media operates in the same way. Protestors in the #SOSBlakAustralia campaign, for example, were disparaged in the media and referred to as 'selfish rabble' who were inconveniencing upstanding citizens trying to get to work (Carlson & Frazer 2021, p. 244).

Global recognition and making fun of colonisers

Social media provides a platform for Indigenous groups to counter colonial discourses and to come together globally to demonstrate the pervasive nature of colonial violence with which we are all too familiar. It is a fact that Indigenous peoples globally are masters at using humour to demonstrate our resistance. Humour and having fun on social media is not only playful and productive as noted by Carlson and Frazer (2021, p. 121) it is, as they argue, 'an affective force – bringing people together, breaking down boundaries, reifying others, and circulating pleasurable feelings across and between bodies'. While the experience of fun is often intimately personal, its collective expression can have profound social effects – '[i]t is a multi-dimensional, multifunctional social phenomenon' (Fincham 2016, p. 5).

The long history of oppressive policies targeting Indigenous people globally has meant that Indigenous 'fun', 'joy' and 'humour' are invariably political (Carlson & Frazer 2021). For Indigenous people, fun often plays important social and political roles in sustaining a sense of a distinctly Indigenous identity. As noted by Fincham (2016, p. 3) 'the role of fun for making situations at worst tolerable and at best enjoyable is clear'. Berglund (2016) provides an overview of the Native American comedy troupe, the 1491s, and their use of social media, in particular, YouTube, to counter colonial discourse stating, 'One of the crucial ways that the 1491s push back against the persistent forces of colonialism to further empower Indigenous youth and others is by highlighting the talents, resourcefulness, and resilience of Indigenous peoples' (Berglund 2016, p. 554).

Of course, 'making fun' of colonisers can also work to produce and sustain a sense of group identity and belonging at both the local and global level. Torres Strait Islander scholar Martin Nakata (2007, p. 12) observed that Indigenous humour 'reveals the ignorance of outsiders of how we operate in and understand our world and many a merry laugh we have all had at whitefellas' expense'. Similarly, Mi'kmaw scholar Katelyn Copage (2019, p. 188) claims that: '[T]hrough humour, the narrative of who is laughing at who is changing. For a long time, Indigenous peoples have been the butt of the white man's jokes. But now, we are changing that narrative to laughing at and with ourselves, and one another.'

A 'Karen' has become a globally recognised term and demonstrates the way in which some fun transcends nation-states and becomes universally understood by collectives of peoples. On a Facebook post on the 'Decolonize Myself: A First Nations Perspective' page a meme was posted that read:

INDIGENOUS In'dıdz ə nas in-dij-uh-nuhs (Adjective) It means my ancestors were here on Turtle Island longer than yours Karen.[3]

A 'Karen' is referencing a white woman who exhibits behaviours that stem from their privilege – calling police on Black and Indigenous peoples while faking fear for their lives or making racist comments or being violent with no fear of authorities. Often videos of white women behaving like a 'Karen' are shared by Indigenous people on YouTube and other social media platforms. There is a global recognition amongst Indigenous peoples about what a 'Karen' is. In 2020, a 'Karen' was filmed harassing and assaulting a group of

Native American protesters who were part of a group called Defend Kumeyaay Land who were protesting the continuing construction of Trump's border wall on their homelands.[4] Online people referred to the woman as 'Border Wall Karen'. Similarly, in 2021 a 'Karen' was filmed calling Native American women in a bar 'rez bitches'. When they began filming the incident, she got upset telling them to go back to 'the reservation'.[5]

Similarly, in 2019 in a small country town in New South Wales an Aboriginal family was harassed in their own home by a 'Karen'. Their neighbours, a white couple, took offence to the family displaying the Aboriginal flag outside their own home. The Aboriginal flag is one of three official Australian flags. The white woman tried with all her strength to pull the flag down with no luck. The Aboriginal family filmed the assault and in the footage you can hear them say to the woman that the flag is 'too strong for you Karen'. The white couple then went on to badger the family about their Aboriginal identity and demanding they remove the flag. The irony that the white woman's actual name was Karen was not lost on social media.

Kira Djnalie whose parents were the victims posted the video on social media gaining much support from Aboriginal and Torres Strait Islander people and other Indigenous people globally. Djnalie created a range of t-shirts available through their RedBubble page and memes shared across social media about the event.[6] One t-shirt has an image of a white silhouette hanging on to the Aboriginal flag with the words 'too strong for you Karen'. The local government MP Ali Coper in a show of support, shared an image of an Aboriginal flag draped over the gate to her office. The post was accompanied by the hashtag #TooStrongForYouKaren.

In the many examples where this pejorative term has been used it is always in reference to a white woman who uses white privilege to try and cause harm to Indigenous people. In places like the US and so-called Australia the threat to call the police is real and there are countless stories of Indigenous peoples being killed by police after being wrongfully accused or identified as a supposed threat. According to the Centres on Juvenile and Criminal Justice, the 'racial group most likely to be killed by law enforcement is Native Americans'[7] and across this continent the deaths of Aboriginal and Torres Strait Islander peoples at the hands of law enforcement is constant (Reid 2022). While there is fun to be had at the expense of such people, and much room for resistance and frivolity, it is of course the case that what we laugh and poke fun at always has the potential to harm us. Our laughter and fun, therefore, carries danger. But we still do it with pleasure whenever we can.

Affective publics of possibility

Social media provides platforms where Indigenous people are busy sharing ideas about the future with other Indigenous peoples globally. It is on these platforms where Indigenous people share their good news, hopes and ideas for a future where we are thriving. While social media can be traumatic as Indigenous people bear witness to much discrimination, racism and online hate (Carlson et al. 2017), we also sustain networked structures of joyful affect in what Papacharissi (2016) calls affective publics produced through sharing success, achievement, good news stories and hope.

Recently Hawaiian ethnoecologist scholar Katie Kamelamela tweeted that they had accepted a position at Arizona State University. They posted: 'Aloha mai, I am excited to TW announce … I have signed to be an Assistant Professor at Arizona State University, College of Global Futures, School of Ocean Futures. I will be teaching courses and conducting research remotely from Hawaii' (@kteabam, September 2022).

This post resulted in much discussion on Twitter in relation to the concept of working remotely, being Indigenous and thinking about new ways to connect, educate, collaborate that might not require you to leave your community or homelands. What followed was a series of tweets by Cheyenne-Chicana scholar Desi Small-Rodriguez who wrote with much excitement about the possibility of working in the academy while also being able to stay living in your community and not having to relocate for employment opportunities: 'Indigenous colleague got hire by @ASU as Asst Professor & can work remotely teaching & researching from their home community! I read this & cried. Yes! Why can't this be an option at more unis? This would be a helluva game changer for recruiting/ retaining Indigenous faculty!' (@native4data, 1 September 2022).

Recruiting Indigenous scholars is difficult. Most universities offer Indigenous focused courses yet there still remains very few

Indigenous peoples with the required qualifications to take up the opportunities. While many settlers occupy positions teaching Indigenous content, students overwhelmingly state they much prefer being taught such topics by Indigenous scholars. It should also be noted that institutions built on the homelands of Indigenous peoples should also do more to support local Indigenous peoples to gain the necessary qualifications and build careers. This idea if more widely accepted, however, would definitely be a game changer. Indigenous people are often reluctant to take up opportunities that require relocation. While many do, overall it remains a significant barrier and particularly if the individual has strong ties to their community and has many obligations and responsibilities. As Small-Rodriguez tweeted: 'This hits hard today as I leave my reservation back to LA for the academic year. Leaving behind not only relatives, but critical opportunities for research & teaching in the places & spaces where tribal sovereignty remains, where Natives are majority, where we are not invisible' (@native4data, 1 September 2022).

Without a doubt there are lost opportunities. Many institutions seek to develop strong relationships with Indigenous communities understanding the value that is gained by doing so. Many do not as Small-Rodriguez notes in this tweet: 'My family & I r home on the Rez bc of this. Sadly the local university is also limited to hiring Indigenous faculty – they're not ready for us. Alternatively, we r making sacrifices to create our own research group within our communities with a few PhD natives & knowledge keepers' (@native4data, 1 September 2022).

Small-Rodriguez goes on to 'imagine otherwise', a concept that Cherokee scholar Daniel Heath Justice authored insisting that to imagine otherwise is an act of visioning that plants the seeds of the future which is not yet here. They argue, 'we can't possibly live otherwise until we first imagine otherwise'.[8] Such imaginings and contemplations include a world filled with possibility and free of the oppressive forces of colonialism: 'Imagine an entire team of Indigenous faculty spread across the Indigenous world in their home communities connected through one institution delivering courses, leading research, creating life changing opportunities for students & communities! This is possible! Let us do it!' (@native4data, 1 September 2022).

As Māori scholar Linda Tuiwai-Smith (2012, p. 255) argues: 'One of the strategies that indigenous peoples have employed effectively to bind people together politically, asks that people imagine a future, that they rise above present-day situations which are generally depressing, dream a new dream and set a new vision.' Digital technologies such as social media provides many possibilities and opportunities. As the world still grapples with COVID-19, our reliance on technologies has also create different, new and innovative ways to connect with each other, to work and to enjoy life. Some of these transient innovations will likely remain with us and has the possibility for institutions like higher education to also imagine otherwise. As argued by Daly and colleagues (2020, p. 150):

> we will have a unique opportunity to rebuild, reimagine, and retool our societies and educational systems and hopefully make significant investments in a global public good. Rather than pull back further into our individualistic shells, we have the opportunity to become even more communal and better linked, and social media and technology will have an important role to play.

Social media platforms provide a foundation for Indigenous peoples globally to develop networks. These connections often begin on a local or small scale but evidence shows their rapid development, the effects of which often produce change – in ideas, actions and importantly, the imagining of future possibilities. Although there are pitfalls, as mentioned, where racism and colonialism infect online spaces, the benefits of Indigenous solidarity that have accrued around social media sites are vast. Users once disconnected in any 'real' sense now attract friends, colleagues and like-minded others on a global scale once unimaginable. Our networks are now in situ, immense and thriving and in many respects, organised and controlled by us.

Notes

1 In this chapter I use the term 'Indigenous' as a global identifier. I use specific terms such as 'Aboriginal' or 'Native American' when speaking about collectives in one specific place and when appropriate I use local specific terms.

2 I make the point that this is a continent not a country. 'Australia' as it is now referred was built on a legal fiction of *terra nullius* (nobody's

land) and claimed for the British Crown, despite being home to hundreds of self-identifying nations.
3 See www.facebook.com/decolonizemyself/photos/a.422532081229653/2271399169676259/
4 See www.youtube.com/watch?v=QeQjRK4TKIc
5 See www.youtube.com/watch?v=TWy-g1eLBP4
6 See www.pedestrian.tv/news/too-strong-for-you-karen-merch/
7 See statistics from the Center on Juvenile and Criminal Justice statistics at www.cjcj.org/news/8113
8 See https://danielheathjustice.com

References

Arias, A. (2019). *Indigenous Interfaces: Spaces, Technology, and Social Networks in Mexico and Central America*. Tempe: University of Arizona Press.

Barker, A. J. (2015). 'A direct act of resurgence, a direct act of sovereignty': Reflections on idle no more, indigenous activism, and Canadian settler colonialism. *Globalizations, 12*(1), 43–65.

Belton, K. A. (2010). From cyberspace to offline communities: Indigenous peoples and global connectivity. *Alternatives, 35*(3), 193–215.

Berglund, J. (2016). 'I'm just as Indian standing before you with no feathers popping out of my head': Critiquing Indigenous performativity in the YouTube performances of the 1491s. *AlterNative: An International Journal of Indigenous Peoples, 12*(5), 541–557.

@BundjalungBud (2022). Blackfulla Twitter connects different mob from all over the country & that's worth celebrating. *Pedestrian*, 8 July. www.pedestrian.tv/news/blackfulla-twitter/?fbclid=IwAR1_TmPPR1_Q0xk4IkCJdSTmFAM0GbML2PabotgnjyLErNjgV-_QnlBW0VE

Carlson, B. (2013). The 'new frontier': Emergent Indigenous identities and social media. In Harris, M., Nakata, M. & Carlson, B. (Eds), *The Politics of Identity: Emerging Indigeneity* (pp. 147–168). Sydney: University of Technology Sydney E-Press.

Carlson, B. (2016). *The Politics of Identity: Who Counts as Aboriginal Today?*. Acton: Aboriginal Studies Press.

Carlson, B. (2021a). Place-online lessons from Indigenous knowledges. In Lewis, P., & Guiao, J. (Eds), *The Public Square Project: Reimagining Our Digital Future* (pp. 58–67). Melbourne: Melbourne University Press.

Carlson, B. (2021b). Internet users: Learning to trust ourselves. *Australian Feminist Studies*, special issue: Gender-Technology-Trust: Feminist Reflections on Mobile and Social Media Practices, Hardley, J., McGrane, C., & Richardson, I. (guest editors).

Carlson, B., & Berglund, J. (2021). *(Des) Indigenous People Rise Up: The Global Ascendancy of Social Media Activism.* New Brunswick: Rutgers University Press.

Carlson, B., & Frazer, R. (2015). 'It's like going to a cemetery and lighting a candle': Aboriginal Australians, sorry business and social media. *AlterNative: An International Journal of Indigenous Peoples, 11*(3), 211–224.

Carlson, B., & Frazer, R. (2016). *Indigenous Activism and Social Media. Negotiating Digital Citizenship: Control, Contest Culture.* Lanham: Rowman & Littlefield International.

Carlson, B. and Frazer, R. (2018). *Social Media Mob: Being Indigenous Online.* Sydney: Macquarie University.

Carlson, B., & Frazer, R. (2021). *Indigenous Digital Life: The Practice and Politics of Being Indigenous on Social Media.* Basingstoke: Palgrave Macmillan.

Carlson, B. L., Jones, L. V., Harris, M., Quezada, N., & Frazer, R. (2017). Trauma, shared recognition and Indigenous resistance on social media. *Australasian Journal of Information Systems, 21.*

Castells, M. (2013). *Communication Power.* Oxford: Oxford University Press.

Christensen, N. B. (2003). *Inuit in Cyberspace: Embedding Offline, Identities Online.* Copenhagen: Museum Tusculanum Press.

Copage, K. (2019). The transformative spirit of Indigenous humour: Redskins, tricksters and puppy stew. *Antistasis, 9*(1), 186–204.

Daly, A. J., Fresno García, M. D., & Bjorklund, Jr., P. (2020). Social media in a new era: Pandemic, pitfalls, and possibilities. *American Journal of Education, 127*(1), 143–151.

Deschine Parkhurst, N. (2021). From# Mniwiconi to# StandWithStandingRock: How# NoDAPL Movement disrupted physical and virtual spaces and brought Indigenous liberation to the forefront of people's minds. In *Indigenous People Rise Up: The Global Ascendancy of Social Media Activism.* New Brunswick: Rutgers University Press, pp. 32–46.

Dreher, T., McCallum, K., & Waller, L. (2016). Indigenous voices and mediatized policy-making in the digital age. *Information, Communication & Society, 19*(1), 23–39.

Duarte, M. E. (2017). *Network Sovereignty: Building the Internet across Indian Country.* Seattle: University of Washington Press.

DuBois, T. A., & Cocq, C. (2019). *Sámi Media and Indigenous Agency in the Arctic North.* Seattle: University of Washington Press.

Fincham, B. (2016). *The Sociology of Fun.* Basingstoke: Palgrave Macmillan.

Goldblatt, H. (2020). A brief history of 'Karen'. *New York Times*, 31 July. www.nytimes.com/2020/07/31/style/karen-name-meme-history.html

Hefler, M., Kerrigan, V., Henryks, J., Freeman, B., & Thomas, D. P. (2019). Social media and health information sharing among Australian Indigenous people. *Health Promotion International*, 34(4), 706–715.

John, S. (2015). Idle no more: Indigenous activism and feminism. *Theory in Action*, 8(4), 38.

Johnson, D. M. (2011). From the tomahawk chop to the road block: Discourses of savagism in whitestream media. *American Indian Quarterly*, 35(1), 104–134.

Kamelamela, K. (@kteabam) (2022). 'Aloha mai, I am excited to TW announce … I have signed to be an Assistant Professor at Arizona State University'. *Twitter post*, 1 September. https://twitter.com/kteabam/status/1565074611460444166

Lang, C. (2020). How the 'Karen Meme' confronts the violent history of white womanhood, *Time*, 6 July. https://time.com/5857023/karen-meme-history-meaning/

Lee, M. (2022). Navigating the social media space for Māori and Indigenous communities. In *Research Anthology on Usage, Identity, and Impact of Social Media on Society and Culture*. Hershey: IGI Global, pp. 879–893.

Lindgren, S., & Cocq, C. (2017). Turning the inside out: Social media and the broadcasting of Indigenous discourse. *European Journal of Communication*, 32(2), 131–150.

Lumby, B. (2010). Cyber-indigeneity: Urban indigenous identity on Facebook. *The Australian Journal of Indigenous Education*, 39(S1), 68–75.

Morozov, E. (2009). Iran: Downside to the 'Twitter revolution'. *Dissent*, 56(4), 10–14.

Nakata, M. N. (2007). *Disciplining the Savages, Savaging the Disciplines*. Acton: Aboriginal Studies Press.

Papacharissi, Z. (2016). Affective publics and structures of story-telling: Sentiment, events and mediality. *Information, Communication & Society*, 19(3), 307–324.

Reid, T. (2022). How much longer can the law justify killing Aboriginal people?. *The Sydney Morning Herald*, 14 March. www.smh.com.au/national/how-much-longer-can-the-law-justify-the-killing-of-aboriginal-people-20220313-p5a46n.html

Rice, E. S., Haynes, E., Royce, P., & Thompson, S. C. (2016). Social media and digital technology use among Indigenous young people in Australia: A literature review. *International Journal for Equity in Health*, 15(1), 1–16.

Tuiwai Smith, L. (2012). *Decolonizing Methodologies: Research and Indigenous Peoples*. London: Zed Books.

Virtanen, P. K. (2015). Indigenous social media practices in Southwestern Amazonia. *AlterNative: An International Journal of Indigenous Peoples*, 11(4), 350–362.

Wilson, A., & Zheng, C. (2021). Shifting social media and the Idle No More movement. In Carlson, B., & Berglund, J. (Eds), *Indigenous Peoples Rise Up: The Global Ascendency of Social Media Activism* (pp. 14–31). New Brunswick: Rutgers University Press.

Wilson, A., Carlson, B. L., & Sciascia, A. (2017). Reterritorialising social media: Indigenous people rise up. *Australasian Journal of Information Systems*, 21, 1–4.

Wolfe, P. (2006). Settler colonialism and the elimination of the native. *Journal of Genocide Research*, 8(4), 387–409.

10

Indigiqueer futures: a conversation between Indigenous non-binary academics

Percy Lezard, Madi Day and Sandy O'Sullivan

Please note that this chapter includes names and discussion of people who are now deceased.

This chapter is a Zoom conversation between non-binary Indigenous academics in October 2021. Percy Lezard (PhD) who joined from Tkaronto, the territory of many nations including the Mississaugas of the Credit, the Anishanabeg, the Chippewa, the Haudenosaunee and the Wendat peoples[1] and Sandy O'Sullivan (PhD) who joined from the land of the Gubbi Gubbi people. Madi Day prepared the questions and facilitated the conversation from Gadigal Country. In this chapter, we present a refined version of our conversation about the realities and complexities of being both non-binary and Indigenous (and the challenges of other intersections including disability) in the academy. The chapter includes reflections and narratives from Percy and Sandy's lives as Indigenous non-binary peoples and their journeys to academia. We also consider the relationship between activism and academia, gender and colonialism, and look to the future of Indigenous Studies.

Although we have refined the piece for academic purposes, we have also left much of the conversation intact. This means that some of the narratives are non-linear and there is use of colloquial terms. We also use terms that change in meaning depending on use, context and territory. This chapter uses the terms Indigenous and First Nations throughout to refer to First Peoples of territories occupied by settler colonial states named Australia and Canada. We also refer to Aboriginal people as the First Peoples of the mainland continent colonists call Australia. In this context, we use

Indigeneity as a global term to communicate shared experiences and relationships with homelands, kin and histories. In conversation, we use non-binary, queer and gender diverse colloquially to refer to our experiences of being outside and beyond Western colonial binaries of gender. Using queer in this manner can be contentious. At the same time, communities that are diverse in terms of gender and sexuality (aka not heterosexual or cisgender) cannot be easily siloed apart. Particularly, when we share other experiences in common like Indigeneity. We also use the Aboriginal English term mob throughout to refer to communities of Indigenous peoples including queer, transgender and non-binary mob.

The term Indigiqueer, used in the title of this chapter was coined by TJ Cuthand to describe part of the Indigenous program for the Vancouver Queer Film Festival in 2004 (Cuthand 2017). Indigequeer/Indigiqueer is in use by Indigenous writers, including Joshua Whitehead (2017), and speaks to a rich body of artistic, activist and academic works that are connected through resistance to colonial enforcements of gender and sexuality in European settler societies including Canada, Australia and the United States of America. We have included a bibliography rather than a reference list at the end of this piece to invite readers to some of these works. The term Two Spirit is in use in continental North America. However, as Percy discusses later in this chapter, it has been used by some to narrow definitions of community and identity, and by others with more expansive meaning. It is not an appropriate term for all Indigenous queer and transgender people and is not used by peoples of Oceania. More recently, Indigenous queer and trans works of futurism from Australia are gaining traction and joining global conversations about resistance and resurgence (Simpson 2017). While we do not have time to discuss this further in this chapter, we invite you to the works of key writers including Arlie Alizzi, Claire G. Coleman, Mykaela Saunders and Ellen van Neervan in the bibliography. Writing into an increasingly globalised and future-thinking space, we use Indigiqueer to refer to relationships, innovations and conversations across time, cultures, lands and seas.

Percy Lezard and Sandy O'Sullivan are public intellectuals who speak, write and research into this space. Madi Day is an Aboriginal transgender researcher who is privileged to enjoy mentoring and leadership from Percy and Sandy as they navigate academia as an early career researcher and PhD candidate.

Percy Lezard is an outma Sqilx^w scholar and Program Coordinator (Chair) of Indigenous Studies at Wilfred Laurier University. They are an expert in Indigenous health, social work and organising, gender-based violence in Two Spirit and Trans communities, Two Spirit pedagogies and Indigenous research methodologies. They recently worked on the MMIWG2SLGBTQIA+ Action Plan – a plan by the Government of Canada to address a national crisis of Missing and Murdered Indigenous women, girls, and Two Spirit and lesbian, gay, bisexual, transgender, queer, questioning, intersex and asexual peoples (Lezard et al. 2021). The resulting report is globally relevant to Indigenous non-binary, transgender and queer peoples as it is speaks directly to gender binaries and gendered violence as related colonial impositions.

Sandy O'Sullivan is a Wiradjuri transgender/non-binary Professor of Indigenous Studies, and an Australian Research Council (ARC) Future Fellow. Since 1991 they have taught and researched across gender and sexuality, museums, the body, performance, design and First Nations' identity. Sandy was the inaugural director of the Centre for Collaborative First Nations' Research at Batchelor Institute in the Northern Territory and was recently Deputy Head of School of Creative Industries at the University of the Sunshine Coast. Their 2020–2024 ARC Future Fellow project titled *Saving Lives: Mapping the Influence of Indigenous LGBTIQ+ Creative Artists* explores the unique contribution and influence of queer artists to understand how modelling complex identities contributes to the wellbeing of all First Nations' peoples.

Madi Day: I'm conscious that I am entering this space as a beneficiary of years of hard work, doors kicked in and paths carved out. So, I wanted to start the conversation today by asking if you could each tell us about your journey into academia.

Sandy O'Sullivan: Sure ... it was a weird journey into it – unlike many of my non-Indigenous colleagues. Non-Indigenous colleagues went to school, and then finished school, and then went to university, and then went on beyond that. Some of them worked in other jobs before they did their PhDs and then came back. But for me, I left school at thirteen and worked in a laundromat and a music store and then worked as a musician when I got to about fifteen.

And then I went to uni[2] in my 20s. And then stayed, if you like, but I'd had ten years of not being in education, more than that, before I then started.

I had never written an essay, or even a sentence, because I couldn't read when I left school, so I'd never written anything before apart from notes and things like shopping lists. When I started uni I got in with adult entry, which meant that I didn't have to do anything to get in except for pass. Because they required it for people who were doing anything other than creative practice, but if you are a creative practitioner, you could do it by audition. So, I did an audition to get into uni and then turned up thinking that I was going to be doing all of this creative practice stuff, which I was, but in addition to that I had to learn how to write. I was really scared of writing because I'd just never done it, and so I had to learn that process and understand a little bit more about, you know, what it meant. We just didn't have ... you know, now I look at my family, we've got these people with PhDs in my family but that didn't exist, I mean that's recent. So, I was the first person to get a PhD as an example. Mum got one afterwards, but she had left school at thirteen as well. David[3] was the only person in the family that had gone through all the way to, you know, had gone through high school and into uni, but he was the first person in our family ever that did that in the 70s. It was relatively uncommon in my experience as an Aboriginal person who's gone through that space, it was completely normal. I mean there were plenty of other people doing PhDs along with me who left school at thirteen. There were lots.

What we're seeing now is we're, finally, now seeing people who actually finished school, who are going through and doing it and it's wonderful to see. It really is. It's the dream. I don't want people to have to have 'life experience'. Like you can get life experience while you're working towards stuff. You don't have to go and work in laundromat to get it. It's a nonsense that's about ... how privilege works and doesn't work, and so in a whole lot of ways I'm really glad that I had that time to spend with my craft. It had nothing to do with community. If you're not connected to community at any point in academic work, then there's some sort of mistake. It wasn't separate time with community and time with the academy. It's time with the community for fifty-five years. But I think the rhetoric for a lot of other people, people who talk about us, it becomes that.

And so, I've always been loath to talk about the 'I left school at thirteen' narrative because a lot of it becomes this kind of fantasy of, you know, poor little kid that didn't know how to read! Suddenly like – that's not what happened! What happened was I went and did other stuff and then I did this stuff, and then all of it was community connected.

So, yeah. I mean that's the journey and I loved it. I loved the reading when I learned how to, and I loved hearing other people's stories and reading was that for me. It was being able to read how other people comprehend the world rather than just put my own stuff out there, so it wasn't self-centred, but it was certainly centred in myself in the sense that I was really interested.

Madi Day: Brilliant, thank you. Percy, how does your experience relate to that?

Percy Lezard: Well, my experience here, as a First Nations person here in Continental North America was I already had colonial systems engaged. I already had systems engaged on me and my additional layer was that the moment I was born, and they wrapped me, I was placed into child welfare. That's the phenomenon here of the Sixties Scoop[4] or, as Raven Sinclair (2007) says, multigenerational stolen folks, right? And in and out of care until the age of eighteen.

So, I have been working labour, hard labour since I was six years old. And knew how to drive since I was six years old. And been raising my siblings and children since also at six years of age. And my older sibling, who's thirteen months older than me, was the last person in my paternal and maternal lineage to have gone to residential school. And my first language is ASL[5] so that has always been difficult because I think in ASL and I also write in ASL, so I'm seen as less than. Not only because the way I think in the subject position and all those things and spatiality of my signing doesn't transfer so well. That's been my experience. When I was in care or back on the reserve and working like up in the mountains logging, falling trees, labour stuff, or working in the orchards all season. Part of that was, up until I was eight, when I was on reserve, I had to go to the creek and get water and use an outhouse, right, you didn't have electricity. So, those are the things that I had to do and to, I guess, escape or just to get a sense of not having to be in that space, I became an athlete. Anything I did, I excelled as an athlete.

Grade two I was playing with the grade seven folks. And just anything – track and field – because we had a lot of energy, my parents
would make us get up and go, regardless of the time of year, like my
learning is also with the Land, on the Land, in our culture.

I was the first to go to public school, high school, to go to a
college program, my undergrad and my PhD. From my mother and
my father, I was the first to successfully do those things. My parents
went to residential school.[6] Once folks saw my brown skin and it
was often in clothes that didn't fit, and I didn't like what they called
me, you know, at that time I didn't know. I didn't like being dead
named or that wasn't my name. I was always getting sent to the
office. Oppositional defiance I think they call it, but I'm just like
'just don't call me that name, that isn't my name, I go by Percy,
that's who I am'. I didn't know that's what I was responding to or
reacting to that I didn't have the words as an eight, nine, ten, eleven,
twelve, thirteen, fourteen-year-old. They'd just go 'okay, we'll just
make this person play sports' and I would. They didn't actually
care if I could read or write. I now know, because my partner's a
literacy worker, that I was functionally illiterate. I had a phenom-
enal memory, and now I know why. I have ASL and that's how
I engage with the world – spatial – and I play off cues of people's
non-verbals, and that helped me later to be formally trained as a
social worker. I didn't have to do a lot of the work that other people
had to do because I was already a first responder and able to read
the body language and non-verbals, and because of colonialism was
able to work through crisis situations and recognise mental health
and wellness.

Everybody knew before me. I didn't have the words, but I knew
I was not going to have a relationship with a cis man. And that
I was going to have many children, but I was not going to bear them
myself. And my family is like 'uh huh okay'. I would be like 'yeah,
I have a girlfriend in school, I play all these sports'. I was very well
liked and had a lot of friends. Then my cousin had shared 'you're
gay'. I'm like 'okay, I don't know what that means'. I was told
I wasn't going to live past twenty. Twenty came and went. I travelled
because of the Jay Treaty. With my status card I didn't need a passport to get into the States. If I had my status card,[7] I could just come
and go as I please and I did that, and within Vancouver. Because
I was like 'okay, if I'm going to date, these are all my cousins and I'm

not going to date my cousin', right? Because when I said those words 'I'm gay' or tried to figure out those words, my family as a whole had a huge reaction to me. They didn't honour and celebrate me, they immediately were triggered back to their responses of having gone to residential school or day schools, and the people who caused them harm were people of the same sex, like nuns and priests who are the same sex. And so, at that time I also thought 'Okay, you say I'm a gift but you're not understanding, you think I can't be around my younger siblings because I'm going to abuse them. What you're talking about now, I think, is about power and control, and who I am is a gift, why are these not matching?'[8]

Everything in my reality from like six years of age, 'Why are people calling me this and it doesn't match? Like what's going on? What is with this?' Again, colonialism. Just having access to those things. Then I went to San Francisco, met a lot of people, and started to engage in poetry and spoken word.[9] Met like Chrystos, Beth Brant, Connie Fife, a lot of Indigenous creatives.[10] Then found out who my family was, and met recently passed, Lee Maracle.[11] Just getting in with creative folks, and playwrights, and poets, and stuff. I didn't write stuff down, I just thought it, remembered it, and spoke it. No one ever said go to school, no one ever said continue your education, make something of yourself. No, it's just get paid. Pay for gas, insurance, fix something on the rez vehicle, make sure we have some staples for the family, and that's what I did. I started working as a counsellor for the school because I could work well with others who are in distress or trying to work through communication or conflict. I figured 'Okay, well, I went to San Francisco, let's get a coin', and then it came up tails, and I came to Toronto, and I've been here since 98 and I thought 'Okay, so they're telling me in this province, Mike Harris said it's a hand up, not a handout.[12] Well, crap. I've been able to do all this helping work and get paid for it, but they want to see accreditation.' That's when I decided to go to school, college, to get something after my name, to be able to continue to get jobs and piecemeal work. I had upwards of, at one time, four part-time positions in various shelters, frontline work, helping, labour, moving and other illegal stuff.

I got into school. Then the first assignment came, was worth 40 per cent of the mark. I got a zero because it was written component, but Professor Cameron saw Percy; A+ speaker in the class, engagement, critical, and Percy's paper; zero, nothing and saw that again, there's something not fitting. Let's go up to the fifth floor of George Brown College where the accessibility services were. They're like 'Hey Percy. You have an appointment here' and I'm like 'What do you mean I have an appointment?' They talked with an intake person, they did a psycho educational assessment on me, I felt poked and prodded. It was all, now looking back, was very Eurocentric. I didn't do well on certain components. I did well in others, and they gave it back to me and said I was gifted and, of course, like institutions do, you have all these learning disabilities but you're very gifted and threw a lot of money at me to get all these fancy dancy software programs. Once I started to learn how to read, I read a book a day. Once I learned how to write because I had a team of folks to … peer tutors and whatnot, they taught me how to write. Then I thought 'Okay well why am I just here getting my college degree? Why don't I go for an undergrad? Nobody has an undergrad in my family, all my family has gone for one year-two year certificate programs in college so let me go check it out … Oh, what do I want to do? Social work. I'm working in that right now, I have four jobs, I'm going to school.'

I got in, and again I didn't do so well, and then again went to another accessibility services. They threw more money at me, and I got more skills to be in an undergrad and I thought 'Heck. Why not go do a Masters?' And I went to University of Toronto and did a Masters. My God. Wow. I thought 'pay back for what you did to my parents and my older siblings; I want to get into a PhD Program.' And I got in! I was like 'Okay. You just think and talk. Well, I think, and I talk, and I've always asked why are things the way they are? And you want me to source other people every time?' At that time, I started teaching at the college level and university courses. I was already prioritising Black, Indigenous, racialised scholars. Coming into, what does Queer Studies mean? What does Indigenous Studies mean? I live those things every day. What more can we do, right? Just coming in and having those conversations with folks about pushing back against whiteness and white supremacy with other Black, Indigenous and racialised folks whilst we're Indigiqueer and gender diverse. I started that process, and I was the only one in my journey. It wasn't until my third year of my social work degree that I met an Indigenous scholar. Everybody else was white, cisgender and able bodied. It wasn't until I had a guest lecture in the second to last course, I needed from our coursework for my PhD that I had access to someone who is racialised and gender diverse. I've never had anybody who was part of my identity as someone who is disabled or visibly shared with us their disability. Indigeneity, and queerness, and all my intersecting identity.

I've never seen myself well represented in any of the texts that I was reading, other than what now I'm able to see as a trauma porn lens. I've never seen anything for me, or about joy. That really made it that much more difficult to want to complete my PhD because people a) saw my confidence as knowing unmentorable but really, I had no idea, I've never done it, nobody in my family has done a PhD. So, that has been my journey being in the institution, but it wasn't until 2015, after teaching since 2007, I was like 'Okay, this is what I want to do.' I didn't see me or how I would speak or think in the text, but I want people to have access and I've had people take multiple courses with me because I reflected their identities as Indigenous, disabled … because I'm outwardly. I say in the first class, 'This is who I am, this is my experience, and this is the approaches we'll take, and this is how it will be. You may not like it; it may discomfort you but if you're not discomforted then I'm not actually doing my job. I'm not going to hold a space for you folks, I'm going to role model for you a different way of coming into learnings.'

Sandy O'Sullivan: Thank you!

Madi Day: Thank you. That brings me to the next question: what do you see as the relationship between activism and academia?

Sandy O'Sullivan: I think there's a relationship between anything and anything. I don't think that you can talk about the experience of being a person and kind of settle it into silos. The problem with the academy is that it does that too much and actually it's not very successful when it does it. Interestingly, it stops being very functional. One of the biggest problems with higher education is it's not very functional because it's not following the regular path of how to be in the world. It's doing all these disruptions of that, and so, in a sense, activism is an obvious idea that should be carried by an institution that's about learning. Not about teaching but about learning. It's why privileged people have used universities as sites of activism. It's why you saw … very white centred, centrally centred activisms that have occurred from Bluestocking[13] through to a whole lot of different processes of civil rights. But it was white centred – it was what mattered to them, and it was what mattered in this kind of lens of who has the power. I don't know that the academy knows how not to do that. Like, I think it still expects that activism will comply with the broader principles that are colonial. From my perspective, it's not anything more than a gathering place for people who are the same. In other words, I've seen it as a site of being able to connect with people who have the same interests, but we don't necessarily have the interests of the academy. I think activism in our institution and in our department comes up as very much about challenging the institution and requiring the institution to hear our challenge. It's absolutely of the world as well, because it has to be and it's sort of forcing the academy back into the world. That's the relationship, for me.

Activism is such a white idea. It just is. It's a power idea. It's that centralising power of 'how can I get more power'. I'm not romanticising Indigeneity or own community because I think sometimes that happens in this notion of 'we have power, and we don't'. We do and we don't and sometimes there can be a kind of overstating of the 'do' in a way that I think a lot of non-Indigenous people see us as activists, when in fact what we're trying to do is survive and also get people to recognise our complexity. Or even the D word, our diversity, you know? But complexity is more what I mean. The reason that I've been writing a bit recently about allyship is that it really worries me that people so easily fall into the idea of being allies, rather than the practice of supporting other people's voices or other people's ideas. Peoples that they don't understand, you know, instead of trying to get them into the box of how they understand us. I think, especially for Blakfellas here, I think there is a real problem at the moment with the perception of how we operate as activists. Different to how it was, for instance in the 70s and 80s.

I didn't do much in the way of activism in the 70s, because I grew up in Queensland and we weren't allowed to. But it doesn't mean that you still don't do things that are, in some ways, activist. As soon as I left Queensland in the 80s, I did start to really engage in protest and I don't mean protest like I turned up to marches, I mean, yes, but also no. I mean real, genuine protest where it was about seeing things that were happening and kind of going 'wait that's happening to us!' And this was the first time, you know this, right? But Stolen Generations[14] … I mean the most remarkable thing about Stolen Generations is that so few of us that were actually subjected to it, knew about it. Knew that it was widespread, you know? Knew that it was something that was happening to other people as well. That there was this comprehension that it was only happening in our own families and that it was only happening to ourselves. Part of that is why I really love social media now because it's this way of challenging some of that stuff. It's that way of decentring the power in that way. So, yes. I don't know about unis. I think they're the worst place for it, but they also have this kind of fantasy of it.

Percy Lezard: Various colleagues, contract lecturers, support staff, admin people, have said 'Oh, it's okay to do that out there, but here let's just teach people and not get them upset.' My family was radical in the sense that they're part of Red Power and AIM, and they collaborated with Black Panthers. And shut stuff down. And had conversations. And would go up to the hills and get deer, elk, moose, fish, harvest stuff and feed everybody. Nothing we have is not just ours. We take what we need and share it with everybody, and nobody goes without and if there's only just one roast, then all hundred of us have to eat off that roast, even if that means we just get a little bit, but everybody has to eat. So, it's been my experience that the institution wanted me as an Indigenous person, but only wanted me to perform Indian and not actually *be* Indian. I was seen as and labelled as a threat. Even though I was taken, I have a language, have a land, have a people. And that was a threat and they saw that as maybe activist. I'm like 'I'm just being in the world.' And I'm in the institution and I'm teaching. I don't dance, I don't sing, I don't smudge. I say I'm not interested in your land acknowledgement if you're not going to give the land back. Or acknowledge that you're going to transfer over onto the occupied territories of the people's whose land that you didn't steal yet when there's outside your doors Black and Indigenous people who are houseless with deteriorating mental health because of ongoing colonial violence.

I think they don't like it when I actually want to raise up students. They actually say 'you shouldn't do that; you shouldn't be affirming and supportive of them' like student groups who are active and wanting to push back against anti-Black racism, or cissexism, or ableism, or anti-Indigenous racism. The institutional powers will say: 'Students couldn't have possibly come into this' and I'm like 'well, I used my code, and we went into a classroom, what's wrong with that? They're not causing harm to anybody; doesn't that fall under your words of academic freedom? Is this not what we're here to support people to do? I'm actualising things that you want to do.' Ever since I started in 2000, I've non-stop gotten every type of complaint filed against me by students and colleagues. Knock on wood. It hasn't happened this year but last year, I had a gaggle of ten students who didn't like the way I said, social work is a colonial project. If we go back to the origin stories, it already excluded Black and Indigenous people. But yeah, those are the folks in the Canadian context that are overrepresented in helping sector and they thought I was unsafe, I was angry, I was targeting them, and I'm like well I'm a social worker myself. Me opening my mouth, the institution labels me as a threat, and a target, and an activist for just breathing. I'm going to continue to build relationships with students and community. They don't like that everything I do I get direction from community. I get that I signed a contract with you, but if community says no, I'm not doing it. They don't like that. I prioritise my relationships and my agreements because I really take my agreements or Treaty responsibility serious, and they are trying to figure those things out.

Sandy O'Sullivan: Academic freedom stuff is such a weird one because, it's like in Queensland we've got this slogan that they started about twenty-five years ago that's 'The Smart State' and it's like you only call yourself the smart state if you think you're not. I think the same thing is true with academic freedom. I think you just start to define it when you know that there isn't such a thing. It's such a worry what they mean too, that it then has to align with policies, and it can't. Policies are always going to mean that you have to play the game of sitting within those spaces, but I mean there's no point in not doing resistance. There's no benefit to it in the broader sense for us as people and as a people. That's how the system wins, and the system wins anyway, it doesn't need help from us. That activism stuff, it's such an interesting problem of this ideal of it rather than the idea of it. So, rather than it just being a prompt to become something of its own. This idea of 'I'm an activist', or 'I'm intersectional', or 'I'm interested in all of this support of others', instead of just actually demonstrating it. What we expect, and what we require from our colleagues, for instance in the academy. The best thing for me about working at Macquarie University has been my colleagues who do this all the time. I don't just mean Bronwyn[15] as a leader within the space. I mean it is amazing to have two full professors in a space. Only 1 per cent of academics become professors[16] in this country, and to have two Aboriginal academics who are professors is remarkable. Bronwyn made that happen. So, it's all of my colleagues. I had thirty years without a good cohort, and I've had a year with a really amazing cohort. I have had good colleagues over the years but that's activism. It's not event based, it's not just Trans Awareness Week. I mean all of those things matter because they do, but it's the activism of the everyday; of the building a curriculum, of the engaging with students, of all of that you just said Percy, about the idea of handing over a room to students and trusting them. Not overseeing them, not policing their boundaries, but kind of allowing them to misbehave in the broader sense of the academy. It's such a powerful thing. This wasn't the situation thirty years ago at all here. There wasn't any possibility of that, and it really was a journey to get here. Having said all of that, there were wonderful things along the way. There really were. There were wonderful people along the way that really moved it forward, and some of them were really complicated people who I have real issue with, but they did really amazing work.

We're in that scale they use that is all about ticking enough boxes and they worry about the Indigenous box as well. So, just like you were saying about them wanting you to perform Indian – they don't even want the performance of it, they want the performance of what they want, you know? I find that to be enormously difficult, but I think in terms of being outside of the binary, it's particularly difficult because they, you know, they really do, even the best of people, really do have trouble with the idea of reconciling the two things as though they need reconciling. Apart from the fact that it's reconciled in one's body, it's also they're not inconsistencies, but it just highlights how tragic their own kind of box-making is. I think that's been the biggest shock for me in the last few years and I'm still getting a lot of people asking me when I found out I was trans, or when I came out. This kind of notion of it being recent is also seen as this idea of destabilising. I've started to say my truth, which is that I've always known but I certainly didn't have a language for it in the 60s. This is everyone but also this language of saying 'you people intentionally erased us so I don't have to show evidence for trans non-binary people existing historically. You have to show me evidence for how you know that all of these people that you're talking about are cisgender.' That's what needs to happen. I think that the turning it around helps because just like the boxes, I don't think they ever think about this stuff. They're supposed to be academics that are using their brains and thinking about stuff so it shocks me ... the lack of inquiry.

Percy Lezard: Further to that, I know the self-advocacy I did for my own PhD changed how they do intake and prioritise communities.[17] I know when I was at many of the universities here in Ontario, it actually made it that much clearer. It is now a clear path for folks here who have had their first tenure track job or first appointment. They don't have to go through twenty-five like I did. Like I did that work because I don't want those people to be treated the way I was, like a zoo. They looked at me in the hallway like I was an animal. I was like 'Okay, I can't hide that I'm visibly Indigenous. I can't hide the fact that I'm not going to go to one of your binary washrooms, I want a single stall washroom.' I didn't want to get into 'I want an all gender.' I'm like 'Okay, I'm going to just name and if you're not able to support me and if you're not ready, then I don't want to be there.' I also started to, in my interviews, interview other people like 'Okay, you're not just going to ask me all these questions of how it can benefit you, how are you going to actually support me? What are you going to do and how are you going to ... because you are benefiting from my connections to community and people on the ground because those are people you can go to get your interviews. How are you actually going to honour and celebrate me being here and all my identities?'

A previous university I had worked at wanted that, and I was very grateful to be there. I loved being there. I'm still grieving that because I was in classrooms where it was 95 per cent Indigenous and I'm including Afro-Indigenous and around 40 per cent of those folks were trans, Two Spirit, non-binary, disabled. They lived their life like I did. I also had been chronically houseless and until I moved to Manitoba in 2018. That's the first time I moved where

I wasn't living on the streets or having to engage in survival street economies. I loved being there. I love the communities and community members that I met. I had access to Two Spirit Elders and trans Elders all the time. I had access to ceremony, and there were times I was in a circle with sixty Two Spirit, trans folks. The youngest person was six and the oldest person was like seventy like that is wonderful medicine. So, I'm just trying to make it easier and not so violent for those coming after me and supporting folks in community with similar literacy levels as I did. To say 'It can happen, it's not an easy journey, but I can support you' or 'Here's a roadmap, and this is what I did to survive'. I now want to thrive, and thriving doesn't mean just getting a crap load of money and lots of research projects.

Thriving is not experiencing violence in terms of misgendering or dead naming or having to talk about somebody else. Just being able to have relationships with people that are not mining me, they're not trying to extract but just actually meaningful relationships and conversations and time with people. That's what I would like and that's what I'm building towards. There's quite a few Two Spirit folks, more than there was twenty-five years ago, in administrative positions. I don't want to be the only one. I just want to say 'we can be in these positions, if we want'. They're violent because we're asked to push out people. I want to be very real – these positions are meant to push out people if they don't function in a particular way that benefits the institution. I named when I interviewed for this, I said 'I'm going to centre the Dish with one Spoon,[18] I'm going to centre myself as a fire keeper, and I'm going to raise up community if that's what they want, and I'm going to always make decisions with them giving me direction, are you okay with that? Because I got a paddle and if we're going to go down our two canoes, then let's get to work, let's start paddling'. And so yeah, they were ready.

Madi Day: When you were talking before, I was thinking about legitimacy as a kind of colonial and institutional violence. I'm thinking about the ways that happens, specifically for non-binary and queer mob, and I was wondering if either of you have any reflections on that.

Sandy O'Sullivan: Yeah. I think that what I'm seeing is that the binary stuff gets incredibly reinforced. Sadly, this has happened across our communities as well because of the push from the federal government on this continent to manage funding. State governments too, manage funding that is really top down so that people behave in colonial ways. They'll talk about men and women and they'll get funding for men and women, and anybody else is just not comprehended and that's a choice. That's a choice that community organisations are making, and communities are making, and I think it's a wrong choice. I think it's unfair and I don't think that there's a community out there that wants to exclude people. I think there's individuals that are transphobic, but I don't think that there's a community that's doing work to exclude. I think they're not doing the work to include.

I think universities think that they're at the forefront of this stuff. I think universities think they're really groovy about being trans inclusive, but they are not. They're hopeless! They're barely tolerating me, and it's really obvious. I mean, I've seen the looks on their faces, and it really reminds me of when I did the museum's work of repatriation. I was at Harvard – I was there giving lectures and I was over at the museum, The Peabody there, and the Lead Curator saw me coming in the front door and ran out the back door when they saw me.[19] They saw me as a threat. How are you supposed to transform anything if you're doing this dickish stuff? How are you transforming anything by having a meeting that follows an agenda and nothing other than what's on the agenda? What a shitty way to manage a world, and this is what colonials do. They manage worlds so that they have an agenda that they tick the box against. So, of course, people outside the binary are really confusing for them.

Percy Lezard: In the National Action Plan[20] I had to fight and I never thought I would have to fight within my own circle. They actively excluded trans folks and experiences of gender diverse folks and the ways violence happens against trans folks. The project initially was Two Spirit, meaning cisgender. And I'm like yes, we need to look at the whole experience of our communities when it comes to gender based violence, and there was a lot of arguments with folks who have a national profile. They refused and were like well that's included. No, no, no, no, because you continually are centring your experience as a Two Spirit cisgender man. The hierarchy. You continue to erase me and the other folks here who are gender diverse and pushed away some gender diverse folks from continuing to work with the circle. I'm like, no, no, we need to stop because again you're prioritising the cisgender portion of the acronym and you really need to think, you really need to have it be about everybody. Last week, I did a review for Canadian Institute for Health Research. Again, they had it as only men and women. I'm like, 'Okay so you've just completely erased.' You harass me for six months to be part of this because of that document[21] that you read, right? Yet you still have funding pools that are just for Indigenous men and Indigenous women. You're not even considering us, you're not even able to support Indigiqueer gender diversity, so this is still a lot more work that you need to do because half you folks continue to misgender me. Like if we can't get past that and you're not able to hear my critique or wanting to push back on, 'Okay, we have all these projects that are supposed to give feedback, funding proposals that are three, five, seven years in length, but it's still for cisgender men and cisgender women like what about the rest? Like how are the health outcomes for my communities going to be supported,' right? And so, before the next thing we need to really hash that out. So again, I'm going to be engaging in conversations with these folks around how support outcomes for trans and non-binary folks, particularly Indigenous folks. Whenever that comes around, I think it's in two months, I'm going to hash that out again.

Sandy O'Sullivan: The problem is that they can be inclusive and it's still excluding, you know, by just the nature of that process. I mean the fact that we've all got really shared experiences with this is one of the things that worries me more than anything else, but it also reinforces the work that can happen.

It's actually why your report has been so important because the shared experiences. That's not a shared experience because there is no pain in Indigeneity, you know. The shared experience is the colonial action and the colonial resistance as well. The resistance to that coloniality and, of course, an ultimate resistance to coloniality, even if it's accidental on our part, is being outside of the binary. Its forcing them to consider that they got it wrong for their own people, you know, that they fucked up their own people. They have. There's not a world out there that doesn't have people outside of the binary, they just managed to fuck up their people first and then do it to everyone else. And then consistently keep doing it because it's not over.

Madi Day: This brings me to my next question on the relationship between colonialism and gender. Percy is shaking their head.

Sandy O'Sullivan: I mean it's an entire function, surely, to control gender. It's all I talk about,[22] but I think my final moment on it would be to say, there is no reason why this has been maintained in terms of the colonial project, except that it is so functionally a part of it and the colonial project is there to ensure that settlers feel like they are the ones in control. And while that happens, there will never be anything that sits outside of what they want to and feel capable of controlling. It's exactly to purpose for them.

Percy Lezard: When I was at my position at a University in Manitoba, I loved it. I was able to actualise and be met by other people who raised me up and I was able to consensually, reciprocally, mutually benefit. When I was pushed out with violence and threats because I was all of me; Indigenous, Sqilx, Two Spirit, gender diverse, disabled, critical, supporting community. I felt hopeless. I felt as if I did not want to live anymore. I had no choice. I had to convince myself that there's hope.

So, I continued to support young folks, I continued to support people in community and continued to hold space for folks when they said, 'I don't understand what this means'. And I'm like, 'Okay so let's find it in our language and then we'll find it on the land and examples.' And then my people started to say it's in the English translation that we put things into the binary. Our language is inclusive, it has no men or women and I'm like, 'Okay, I have hope because our language speakers, our language, my existence, I am there. It's resurgent, picking up.' So, I am trying to find sites of hope to recover my ancestors as trans folks and non-binary folks in the language. I need to imagine that every day is not a dystopia, it's not my apocalypse. I need to reimagine the future as much as possible.

So, I don't constantly want to be preoccupied with continually thinking of gender in the colonial project. I need to find places of hope. That's my response and it's ever growing and ever evolving.

Madi Day: Thank you. Mariame Kaba says that hope is a discipline[23] and I think I cling to that in terms of abolishing colonialism and other possible futures in my own context. I find hope in the lives of role models like you two, and in anti-colonial and Indigenous theory and research. My final question is, what would you like to see from Indigenous Studies in the future?

Sandy O'Sullivan: Indigenous Studies, for a start, needs to be something that's entirely in and part of community. It can't be disconnected from community and not some fantasy of community. That's reality. Not everyone in community wants anything to do with the university either so it's not that. It's about being in service of communities, not drawing from communities.

Percy Lezard: I would love the opportunity to be mediocre. I'm serious. White people get to get $5 million grants to be mediocre and not actually engage in meaningful relationships with Indigenous people, trans people, Two Spirit people, and then they get promoted, right?

I look forward to the day where I can be mediocre, and I don't have to be the first person! I don't want to be the first. I get that it's my internal governance system as a hereditary Chief. I get that it's part of my responsibilities as a Firekeeper but sometimes I just want somebody else to have to take the knocks and the kicks and the words and being pushed out, and I can just be mediocre and mediocre is brilliant, right? And it's okay if it's not brilliant because Indigenous people should be afforded the opportunity to go, 'Oh yeah that's shit,' and that's okay! You're still not less than. You're just going to figure it out and that's, you know, that's truly how I would like to be.

I think one thing I would like, and I don't know if institutions will have the capacity or want to do this, I would love to be on our homelands. I don't want to be 7,000 kilometres away from my people. I want to be able to bring all of that I've learned and share it with my own people. And the beneficiaries are not people from other nations. I would love an opportunity to be able to do Indigenous sovereignty. Indigenous, no, Sqilx epistemologies, anthologies, axiologies on my own homelands with my own people.

Those are some things. If people want to be in these positions, that is a choice, and they can change it anytime they like. I would like those people to be Indigenous because I know in the program there's only two Indigenous people out of six and I'm trying to bring in two more relatives so those white folks can leave, and it can be Indigenous people having conversations and being mediocre if we want. Not having to be twenty times as better as a non-Indigenous person. We can just be and have conversations that are comfortable, uncomfortable, funny, whatever and not have to be excellent, and not have to be ten times better, and not have to attract about ten times more money to get the same legitimacy as the non-Indigenous folks. So, I'm looking forward to 'mediocrity' that is afforded to non-Indigenous people.

Sandy O'Sullivan: Me too. I hear you. I mean, not to load it up with 'it has to all work and it's all got to be right ...' none of that stuff. It's not like all bad, all good. These spaces are spaces that need to work and if they're not working, they need to go away. That's unis. They need to stop being just to maintain the colonial project, and they need to actually serve people. Yeah, and look at what we've done, the three of us. Look at the fact that we've actually done that. We continue to do it for other people, so we know that there's something in that, you know, in those spaces of resistance.

Notes

1 Tkaronto (Toronto) is also covered by Treaty 13 signed with the Mississaugas of the Credit, and the Williams Treaty signed with multiple Mississaugas and Chippewa bands. What should also be noted is an agreement/Treaty called 'Dish with one Spoon' existed between the Huron Wendat, Haudenosaunee and Anishinaabeg peoples prior to the arrival of white settlers/occupiers. This was an agreement between First Peoples to share territory and protect the land in the spirit of peace, friendship and respect still holds today.
2 Short form for university.
3 Dr David Hardy is Sandy O'Sullivan's brother. He was also an influential queer Aboriginal academic. David passed away in May 2022. He is sorely missed.
4 Sixties Scoop is a term coined by Patrick Johnston (1983). It refers to a period between 1960 and the mid 1980s where Canadian child welfare took thousands of Aboriginal children from their families and placed them with settler families. It's important to note that Sixties Scoop refers to a particular period of child removal and that Canadian child welfare continues to remove Aboriginal children from their people. Please see the work of Raven Sinclair (2007) for more on the Sixties Scoop and the impact on Aboriginal children and their communities.
5 American Sign Language.

6 For extensive information about the legacy of Canada's Residential School system, please go to https://nctr.ca/education/teaching-resources/residential-school-history/

7 In colonial Canada, Indigenous peoples are still governed by the Indian Act which provides 'status' to First Nations people. www.sac-isc.gc.ca/eng/1100100032374/1572457769548

8 Alex Wilson (2008) has also written about the impact of abuse in residential schools on Indigenous families' understandings of same sex attraction. Wilson also notes how residential schools were particularly violent for children who could not easily conform to strict colonial gender roles and heterosexuality (ibid. pp. 194–195).

9 Lezard, P. (2000). The dark land of the silent. *Fireweed*, 57, 15.

10 We cite some of the creative works from these writers in the bibliography for this piece.

11 Lee Maracle was a revolutionary Indigenous poet and writer. We acknowledge and pay respect to her passing in November 2021.

12 Percy is referring to former premiere of Ontario, Mike Harris' comments about welfare during a televised leaders debate in 1995.

13 Bluestocking refers to a society and broader campaign focused on white women's access to university in eighteenth century Britain. University unions in the United Kingdom and Australia observe Bluestocking Week – a week dedicated to women's contributions to higher education.

14 Stolen Generations refers to period of policy between the 1910s and 1970s where Australian federal and state bodies as well as religious institutions stole Aboriginal children from their families and placed them in institutions and homes, and with settler families. Although the policies themselves have been officially abolished, many Aboriginal people argue this culture of child removal is ongoing. For more on Stolen Generations and the impact of removal on Aboriginal people please see Stephanie Gilbert's work (2019).

15 Bronwyn Carlson is a prolific scholar and advocate for Indigenous peoples' participation in higher education. She is the Head of Indigenous Studies at Macquarie University.

16 Professor is the highest academic rank in Australian universities. Aboriginal and Torres Strait Islander people are currently underrepresented at this level.

17 Percy's PhD thesis explores the use of relational methodologies as abolitionist frameworks for engaging with Indigenous communities in both educational and social work settings.

18 For details of this treaty which was between Indigenous peoples prior to the arrival of white settler/occupiers, please read: https://circles forreconciliation.ca/wp-content/uploads/2020/04/Respect-Trust-Treaties-Reconciliation.pdf

19 Sandy has done significant work in the museums space including in repatriation and challenging the symbolic annihilation of Indigenous and queer people in these sites. Their writing on this work is included in the bibliography.

20 Percy is referring to their work on the MMIWG2SLGBTQQIA+ National Action Plan.

21 Lezard, P., Prefontaine, N., Cederwall, D. M., Sparrow, C., Maracle, S., Beck, A., & McCleod, A. (2021). 2SLGBTQQIA+ Sub-Working Group MMIWG2SLGBTQQIA+ National Action Plan Final report. https://scholars.wlu.ca/indg_faculty/1/

22 Sandy is currently working on a book as part of their ARC Future Fellowship on the colonial project of gender. There are further references to their existing writing on this topic in the bibliography.

23 See Kaba, M. (2021). *We Do This' Til We Free Us: Abolitionist Organizing and Transforming Justice* (Vol. 1). Chicago: Haymarket Books.

Bibliography

Alizzi, A. (2017). Becoming-with and together: Indigenous transgender and transcultural practices. *Artlink*, 37(2), 76–81.

Brant, B. (1985). *Mohawk Trail*. Ithaca, NY: Firebrand Books.

Brant, B. (Ed.). (1988). *A Gathering of Spirit: A Collection of North American Indian Women*. Women's Press Literary. Ithaca, NY: Firebrand Books.

Brant, B. (1993). Giveaway: Native lesbian writers. *Signs: Journal of Women in Culture and Society*, 18(4), 944–947.

Brant, B. (1997). The good red road: Journeys of homecoming in Native women's writing. *American Indian Culture and Research Journal*, 21(1), 193–206.

Chrystos. (1988). *Not Vanishing*. Vancouver: Press Gang.

Chrystos. (1991). *Dream On*. Vancouver: Press Gang.

Chrystos. (1995). *Fire Power*. Vancouver: Press Gang.

Coleman, C. G. (2017). *Terra Nullius*. London: Hachette UK.

Coleman, C. G. (2019). *The Old Lie*. Sydney: Hachette Australia.

Cuthand, T. J. (2017). Indigequeer/Indigiqueer. *TJ Cuthand*. www.thirzacuthand.com/2017/05/12/indigequeerindigiqueer/

Fife, C. (1993). *The Colour of Resistance: A Contemporary Collection of Writing by Aboriginal Women*. Toronto: Sister Vision Press.

Fife, C. (2001). *Poems for a New World*. Vancouver: Ronsdale Press.

Gilbert, S. (2019). Living with the past: The creation of the Stolen Generation positionality. *AlterNative: An International Journal of Indigenous Peoples*, 15(3), 226–233.

Ismail, R. & van Neervan, E. (Eds). (2022). *Unlimited Futures: Speculative, Visionary Blak and Black Fiction*. Perth: Fremantle Press.

Johnston, P. (1983). *Aboriginal Children and the Child Welfare System*. Toronto: Canadian Council on Social Development.

Kaba, M. (2021). *We Do This' Til We Free Us: Abolitionist Organizing and Transforming Justice* (Vol. 1). Chicago: Haymarket Books.

Kelada, O., & Alizzi, A. (2019). Beyond the wonderland of whiteness: The Blak wave of Indigenous women shaping race on screen. In Collins, F., Landman, J., & Bye, S. (Eds), *A Companion to Australian Cinema* (pp. 107–130). Hoboken, NJ: Wiley-Blackwell.

Lezard, P. (2022). *Sqilx w Educator Rising: Relationality as Methodology in a Social Work Abolitionist Framework*. Doctoral dissertation, University of Toronto.

Lezard, P., Prefontaine, N., Cederwall, D. M., Sparrow, C., Maracle, S., Beck, A., & McCleod, A. (2021). 2SLGBTQQIA+ Sub-Working Group MMIWG2SLGBTQQIA+ National Action Plan final report. https://scholars.wlu.ca/indg_faculty/1/

O'Sullivan, S. (2007). Human remains: Anthropodermic bibliopegy and the appeal of the extreme in challenging the continuing external management of Indigenous remains. *Ngoonjook* (*30*), 80–85.

O'Sullivan, S. (2013). Reversing the gaze: Considering Indigenous perspectives on museums, cultural representation and the equivocal digital remnant. In Ormond-Parke, L., et al. (Eds), *Information Technology and Indigenous Communities* (pp. 139–150). Canberra: Aboriginal Studies Press.

O'Sullivan, S. (2015). Queering ideas of Indigeneity: Response in repose: Challenging, engaging and ignoring centralising ontologies, responsibilities, deflections and erasures. *Journal of Global Indigeneity*, 1(1), 5.

O'Sullivan, S. (2016). Recasting identities: Intercultural understandings of First Peoples in the national museum space. In Burnard, P., Mackinlay, E., & Powell, K. (Eds), *The Routledge International Handbook of Intercultural Arts Research* (pp. 35–45). London: Routledge.

O'Sullivan, S. (2021). The colonial project of gender (and everything else). *Genealogy*, 5(3), 67.

O'Sullivan, S. (2022). Challenging the colonialities of symbolic annihilation. *Southerly*, 79(3), 16–22.

Saunders, M. (2018). Living and dying countries: Ecocide, consciousness & agency in First Nations futurism. *Postcolonial Studies Association*, 7, 7–9.

Saunders, M. (2019). Goori-futurism: Envisioning the sovereignty of Minjungbal-Nganduwal country, community, and culture through speculative fiction. Symposium: Proceedings of the SFRA 2019 Conference. *Review*, 3, 59–64.

Saunders, M. (2022). Everywhen: Against 'the power of now'. *Griffith REVIEW* (76), 115–125.

Saunders, M. (Ed.). (2022). *This All Come Back Now: An Anthology of First Nations Speculative Fiction*. Brisbane: University of Queensland Press.

Simpson, L. B. (2017). *As We Have Always Done: Indigenous Freedom through Radical Resistance*. Minneapolis: University of Minnesota Press.

Sinclair, R. (2007). Identity lost and found: Lessons from the sixties scoop. *First Peoples Child & Family Review: A Journal on Innovation and Best Practices in Aboriginal Child Welfare Administration, Research, Policy & Practice*, 3(1), 65–82.

van Neerven, E. (Ed.). (2021). *Flock: First Nations Stories Then and Now*. Brisbane: University of Queensland Press.

Whitehead, J. (2017). *Full-Metal Indigiqueer: The Pro(1,0)zoa*. Vancouver: Talon Books.

Wilson, A. (2008). N'tacinowin inna nah': Our coming in stories. *Canadian Woman Studies/Les Cahiers De La Femme*, 26(3). https://cws.journals. yorku.ca/index.php/cws/article/view/22131

11

Bio-power, the governmentality of killing and Indigenous people's resistance: imposition of the Armed Forces (Special Powers) Act, extra-judicial execution and Indigenous women's resistance in Manipur, northeast India

Binalakshmi Nepram

Wars are no longer waged in the name of a sovereign who must be defended, they are waged on behalf of the existence of everyone, entire populations are mobilized for the purpose of wholesale slaughter in the name of life necessity; massacres have become vital. It is as managers of life and survival, of bodies and the race, that so many regimes have been able to wage so many wars, causing so many men to be killed. (Foucault 1984, p. 260)

Introduction

For over sixty-two years, unknown to the world since 1958, the Indian government has imposed a martial law called the *Armed Forces (Special Powers) Act*[1] (AFSPA) on 45 million Indigenous peoples who live in the region of Manipur and Northeast India. The *Armed Forces (Special Powers) Act* is a British colonial Act that was imposed in 1942 to thwart Mahatma Gandhi's 'Quit India' movement.[2] Manipur and parts of Northeast India were independent Asiatic nation-states, and some of the Indigenous peoples there were never a part of what is now referred to as India. However, they were taken over by the newly formed Union of India after British colonial rule ended on 15 August 1947. The government of India then used the same Act and enforced it on Indigenous peoples of Manipur and Northeast India in 1958. After independence, the Indian government put over 300,000 armed forces personnel in the Indigenous region of Manipur and Northeast India and imposed martial law. In addition, the histories of 45 million Indigenous peoples have been deleted from the curriculum of modern India and rampant racism continues against the Indigenous peoples living in Manipur and Northeast India. Violence against Indigenous peoples is a global issue as Teltumbde (2009, p. 16) articulates: 'Whether it is Australian attacks on Indians or atrocities committed on a dalits by Indians, or discrimination and oppression of the people of the north-east, they are basically issues that concern humanity and cannot be prevented from being internationalised' (2009, p. 16).

To protest the violation of their rights, Indigenous women of Manipur started a movement in the 1980s called 'Meira Paibi', which in Manipuri Indigenous language means 'women with bamboo torches' because they patrol the streets of Manipur all night with flaming bamboo torches. Women of Manipur conduct sit-ins, protest marches and have led a nude protest to confront the military's sexual assaults. Together with the Meira Paibis, a sixteen-year hunger strike, known to be the world's longest of its kind, was waged by Irom Sharmila to protest against martial law (Kakoty 2019). In addition to Irom Sharmila's case, the self-immolation and death of Pebam Chittaranjan Singh on 16 August 2004 was also a protest against the militarisation of Manipur by India (Kakoty 2019; Teltumbde 2009).

The Indian state dealt with the various protests with an iron hand. The Irom Sharmila hunger strike case was classified as a criminal act. She was confined in a hospital for sixteen long years and force-fed through a nasal tube into which rice, lentils and water were injected thrice daily. The Indian government of also imposed the *National Security Act* on mothers of Manipur who protested nude against the Indian paramilitary following the rape and killing of Thangjam Manorama by Indian armed forces in July 2004 (Basnet 2019; Kakoty 2019). The armed forces have a wide range of powers afforded them and they inflict horrifying violence upon the people. Teltumbde (2009, p. 16) argues that:

> The AFSPA gives the armed forces wide powers to shoot to kill, arrest on flimsy pretext, conduct searches without the warrant, and demolish structures in the name of 'aiding civil power'. Equipped with

these special powers, soldiers have raped, tortured, 'disappeared', and killed Indian citizens for five decades without being held accountable. (2009, p. 16)

In this chapter, I draw on Michel Foucault's theory of biopower and the governmentality of killing to explore the history and racialised intent behind the colonial occupation of Manipur and the imposition of AFSPA. In addition, I will be using Achille Mbembé's 'necro-politics' (2019) to build and strengthen how this oppression has deepened over the years with massive military camps and control structures. Women using their bodies to resist militarisation by fasting and using their bodies as sites of protest against the martial law echoes similar arguments made by Banu Bargu's (2014) *Starve and Immolate: the Politics of Human Weapons*, particularly the concept of 'necro-resistance' which demonstrates the strong and sustained resistance continuing today.

Bio-power by Indian state in Manipur, Northeast India

We live in a world where freedom, dignity and equality are cherished yet hardly realised by many and particularly Indigenous peoples. The British left India after 200 years of colonial rule, and people in India celebrate 'Independence Day' every year on 15 August. Immediately after the British departure, the Union of India annexed Manipur on 21 September 1949 and then imposed AFSPA. AFSPA is a remnant of British colonial legislation introduced 1942 to thwart Mahatma Gandhi's 'Quit India' movement. According to AG Noorani (2015, para. 2):

> On August 15, 1942, that most illiberal of Viceroys and Governors General, Linlithgow, promulgated The Armed Forces (Special Powers) Ordinance, 1942, under Section 72 of the Government of India Act, 1935. Its avowed object was 'to confer special powers upon certain officers of the Armed Forces', chief among these was a licence to kill.

The imposition of martial law on Indigenous peoples in Manipur and Northeast India has led to over 20,000 people being killed (Human Rights Watch 2008), and numerous incidences of rape, arrests, torture and extra-judicial executions. Under AFSPA, armed forces personnel have the ability to commit any crime with complete impunity. AFSPA is a 'technology of killing' as described by Michel Foucault (1984), it is the 'governmentality of killing'. Inferring from Foucault (1984, p. 14) one can call the political structures, the new regime of control that evolved with the Indian military in full control, as a bio-power. Manipur and Northeast India are thus dotted with military camps – 300,000 troops are deployed in Manipur and Northeast India, the majority of them for counter-insurgency operations.

Elements of hegemonic politics by India

In a piece titled *Elements of Politics*, Antonio Gramsci (1992, p. 144) writes that the first element of politics is that 'there really do exist rulers and ruled, leaders and led. The entire science and art of politics are based on this primordial, and given irreducible fact'. About the conception of law, Gramsci (1992, p. 246) writes 'If every state tends to create and maintain a certain type of civilization and of citizen, and to eliminate certain customs and attitudes and to disseminate others, then the law will be instrumental for this purpose (together with the school system, and other institutions and activities).' The law is the repressive and negative aspect of the entire positive, civilising activity undertaken by the state (Gramsci 1992). In the article 'Annexation of Manipur as the 19th State of India', Malem Mangal Laishram writes:

> The situation of Manipur from 1949 onwards has been that of an occupied territory followed by the ultimate annexation or incorporation by the Union of India in 1972. From the standards of international law and particularly under the legal order of the UN Charter and international humanitarian law, India's continued unlawful presence in Manipur represents an illegal territorial regime with intention to change the international status of the territory of Manipur as well as its government system and demographic characteristics. (Laishram 2020, p. 352)

It is in this repressive and negative aspect that the Indian nation-state has long tried to subdue the arts, culture and significance of Indigenous peoples who live in Manipur and Northeast India.

The gaze of the Indian state

Besides the cultural hegemony practised by India, one also sees what Jurgen Habermas (1991) describes as a 'gaze'. According to Habermas (1991, p. 245): 'A gaze that objectifies and examines, that takes things apart analytically, that monitors and penetrates everything, gains a power that is structurally formative for those institutions.' The gaze, as explained by Habermas, is also a phenomenon that the Indian state employs in regard to the Indigenous people in Manipur, which has led to the rupturing of bonds between different ethnicities. It is as if someone is constantly monitoring us. It makes us an object of the state, which is constantly planning ways to control us.

The control of the Indian state aims to paralyse the people. This has resulted in misunderstandings and tensions between ethnic groups, in which each ethnic group has been made isolated by the Indian state and monitored as a kind of controlling mechanism. For every twenty Manipuris, there is one Indian army personnel in the region. There are 350 military stations all across Manipur and military checking is conducted on many of the roads in the occupied territories.

State-sanctioned killing and the panopticon

Michel Foucault's (1984, p. 262) notion of the 'power over life' evolved in two basic forms. First, what is done on the human body to the group and to the individual person. This is the 'anatomo-politics of the human body'. Second, centred on the body 'as a machine, its disciplining, the optimization etc' and 'species body – the body imbibed with the mechanisms of life and serving as the basis of the biological processes, propagation, births, mortality, level of health, life expectancy – their supervision effected through an entire series of interventions and regulatory controls – a bio-politics of the population'.

Foucault (1984) uses the word 'technologies' which is 'knowledge and power' to describe the set of operations, of procedures around the objectification of the body. Some of the disciplinary technologies are listed as workshops, schools, prisons, hospitals, and factories to force a docile body that may be subjected, used, transferred, and improved. Disciplinary controls according to Foucault (1984) are linked to the rise of capitalism.

The introduction of the office of governor, of Hindi language and forcing all to learn it; the introduction of Indian Administrative and Foreign Service and schools in remote Indigenous parts of the region; and the setting up of over 160 dams, prisons, and counter-insurgency schools are some of the disciplinary controls that India's settler colonialism imposed on the people of Manipur and Northeast India. The panopticon is a particular organisation of space and human beings, a visual order that clarifies the mechanisms of power which are being deployed (Foucault 1984). The way in which AFSPA operates, from the Parliament of India to the structures on the ground, is how the panopticon works.

The state of exception and necro-politics

Politics is the work of the death, wrote Achille Mbembé and Libby Meintjes (2003). Mbembé and Meintjes (2003) concur that that sovereignty consists of the will and the capacity to kill in order to live:

The sovereign right to kill is not subject to any rule in the colonies. In the colonies, the sovereign might kill at any time or in any manner. Colonial warfare is not subject to legal and institutional rules. It is not a legally codified activity. Instead, colonial terror constantly intertwines with colonially generated fantasies of wilderness and death and fictions to create the effect of the real (Mbembé and Meintjes 2003, pp. 14–15).

The racism that Indigenous peoples of Manipur and Northeast India face typifies this kind of issue. Since the majority of the people of Manipur have not accepted Indian sovereignty, then as per Mbembé's (2019) logic, they are in a state of war and hence it is as if India has declared war on the people of Manipur and Northeast India for the past sixty-two years. Becoming a subject supposes upholding the work of death. 'Politics is therefore death that lives a human life' (Mbembé and Meintjes 2003, pp. 14–15), and thus, politics is the work of death.

The state of siege

The state of siege is also a phenomenon seen in Manipur and Northeast India. According to Mbembé and Meintjes (2003; Mbembé 2019), the state of siege is in itself is identified as a part of a 'military institution' where:

> besieged villages and towns are sealed off and cut off from the world … Freedom is given to local commanders to use their discretion as to when and whom to shoot. Movement between the territorial cells requires formal permits. Local civil institutions are systematically destroyed. The besieged population is deprived of their means of income. Invisible kill is added to outright execution. (Mbembé and Meintjes, 2003, pp. 29–30)

Why did the Indian government impose an old colonial law on Indigenous peoples?

The question is why do oppressed people also take the structures, the modes and methods of killing as described? Can we answer this through the 'coloniality of power' as persists through the essay by Anibal Quijano (2007)? Quijano (2007) argues that 'coloniality' is the most general form of domination in the world today. He stated that 'Coloniality of power was conceived together with America and western Europe, with the social category of "race" as the key element of the social classification of the colonized and the colonizers' (Quijano 2007, p. 171). According to Quijano (2007, p. 171):

> The process of Eurocentrism of the new world power in the following centuries gave way to the imposition of such a 'racial' criteria to the new social classification of the world population on a global scale. So, in the first place, new social identities were produced all over the world – 'Whites', 'Indians', 'Negroes', 'Yellows', 'Olives' using physiognomic traits of the people as external manifestation of their 'racial' nature. Then on the basis of the new 'geo-cultural identities', were introduced: Europeans, Americans, Asiatic, African, Oceania etc.

This racialisation also justified domination in the way India viewed Manipur. India was the subject and Manipur the object. Terms like 'Chinkies' and 'Momo' have been given to Indigenous peoples of Manipur and Northeast India and many face racial and gender-based violence.

The politics of human weapons and the weaponisation of life

Banu Bargu (2014) refers to the 'politics of human weapons' as the tactic of resorting to corporeal and existential practices of struggle, based on the technique of self-destruction, in order to make a political statement or advance political goals. She uses the term 'human weapons' (Bargu 2014, p. 15). Bargu (2014) backs this up with the concept of 'necro-resistance' as an emergent repertoire of action that is based on the appropriation of the power of life and death into the hands of those who resist. The insurgent's body becomes the concrete battleground of domination and resistance, subjugation and subversion, sovereignty and sacrifice (Bargu 2014, p. 265). Necro-resistance according to Bargu (2014, p. 27) is the '*refusal* against simultaneously individualizing and totalizing domination that act by wrenching the power of life and death away from the apparatuses of the modern state in which this power is conventionally vested'.

Resistance to power: the movement of the Meira Paibis of Manipur

Using the theory of Banu Bargu (2014), in spite of the politics of death that has been going on, Manipuri women who are called Meira Paibis ('women with bamboo torches') have been at the forefront of a strong nonviolent peace and resistance movement since the start of counter-insurgency operations that took place in late 1970s. Women's groups in Manipur have developed many powerful nonviolent actions designed to confront the insurgency that has engulfed the region in the last seven decades. Following are some of the acts of resistance implemented by the women of Manipur.

Nude protest by the women of Manipur, 15 July 2004

On 15 July 2004, twelve mothers from Manipur stripped in front of the Kangla Fort unit of the 17th Assam Rifles Unit of the Indian military in Manipur, India.[3] The women held banners across their bare bodies which read: 'Indian Army Rape Us', and 'Indian Army Take Away Our Flesh'. The protest was in response to the abduction, brutal rape, torture and murder of Thangjam Manorama, a thirty-year-old woman who was falsely accused by the Indian army of being a militant. Still today, those who raped and killed Thangjam Manorama are not punished and the governmentality of killings continues. The mothers used their bodies as a protest site.

Irom Sharmila's hunger strike for sixteen years against martial law

Another example of how the body is used as a weapon can be seen in the Irom Sharmila case. On 4 November 2000, after the Malom Massacre where ten Manipuris were gunned down in Malom Village, Irom Sharmila started a fast to protest against AFSPA (Sharma 2014). The army presence dominates the political and social environments in the border regions of India's northeast. The Indian government has imposed martial law in these regions that are the 'disturbed' regions under the AFSPA, 1958. Special powers conferred to the military included targeting suspicious persons and seizing weapons before 'crimes' are committed.

The Malom Massacre on 2 November 2000 happened when the army shot dead ten civilians at a local bus stand and in nearby fields (Sharma 2014). Two days later, Sharmila started an indefinite fast against AFSPA and two weeks later, the government arrested Sharmila on charges of attempting suicide.[4] The government force-fed Sharmila through a nasal feeding tube and put her in solitary confinement in a local hospital ward of Jawaharlal Nehru Hospital.

Sharmila's hunger strike demonstrates what Banu Bargu (2014) called 'necro-resistance'. Her protest aimed to coerce the government to act and repeal the law. Despite the hunger strike, the government did not change the laws in Manipur and Indigenous women of Manipur continue to demonstrate a strong and sustained resistance to this day.

Conclusion

This chapter has explored Foucault's (1984) work on biopower and demonstrated how India has evolved the state of exception and allowed its military to do the 'governmentality of killing'. It has examined AFSPA as an example of a technology of killing imbued with biopower which sees Indigenous peoples as objects and regulates Indigenous lives. In spite of these challenges, Indigenous peoples have been resilient in the face of oppressive systems and people, epitomised by the rise of an Indigenous women's resurgence throughout the Northeast India, evidenced in movements such as Meira Paibi Movement, the hunger strike of Irom Sharmila and the nude protest by the mothers of Manipur. This legacy lives on despite the governmentality of killing that has been happening for the past sixty-two years. Herein lies the truth: where there's power, there's resistance, giving agency to human lives.

Notes

1 See www.mha.gov.in/sites/default/files/armed_forces_special_powers_act1958.pdf
2 See www.open.ac.uk/researchprojects/makingbritain/content/1942-quit-india-movement
3 See www.indiatoday.in/india/story/if-you-remember-manipuri-women-only-for-nude-protest-against-army-think-again-1436411-2019-01-22
4 See www.reuters.com/article/us-india-rights-army/indias-iron-lady-ends-16-year-hunger-strike-over-military-law-idUSKCN10K17I

References

Bargu, B. (2014). *Starve and Immolate: The Politics of Human Weapons*. New York: Columbia University Press.
Begum, A. A. (2012). Talking about extrajudicial executions in North East India. In Mahanta, N., & Gogoi, D. (Eds), *Shifting Terrain: Conflict Dynamics in North East India*. Guwahati: DVS Publishers.

Foucault, M. (1984). *The Foucault Reader*, ed. P. Rabinow. New York: Pantheon Books.

Gramsci, A. (1992). *Selections From the Prison Notebooks*, ed. Q. Hoare & G. Smith. New York: International Publishers.

Habermas, J. (1991). *The Structural Transformation of the Public Sphere: An Inquiry into a Category of Bourgeois Society*. Cambridge, MA: MIT Press.

Human Rights Watch. (2008). These fellows must be eliminated. www.hrw.org/reports/2008/india0908/index.htm

Kakoty, R. (2019). Bodies at protest and power of the image: Irom Sharmila as an icon. *South Asian Popular Culture*, 17(3), 213–225.

Laishram, M. M. (2020). Annexation of Manipur as the 19th State of India: The Status of the Territory of Manipur in International Law since 1949. *Beijing Law Review*, *31*, 328.

Mbembé, J. A. (2019). *Necro-politics*. Durham, NC: Duke University Press.

Mbembé, J. A. and Meintjes, L. (2003). Necropolitics. *Public Culture*, 15(1), 11–40.

Noorani, A. G. (2015). AFSPA: The license to kill, *Frontline*, 17 April. https://frontline.thehindu.com/the-nation/afspa-licence-to-kill/article7048801.ece

Quijano, A. (2007). Coloniality and modernity/rationality. *Cultural Studies*, 168–178.

Sharma, A. (2014). Irom Chanu Sharmila and the Movement against Armed Forces Special Powers Act (AFSPA).

Teltumbde, A. (2009). Race or caste, discrimination is a universal concern. *Economic and Political Weekly*, 16–18.

12

Queer multi-racial sovereign networks: conceptualising Indigenous and Asian multi-racial identities for understanding the world and futures

Souksavanh T. Keovorabouth

On/Off
Inside/Outside
Reservation/Urban
Native/Non-Native
Reservations determining who we are?
settler-colonial borders confining us
Boxing us in to be disposed
Lands found to be desolate
Displaced/Displacement
Is nothing new to Native peoples.
Blood quantum as colonial design
Meant to define us
To tell us who we are
To argue
To render us to nothingness.
Urban living
Reclamation/Reclaiming
Identities beyond reservation borders.
We craft and mold our teachings
Into our philosophies
Used for our communities
Research/Researcher
Infiltrating western spaces
to declare what is ours.
Our land

Our knowledge
Our communities
We are still here
Belonging/Belong
This is a piece dedicated to all my multi-racial Indigenous folx
Who have never felt enough.
Placed within a percentage
Making us feel alone.
But through our lived and shared experiences and
This ever-interconnected relationship between me and you
We belong

Introduction

I begin this chapter with a poem I wrote about the harmful dichoto-mies that I have experienced as an Indigenous multi-racial person. Through my academic journey and being able to have the oppor-tunity to create kin around the world, I believe that outside these dichotomies lives an imaginary that (re)creates our understanding of Indigeneity. Due to the colonial notions of blood quantum equating to an authentic Indigenous identity, I have always never felt enough. But through traditional teachings, research, listening and having critical conversations with people I care about, I begin to tell my story and connections between my multi-racial Indigenous and Asian identities and bring them into a future where all multi-racial Indigenous peoples can feel they belong.

With the current violent attacks against Asian and Asian American folx[1] in the United States (possibly even around the world) and the constant erasure of Indigenous people, I have found myself critically thinking about my role in the world. As a queer Diné (Indigenous) and second-generation Laotian person in the United States, more than ever I find that all of my identities are under attack by white supremacy. Holding a multi-racial identity, especially a queer multi-racial identity, I feel the harm from all sides that sometimes renders me feeling disposable. But as I step back and listen to ancestral teachings from both Diné and Laos, I know that there is strength channelling through me to create a world where queer multi-racialism is critical for Indigenous peoples, sovereignty and futures.

Settler colonialism has taught Black, Indigenous, People of Colour (BIPOC) to believe that they must live in a world with a singular identity attached to a singular culture – 'such policing serves to alienate past and potential future Indigenous people, or force those who inhabit Indigeneity into a 'prison-house' of identity' (Paradies 2006). While I would argue that as multi-racial people, especially ones who are holding an Indigenous identity, we are unable to separate our cultures because they are not only connected to us on an individual level to those specific cultures. I also argue that we are actually interwoven on a cultural level too.

I aim to highlight the importance of utilising the beauty of multi-racialism as a practice of healing into a decolonial future. For me, I must engage with both my Diné and Laotian cultural identities as a means of manoeuvring throughout the world. I encourage all my fellow multi-racial Indigenous folx to conceptualise their engagement and connectedness between multi-racialism as a practice of healing from settler colonialism. I envision our futures with us in mind, not just as Indigenous but rather us as Indigenous and [insert your other racial identities] at once.

Throughout this chapter, I will engage with Indigenous and Asian scholar-activists works to build a multi-racial praxis of understanding the world and envision a future outside of colonial rule from my own experience as a foundation to encourage others to do so with their Indigenous and other cultural connections. This chapter aims to address the confusion and feelings of being 'not enough' as a means of isolation to turn that into building a harmonious future of belonging for multi-racial folx.

Warning: In the next sections, there will be conversations of violence against Asian/American and Indigenous peoples.

#StopAsianHate, model minority and relationality to my Indigeneity

To my Asian folx
Asian Women,
Queer Asians
First-Generation Asians,
Undocumented Asians

Trans Asian
Multi-racial Asian,
Trans-racial adoptee Asians
Asians with disabilities
Desi Asians
We are seen as non-human
Objects for pleasure
Who must be silenced, erased, and eradicated
But I want to reiterate time and time again that
You are loved and important!
As a queer multi-racial second generation Asian American and
    Indigenous person
I sit in disbelief,
without shock,
The acts of white supremacy
Continuing to dispose of our community
Based on their 'sexual addictions'
Asian women and Queer Asian folx
Seen as submissive, docile, petite
Traits that were subscribed onto our bodies.
Saying it's not racially motivated
But what's more racialized than the sexuality of our very existence?
Do not blame the women
Do not blame their work
Do not blame the victims
For the blood on your hands for having a 'bad day'
'Go back to China' repeated out of their mouths
As though Asian is a monolith with Chinese.
We are not all Chinese,
We are Laotian, Korean, Japanese,
Vietnamese, Cambodian, and Indian to name a few.
While your Model Minority rings true as Myth
Hoping that it has us turn against each other
While fortunately, our solidarities with each other are stronger than
    the hate you have for us.
You love our food
You love our anime
You love our culture
You love our bodies
But do not care of our existence
In this world that you created
For your own benefit

You crave our existence
And being,
as warm dishes
You have served for yourself.
Unasked and unwelcomed
Blaming us for your violent words,
Actions, and fantasies.
We are not the virus,
The Kung Flu or the Chinese Virus or any ridiculous name you've
     come up with,
Rather, your ideologies of who we are
Are the true virus,
The virus that is not only killing us
But manipulating your ytness to think
That WE are the harmful ones.
When in fact, YOUR ytness literally
Murdered our Asian relatives,
Siblings who were silenced
By the power you think you can hold over us
As Asian folx.
It has not only been a year of this hate,
but a lifetime in this country of this anti-Asian violence.
Even on stolen land.
You have persecuted us, murdered us, fetishized us, sexualized us
As though we are disposable dolls for you to throw away when
     you want.
These are Hate crimes
And we will not be your scapegoats any longer!
Nor accept your yt gaslighting.
We need to protect our elders, our women, our children, and our
     queer folx
who are seen as 'vulnerable'
when I would argue, are our most powerful in the community.
Although, I am half Asian='/. These actions impact all of me!
If I am hit or shot or assaulted, It is not half of me, it is all of me.
Such as it is not just half of my community being injured, it is
     all of us.
This is my community, this is my whole being and existence being
     targeted and impacted
Just as any Indigenous issue impacts me!
Just as other multi-racial and trans-racial adoptees are just as
     impacted by these violent acts!

I love my Asian identity
I love my Asian food
I love my Asian features
But mostly, I love my Asian community <3
#StopAsianHate

I wrote and read this poem on my Instagram in the heat of the moment after hearing about many of the Asian hate crimes that were occurring throughout the United States. The COVID-19 pandemic and the rhetoric coming from the most recent previous US president had ignited the continued hate toward Asian and Asian American folx. Between 19 March 2020 and June 2020 alone, approximately 9,081 incidents of racially motivated attacks were documented by Stop Asian American Pacific Islander (AAPI) Hate (The Associated Press 2021). The one event that was most triggering for me, as a second-generation Laotian and queer person, was the Atlanta, Georgia, shooting targeting Asian women in particular. The suspect had reportedly told police that he had a 'sexual addiction' and had therefore been motivated to carry out the shootings at the massage parlours in an attempt to eliminate his 'temptation' (Fausset et al. 2021).

Through this tragic event, again we see the reality that gender and sexuality has been imposed onto Asian bodies, especially bodies that are seen as fragile, docile and able to be easily controlled or disposed of such as undocumented individuals, sex workers and people of low socio-economic status trying to make ends meet. In my mind and my experience as someone who is read as racially ambiguous and often-times described as 'exotic' because of it, I have been sexualised and fetishised for my ambiguity – what Black feminist scholar bell hooks (2015) who was known for her intersectional feminist theories, would describe as 'eating the Other' – mainly by white men. hooks states, 'displacing the notion of Otherness from race, ethnicity, skin-color, the body emerges as a site of contestation where sexuality is the metaphoric Other that threatens to take over, consume, transform via the experience of pleasure' (hooks 2015, p. 22).

As a multi-racial person, this event does not just affect a piece of me but rather all of me. My Laotian identity is not a fraction of my identity in the way that colonialism has defined identities in terms of blood quantum, but as a part of my identity and who I am as a whole person. I was reminded that day, when I heard the news of the shooting of these Asian women, of the ways that my whole body, Diné and Laotian, Queer, and Brown are all potential targets of white supremacy, misogyny, homophobia and transphobia. I mention this instance because of the many traumas that have been going on in the world, especially toward Black, Indigenous and Asian folx at the hands of primarily white men.

In *Queering Contemporary Asian American Art*, Zavé Gayatri Martohardjono, a multi-racial Asian artist argues that, 'our identities are the only things we have; they define us … what are we without these bodies that carry history? And what are the many burdens that come with our skin?' (cited in Kina and Bernabe 2017, p. 146). As multi-racial folx, we feel and experience these traumas across all of our identities. Martohardjono is addressing the histories that we carry with our multi-racial identity, along with the burdens. It is not only one of our histories that we must heal from intergenerational trauma, it is all of these connections that make up our very identity. The traumatic history of Indigenous people in America, and quite frankly around the world, plus the history which is often traumatic as well for Asian/American folx in America. All of these create our past, present, and futures. I'm realising that there is a lot to unpack and heal, not only for my Indigenous identity, which is a constant project of mine, but also (re)connect with my Asian identity to process the harm that has been placed upon these two identities simultaneously.

To these words I would add understanding the impacts of the Model Minority [Myth] (Wu 2013), described by historian Ellen Wu (2013) in the book *The Color of Success: Asian Americans and the Origins of the Model Minority*. Wu traces a host of stakeholders coining the term by inventing a new stereotype of Asian Americans as the model minority – 'a racial group distinct from the white majority, but lauded as well assimilated, upwardly mobile, politically nonthreatening, and definitely not-black' (Wu 2013, p. 2). The model minority has been used to position Asian/Americans in a particular way against Black communities and other communities of colour, by stating 'if Asians can assimilate why can you not?'

Another tactic that is being utilised against Asian/American peoples to hold power over them.

As writer Scot Nakagawa (2018, para. 16) notes, the goal of Wu's work 'was to demonstrate that Asians were suitable for citizenship and able to vertically integrate into the white middle class'. The ability to 'vertically integrate' is based on confounded relationship between whiteness in skin (Xu and Lee 2013). To better understand the model minority as a myth, Claire Kim (1999) originated the *Racial Triangulation Theory*, which depicts the imposed relationship between white, Asian and Black folx. They set up a simple understanding between this relationship: an x and y graph depicting 'superior/inferior' on one axis and 'insider/foreigner' on the other, indicating that Asian folx would be considered foreigner and uniquely between superior and inferior because of the racial inferiority to white but superiority to Black (Kim 1999).

Reflecting on my own experience in relation to Kim's *Racial Triangulation Theory*, there are limitations when addressing multi-racial identity within this triangulation. I have thought a lot recently about questions including: as someone who is second-generation Asian from America, would I be considered American or as a foreigner, in the US, or as a 'foreigner'? While at the same time I am Diné, I'm far beyond 'insider' because what is now referred to as the US comprises our homelands. As I have been pondering this question, it brought great insight into how both my Laotian, Asian identity might ever be having a conversation with my Diné, Indigenous and queer/Two Spirit identity. Mixed race Asian American artist and scholar, Laura Kina states:

> in looking at the binary categories of Black/white and gay/straight, hooks warns against the erasure and deflection of the impact of racial oppression on people of color by attempting to make the oppressions of blackness and gayness synonymous; she urges rather that we find ways in which these experience are linked and yet differ. (Cited in Kina and Bernabe 2017, p. 145)

My identities no longer exist as separate for me; they are so connected as to be forever working with each other to shape my lived experience, through the linkages and the ways they differ to inform each other.

Through my multi-racial experience, my understandings of whiteness also must come into play. In Kai Cheng Thom's (2017) poem in *A Place Called No Homeland* titled 'Dear Now', they are reflecting on their connection and relationship with whiteness. They state, 'someday you will get tired of trying to fuck your way into whiteness, as if going down on him you might, somehow rise above this body you were given' (Thom 2017, p. 44). As someone who is read as Asian in Indigenous spaces, as Indigenous in Asian spaces, and as 'exotic' in all other spaces I have experienced a complicated relationship with whiteness as something I should prize. The ideas of wanting to be lighter or be with someone who is white was implanted in me through media and how society trains us to believe ourselves to only be valuable by whiteness. I found Thom's piece, not only true but also relatable in experience in how my Asian, Indigenous and Queer identity all intermingle together. For the longest time, I was ashamed of my Asian, Indigenous, feminine and Brown skin, until I learned about the beauty and stories of my peoples. I believe through this (re)telling of our beauty and our histories, we are able to trace back to ourselves for future generations to thrive.

By understanding the construction of the model minority as a myth, I make the connection to how I conceptualise my Indigenous futures for generational healing. In *Spiral to the Stars*, Laura Harjo discusses Mvskogee futurity by first dissecting the impacts of settler colonialism, stating: 'settler-colonialism is not a temporality that has passed; it is a far-reaching structure that persists. It shapes our ways of knowing, managing, and exchanging land. Further, it works to dispossess Indigenous communities of their futures – futures imagined on their terms within their ways of knowing' (Harjo 2019, p. 10).

We sometimes feel rendered down to find our value by whiteness is because of the structure of settler–colonialism and how it operates to feel detached from ourselves. It is through this speaking back against these oppressive systems are we then able to imagine futures where these holds are no longer existing. By processing my thoughts and experiences as a multi-racial person and thinking critically about Indigenous futures, I argue to interject queer multiracialism into the conversation because of our unique and distinct and often targeted experiences with settler colonialism and white supremacy. It not only adds to the conversation but allows for a vast array of experiences and positionalities that share the unlimited ways of navigating the world.

Queer Indigenous multi-racial futures

First, I want to make sure that I highlight the importance of queerness, not only as it pertains to diverse gender, sex and sexuality. Queer 'is not situated in the discourse of queer sex but rather as a way to position the mixed-race subject as willfully resisting assimilation into normative whiteness' (Kina and Bernabe 2017, p. 142). Queerness begins to live outside of the hegemonic and heteronormative settler–colonial nation-state that has impacted Black, Brown and Indigenous bodies. Here, we begin to imagine a space and world where queerness lives outside of these violent systems and that with the interconnectedness between Indigenous and multi-racial, another reality where we thrive can exist.

A major issue that multi-racial people face is always being read as a singular racial identity, 'asserting a multi-racial Indigenous identity is neither common nor straightforward because racial loyalty demands that anomalous individuals choose to be either exclusively Indigenous or exclusively non-Indigenous' (Paradies 2006, p. 357). What I mean by this is that even though I live and exist in both realms of my Diné and Laotian identity, I will only be read as one or the other. Andrew Jolivétte names this specific mechanic the 'mixed-race metronomic': 'The mixed-race metronomic subject is socialized to perform a fixed, mechanical identity that never changes and that fits the expectations of both outsiders and insiders' (Jolivétte 2016, p. 76). Through and only through cis-heteronormative structures of white supremacy and settler colonialism, multi-racial people become the mixed-race metronomic subject. This subjugation of being socialised to perform a fixed identity, is a form of erasure.

Due to genocide, assimilation and colonisation, even our Indigenous communities have been impacted by these same heteronormative logics and limitations of the world (Keovorabouth

2021). As queer Cree, Saulteaux and Métis writer Jas A. Morgan reflects on their own queer and Indigenous experience:

> When Indigenous people ask me the question, But why do you have to be queer? Why can't you just be Indian? I know they're actually questioning why I need to be so yt [white], and probably why I have to be such a dyke, too. The question about my need to be 'queer' comes with underlying implications of shame and homophobia, and a little gaslighting on the back end, too – the suggestion that I'm not Indian enough because I have to appeal to colonial gender and sexuality to speak truth to fire. (Morgan 2018, p. 49)

The settler–colonial nation-state has impacted Indigenous communities, and although many still hold to cultural and traditional teachings, we must also face the reality that many are survivors of trauma that has been passed down from generation to generation feeling as though there is no point in healing. That is until now. Some healing is now possible through this speaking back and bringing light to not only Queer identity but also the complexities of Indigeneity and also what it means to be Indigenous and multi-racial.

By including 'queer', in front of the 'multi-racial' identity, to then be 'queer multi-racial' we are able to imagine ourselves living outside of the confinements of the mixed-race metronomic subject because we are then able to begin to create a life outside of the violence of the settler–colonial nation-state's oppressive subjugation of our bodies. As Mississauga Nishnaabeg writer Leanne Betasamosake Simpson states: 'We can choose to uphold white, heterosexual, masculine control over Indigenous bodies, or we can choose to collectively engage in the dismantling of heteropatriarchy as a nation-building project' (Simpson 2017, p. 91). Simpson highlights the core argument for understanding, highlighting, and imposing queer multi-racial into Indigenous futures as it creates a new way of imagining and being in the world. Through this process, I have used my own queer Indigenous multi-racial identity to understand the operation, but I highly encourage other queer Indigenous multi-racial people to envision themselves outside of the confines of settler–colonial rule by imagining futures and worlds where we are thriving.

Indigenous communities have a history of forced removal, displacement and relocation. In the poem 'Prayer 4', Morgan writes: 'when you lose place, because your ancestors did what they needed to do so you'd survive, your body, your community, becomes your home and sovereignty' (Morgan 2018, pp. 85–86). The connections to survivability and trauma lead to our ancestors caring and loving our existence. Our bodies and communities, even ones that we can create ourselves, become our homes. It is through imagining queer Indigenous multi-racial futures where we can fully have home and sovereignty.

In Kai Cheng Thom's poem 'Queer Tribe' in the collection titled *A Place Called No Homeland*, they write:

> where are our elders? Who can teach us how to justice, not just on tumblr but on the dance floor, in our homes, in each other's arms? I think we gotta stop fetishizing survival. We are all survivors that's why we all bleed so much. I used to think blood was so beautiful have to remember we are more than scars. Gotta stop. Fetishizing the dead. Sometimes I need more than ghosts to fill my stomach, my pockets, my bed, my poems need to live for the living. I want to be able to honestly tell the difference between those who didn't make it and those we left behind. (Thom 2017, p. 32)

It is important to understand our past because that informs our present but also helps us navigate the future. Thom brings up a great point in terms of 'fetishising survival' – the whole point of life is to live, without having to just merely only survive. We can acknowledge and embrace our ancestors as being survivors while knowing we still have community surviving from this systemic racism, but we can and are able to live beyond just survival anymore. By imagining queer Indigenous multi-racial futures, we begin to live outside of the notion of needing to or having to survive, but rather, we can actually imagine a world where we in the now and the future can just live and thrive.

Through understanding our histories as Indigenous peoples, I am reminded of Simpson's (2017, p. 6) words: 'It is not happenstance or luck that Indigenous peoples and our lands still exist after centuries of attack. This is our strategic brilliance. Our presence is our weapon.' It is through our queerness, Indigeneity, and multi-racial identities, characteristic of our existence, that allow us to also be brilliant and our presence is also our weapon. Allowing each individual piece of your identities to inform your presence is the only time you will and can be whole. Our communities have always embraced what we now know as 'queer' and 'multi-racial', and it is now time for us to do it for ourselves, to combat the settler–colonial rule that says otherwise. We begin to create and imagine worlds and futures that are inherently queer, multi-racial, and most importantly, Indigenous.

Note

1 Based on the Merriam-Webster definition, 'folx' like 'folks' is a used especially to explicitly signal the inclusion of groups commonly marginalised such as women, queer, trans, non-binary and Two Spirit peoples.

References

The Associated Press. (2021). More than 9,000 anti-Asian incidents have been reported since the pandemic began. *NPR*, 12 August. www.npr. org/2021/08/12/1027236499/anti-asian-hate-crimes-assaults-pandemic-incidents-aapi

Doan, M. C. (2019). *Water/Tongue*. Richmond: Omnidawn Publishing.

Fausset, R., Bogel-Burroughs, N., & Fazio, M. (2021). 8 dead in Atlanta spa shootings, with fears of Anti-Asian bias. *New York Times*, 17 March. www.nytimes.com/live/2021/03/17/us/shooting-atlanta-acworth

Harjo, L. (2019). *Spiral to the Stars: Mvskoke Tools of Futurity*. Tempe: University of Arizona Press.

hooks, b. (2015). Eating the other: Desire and resistance. In *Black Looks: Race and Representation*. New York: Routledge.

Jolivétte, A. (2016). *Indian Blood: HIV and Colonial Trauma in San Francisco's Two-Spirit Community*. Seattle: University of Washington Press.

Keovorabouth, S. T. (2021). Reaching back to traditional teachings: Diné knowledge and gender politics. *Genealogy*, 5(4), 95.

Kim, C. J. (1999). The racial triangulation of Asian Americans. *Politics & Society*, 27(1) 105–138.

Kina, L. & Bernabe, J. C. (2017). *Queering Contemporary Asian American Art*. Seattle: University of Washington Press.

Morgan, J. A. (2018). *Nîtisânak*. Montreal: Metonymy Press.

Nakagawa, S. (2018). Becoming Asian. *Oregon Humanities*, 27 April. https://oregonhumanities.org/rll/magazine/owe-spring-2018/becoming-asian-scot-nakagawa/

Paradies. (2006). Beyond black and white: Essentialism, hybridity and Indigeneity. *Journal of Sociology*, 42(4), 355–367.

Simpson, L. B. (2017). *As We Have Always Done: Indigenous Freedom through Radical Resistance*. Minneapolis:University of Minnesota Press.

Thom, K. C. (2017). *A Place Called No Homeland*. Vancouver: Arsenal Pulp Press.

Wu, E. (2013). *The Color of Success: Asian Americans and the Origins of the Model Minority*. Princeton: Princeton University Press.

Xu, J. and Lee, J. C. (2013). The marginalized 'model' minority: An empirical examination of the racial triangulation of Asian Americans. *Social Forces, 91*(4), 1363–1397.

13

Transnational Indigenous feminisms: four narratives for global Indigeneity

Yi-Chun Tricia Lin, Bronwyn Carlson, Coro J.-A. Juanena, waaseyaa'sin Christine Sy and Alex Wilson

Introduction

This collective was first brought together as a proposed roundtable to present at the 2020 (US-based) National Women's Studies Association (NWSA), to examine collectively Indigenous womxn's boundary-defying and boundary-crossing cultural productions as resistance, resurgence, movement – and world-making – in short, as transnational Indigenous feminist practices. Indigenous womxn's cultural work has always been at the forefront of many social movements, historically and in modern times, as in #MMIWG2S, #IdleNoMore, #NoDAPL, #LandBack and #SOSBlakAustralia. Bronwyn Carlson's narrative below speaks powerfully to what Indigenous boundary-crossing mobilising in the twenty-first century could look like. Women's movements in the US and the world over owe much to Indigenous womxn's cultural work that inspired early feminists on Turtle Island – what we would today call transnational, Indigenous, and feminist (Wagner 2001). This roundtable on transnational Indigenous feminisms, which finally presented digitally in November 2021 as the NWSA 2020 was cancelled due to the coronavirus pandemic and related restrictions, showcases the complex web of the Indigenous feminist and community work, collaborations, movements, and struggles that defy the imperial (neo-) colonial, and neoliberal politics and nation-state boundaries. Together, the four narratives make the case for transnational Indigenous feminisms as a way of life, as a cosmology and epistemology, as a community practice, and as what some understand to be 'sustainable' living and stewardship of earth communities.

Māori scholar Linda Tuhiwai Smith identifies twenty-five Indigenous projects in *Decolonizing Methodologies: Research & Indigenous Peoples* (1999). How might transnational Indigenous feminisms re-articulate and add to the twenty-five projects? waaseyaa'sin Christine Sy offers (re)mapping as one. As such, each of the four powerful narratives is a powerful testimony and a revelation of what transnational Indigenous feminisms look like and the lessons for the non-Indigenous as well as settler–colonial communities aspiring to feminist practices. In 'Indigenous Feminisms: Why Transnational? Why Now?', an introduction for the 2016 *Lectora* special issue 'Transnational Indigenous Feminisms', Yi-Chun Tricia Lin articulates that 'Indigenous feminist work has almost always been transnational, translational, and boundary crossing. It was global long before "global" and "trans-national" became buzzwords – and turned into academic currency' (2016, p. 9). Both waaseyaa'sin Christine Sy and Alex Wilson share narratives of Indigenous womxn's work that is boundary-crossing and has been transnational for millennia. Indeed, Indigenous feminist practices are, at their core, anti-heteropatriarchal, anti-colonial, anti-capitalist, anti-racist and anti-white supremacist. These practices chart out and model a planetary vision often missing in transnational feminist articulations. Wilson's piece underscores that this ancient practice is critically urgent, land-based, and places at its centre care of the land on which nations, human and otherwise, stand.

Coro A.-J. Juanena's narrative offers an intimate account of Indigenous women organising across boundaries and transnationally, through the United Nations forum, the Permanent Forum on Indigenous Issues (UNPFII), which has met annually since 2002. This space of organising, as Juanena calls it, is 'Nomadic Feminist Nation Zero-Risk' – a sacred and safe space. It is important to note that this international platform is a direct result of decades of transnational Indigenous mobilising, which would not have been possible without Indigenous peoples' transnational and feminist networking. The power of global Indigeneity, indeed, is what made possible the creation and ultimate passage of the United Nations Declaration on the Rights of Indigenous Peoples, adopted by the UN General Assembly in 2007.

These transnational feminist practices are taken up by Indigenous folx of all genders, along with their communities. They are among the oldest in the human community, rooted in a cosmology, a way of life that deems all beings as relations, as in the Lakota greeting/phrase/concept 'mitakuye oyasin' ('all my relations' or 'we are all related') or in the Mohawk thanksgiving address. Sy's narrative of a sugar bush mapping provides a 'representation of documentary, photographic, oral, and living evidence of Anishinaabe womxn engaged in sugar bush' and a horizon through which the Anishinaabe womxn's (nation-state) boundary-defying and cross-border feminist practices. The gathering of the four narratives presents a moment for re-thinking, re-angling, and expanding the transnational feminist discourses from and through Indigenous perspectives and practices.

Narrative #1: Bronwyn Carlson, 'Indigenous Digital Humanities: so transnational, so feminist'

For the past decade, I guess my work could be described as Indigenous Digital Humanities. I am interested in the everyday lives of Indigenous peoples here, across this continent now known as Australia, and also other Indigenous peoples and communities around the globe (Carlson & Frazer 2021a; Carlson & Berglund 2021). I am particularly interested in how we use digital technologies, such as social media, to engage in global Indigenous solidarity for issues that are common to us all. Social media has transformed the way Indigenous peoples interact with each other and how we connect with other people at a local, regional, national, and global level (Carlson & Berglund 2021; Duarte 2017a). Facebook, Twitter, and other social media facilitate this interaction and allow users to maintain relationships across vast distances and time zones, thereby increasing social, cultural, and political connectivity and impact.

Even though Indigenous populations worldwide are avid social media users, Indigenous social media research is only beginning to gain traction in academia. The rapid rise of the use of social media as a means of social, cultural, intimate and political interaction among Indigenous peoples and groups is exciting. We have always used technology for our own means (Carlson 2021). While this is not to suggest there is no digital inequality, it does counter any assumptions that Indigenous peoples may have little interest in the possibilities of technology and the online environment (Carlson & Frazer 2018a). Social media, which I have previously written about as a 'new frontier' (Carlson 2013) 'is where Indigenous peoples are busy interacting and networking in what can be argued as a cultural and political reterritorialisation of digital media spaces' (Carlson & Dreher 2018, p. 17).

The widespread adoption of internet technologies such as social media has thoroughly transformed organised politics, protest, and activism. Early writing on digital technology was mostly optimistic about its democratic potential and there were hopes of democratic revolutions, led by the people directly connected through digital media (Carlson & Frazer 2021b, p. 169). While there are crucial questions around whether social media's capacity for 'giving voice' to Indigenous peoples actually results in any substantive change to policies and practices or whether online activism is really just what has been called 'slactivism' (Dennis 2019) – half-hearted, meaningless and ineffective activism – it is difficult to overestimate how important social media has become for many Indigenous movements (Dreher et al. 2016).

Without a doubt, Indigenous peoples globally have less access and often systematic exclusion from political power (Hedgpeth 2020). This includes voter power, capital, proximity to politicians and representation in politics. Instead, political power, for Indigenous peoples, as argued by Carlson and Frazer (2021b, p. 169) 'comes from our relational connections to one another, our irrefutable moral claim to sovereignty, and our immense creativity in political strategy'.

As I write, the world is in the grip of a serious global pandemic. Across this continent, as in most parts of the world, there is an immediate reliance on digital technologies. Connected ecosystems are making it possible for new forms of everyday functioning as more and more people find themselves working from home or are isolated at home. Some everyday activities have become fully reliant on digital technology, as the global crisis plays out and these new ways of being may very well turn into standard operating procedures in the near future (Timberg et al. 2020). We have now been thrust, ready or not, into the digital world.

In lockdown, I was fortunate enough to work in a profession that allowed for me to work from home. During that time,

I connected with colleagues across the globe using Zoom and other digital platforms. Prior to the pandemic, I had been working on two book ideas with colleagues. The first idea was for a collection of papers that spoke to the work Indigenous people carry out in communities and online. The book, a collaboration with my colleague Jeff Berglund at Northern Arizona University, *Indigenous People Rise up: The Global Ascendency of Social Media Activism* (Carlson & Berglund 2021) was realised and published in 2021. This is an international collaboration and includes chapters on Indigenous peoples' community and political activism including significant movements such as #NODAPL (Deschine Parkurst 2021); #SOSBlakAustralia (Carlson & Frazer 2021a); #MMIWG (Moeke-Pickering et al. 2021); and #IdleNoMore (Wilson & Zheng 2021) and many others. These chapters illustrate the impact of social media in expanding the nature of Indigenous communities. Social media has bridged distance, time, and nation-states to mobilise Indigenous peoples to build coalitions across the globe and to stand in solidarity with one another. These movements have succeeded, and gained momentum and traction precisely because of our strategic use of social media.

The second book, *Indigenous Digital Life: The Practice and Politics of Being Indigenous on Social Media*, co-written with colleague Ryan Frazer (Carlson & Frazer 2021b), is centred on the question of how social media has become entangled in the everyday lives of Aboriginal and Torres Strait Islander people. Across this content colonially known as Australia, Indigenous peoples are extremely adept and conversant with the use of social media across all geographical locations. The social media campaign #SOSBLAKAUSTRALIA mentioned above is a prime example and represents the response of Indigenous women from the Kimberley region of Western Australia to the government's plans to cut essential services funding for up to 150 Indigenous communities outside of urban locations (Carlson & Frazer 2016). The #SOSBLAKAUSTRALIA campaign like many others was initiated by Indigenous women. It is true that Indigenous women and the LGBTQAI+[1] community are often at the forefront of community and political activism. This is largely because these cohorts are the most targeted when it comes to violence and they are often the strength of our families. Communications scholar Manuel Castells

(2015) argues that social movements are always about resistance to some form of power and notes that successful social movements are dependent on communication that is autonomous from state or corporate control. Social media has changed the control of communication. Social movements in the contemporary world are generally hybrid in nature and involve extensive use of online tools along with physical occupation of urban spaces. #SOSBLAKAUSTRALIA is a perfect example of a hybrid social movement that called for action both online and offline.

#SOSBLAKAUSTRALIA was a result of what could be described as 'the perfect storm'. Indigenous people and communities had had enough of the repeated failure of successive governments to act in the best interest of Aboriginal and Torres Strait Islander peoples. Tired of the racism, bigotry, oppression and genocide, Indigenous people began a historic social media-driven campaign. The catalyst that set the campaign in motion was then Western Australian state premier Colin Barnett announcing in 2014 that he would close up to 150 remote Indigenous communities (Carlson & Frazer 2016, p. 122). In 2015, Tony Abbott, then prime minister and self-appointed minster for Indigenous Affairs stated on radio that he supported Barnett's decision, explaining, 'What we can't do is endlessly subsidise lifestyle choices if those lifestyle choices are not conducive to the kind of full participation in Australian society that everyone should have' (ABC 2015). This would have ultimately meant the forced removal of Indigenous peoples from homelands they and their ancestors have been caring for and living on for over 60,000 years.

The campaign began with members of the Bieundurry family in Waangkatjungka and a small group of other Indigenous women from the Kimberley area who were making plans on Facebook to hold a rally. Over the evening, the thread gained momentum with many others joining in (Harlow 2001, p. 231). One of those people was Nyikina woman Sam Cook. Sam created the Facebook page 'Stop the forced closure of Aboriginal communities' and hoped to gain at least 1,000 likes. A few hours later, over 2,000 people had already liked the page (Carlson & Frazer 2016, p. 124). The page was shared across the world and other Indigenous people and allies began to post and support the protest. Many Indigenous people here believe that the Australian governments are incapable of finding solutions that are Indigenous-led and that international aid may be the only answer, hence the use of the international code 'SOS' signalling extreme distress and an urgent appeal for help.

Over the next five days, every state and territory had mobilised with dozens of rallies and more than 30,000 people marching in the streets – from remote locations, regional towns, major cities and the capital of Australia. Due to the affordances of social media platforms, in less than thirty days 'SOS BLAK AUSTRALIA, Stop the Forced Closures of Aboriginal Communities' created a social media platform with hundreds of thousands of supporters from across the globe (Carlson & Frazer 2016). As Petray (2011, p. 933) argues, 'the interactivity enabled by Web 2.0 serves to expand the 'virtual we' of Indigenous solidarity, encompassing not just Indigenous people but their supporters, and many sympathetic individuals from around the world'. Harlow (2011, p. 226), who explored the use of Facebook in a protest movement against the Guatemalan government (a country where around 50% of the population is Indigenous), found that Facebook was used 'to mobilise and advance an online justice movement that activated an offline movement'.

Protests in Naarm (which colonisers renamed Melbourne) were a sight to be seen. Thousands descended upon the city business district in a wave of anger, bringing the city to a standstill. The online publication *New Matilda* described the emotional force of the movement: 'The ability to mobilise so many across the country, not once, but twice, within two months of each other speaks to the outrage that will hopefully end up suffocating Barnett's plans to close these communities' (New Matilda 2015, para. 8). However, Indigenous bodies and Indigenous anger on the streets causes great concern to settlers. So, although the Naarm protest was regarded as unequivocally peaceful, the fact that the crowd disrupted activity on two main streets for several hours during peak hour elicited a response by the mainstream media that was decisively antagonistic. The *Herald Sun* labelled the protestors as 'selfish rabble' (see Clarke 2015) and foregrounded the 'selfish' disruption to 'innocent' commuters' homeward journey (Watson 2015). The assumption was that Indigenous people were unemployed and did not positively contribute to society.

Indigenous anger is often referred to as 'off-putting' to non-Indigenous peoples – we are told our anger alienates people. Indigenous activists are accused of divisive behaviour and our anger is deemed 'inappropriate' and unwarranted. But anger fuels people into action as argued by Carlson and Frazer (2021b, p. 55):

> Anger has a palpable affective force. As a response to the unjust suffering of others, it circulates rapidly between bodies, eliciting and consolidating a collective of people against that injustice whose actions and reactions stimulate affect. Anger is a force that demands attention and is therefore capable of generating far-reaching empathy and solidarity on social media.

Social media sites are increasingly used by Indigenous people to connect, interact socially and to politically agitate for social justice. Many Indigenous social and political movements depend on social media sites, such as Facebook and Twitter, as a means of effecting swift and efficient communication between and among Indigenous peoples. More recently, we have seen a huge uptake of platforms such as Instagram and TikTok among Indigenous youth. While we are well-versed on the capitalist drive of social media and the multiple problems with engaging online (Duarte 2017b; Carlson & Frazer 2018b; Carlson & Day 2022), we also see the benefits these platforms provide for us. We weigh this up and make decisions based on how we can use digital technologies for our own needs.

Narrative #2: Coro J.-A. Juanena, 'Nomadic Feminist Nations Zero-Risk: When Indigenous women organise'

In May 2005, I landed in New York to attend the Global Indigenous Women's Caucus (GIWC) for the first time. It was a preparatory meeting for the Permanent Forum on Indigenous Issues (UNPFII) that would be held at United Nations headquarters over two weeks. Three years earlier, the sessions of the UNPFII had begun and it would take place on an annual basis thereafter thanks to the work of Indigenous leaders who had been fighting for the recognition and vindication of this space within the United Nations (UN). In 2007, the Expert Mechanism on the Rights of Indigenous Peoples (EMRIP) was established by the Human Rights Council in Geneva.

Of course, at the same time the Global Indigenous Women's Caucus got together at those sessions.

During all these years, I have been presented and participated in these meetings. In addition, I was able to attend other events around the world organised and participated in exclusively by Indigenous women[2] and all of them share some common characteristics. A good deal of my doctoral dissertation came from there but, over the years, I have realised the enormous value and significance of these events. So, I would like to take this opportunity to unveil and disclose the important contribution that these practices have provided to the transnational Indigenous Women's Movement. These meetings between Indigenous women from all over the world and prior to the United Nations conferences, where Indigenous peoples raise their voices, share a certain singularity that has allowed for the construction of a joint political identity. This has led me to name these spaces of resistance and creation 'Nomadic Feminist Nation Zero-Risk'.

I shall first define the concept of Nomadic Feminist Nation Zero-Risk. Subsequently, I will delve into the different meanings and consequences of this idea. And finally, I will evaluate the impact of this practice of feminist resistance.

In a nutshell, Nomadic Feminist Nation Zero-Risk is a safe place of enunciation, both symbolic and physical, which is self-constructed and self-managed by Indigenous Women.[3] Place of enunciation means the place we speak from, therefore the first consequence of the existence of such a space is that Indigenous women cease to be spoken for by others, and begin speaking for themselves, about themselves and to themselves.

Within the zero-risk frameworks and platforms, their bodies, minds and spirits can express themselves freely and sovereignly, safe from any danger that might put their bodies, minds, or spirits at risk. This implies a place without violence, and not only a territory free from behavioural violence but also from what Johan Galtung refers to as structural (1969) and cultural violence (1990), more subtle forms of violence that prevent individuals, groups, and societies from reaching their full potential. Structural and cultural violence underscore harmful inequalities of power and wealth between different social groups. Nevertheless, we must keep in mind what James Gilligan (1997) points out, that structural and behavioural violence are inextricably related to each other, as cause to effect. So, creating a peaceful place entails constructing a space where, as a collective, they can develop their potential and organise themselves without endangering their own person.

At the same time, Nomadic Feminist Nations Zero-Risk is a symbolic space where Indigenous women create their own nation, a community of Indigenous Women from around the world. There, they establish bonds and mutual alliance to overcome their condition and the control of their own power of representation, using Foucault's term (1990), safe from the technologies of representation from the imperial discourse (Said 1996). These spaces of enunciation enable all of them to construct their strategies of resistance and evaluate possible common alternatives. As a result, their own political identity will be introduced and positioned within the transnational political arena.

On the other hand, through accompaniment and mutual support, the subaltern women inhabit their Nomadic Feminist Nations where the development of their integral and multidimensional empowerment is possible. The empowerment process involves having the opportunity to go through their lives to construct their own story and break with the invisibility that haunts them. At this point, I fully agree with Adriana Cavarero (2005) when she states that having a voice is not only making ourselves visible but also making ourselves audible to others. However, first of all, to become audible as a collective implies mutual and attentive listening based on an ethics of care among those who have suffered similar experiences. In that sense, we can talk about multidimensional empowerment because that includes the empowerment of their souls, minds, and bodies. We can also affirm that there is a process of integral empowerment since it is not only a political empowerment, alien to the planetary community. As daughters of Mother Earth, they are part of her body where they live in harmony with the rest of the sons and daughters of nature. As a collective, they declare themselves to be an interdependent part of different species growing or living together in the universe. Integral empowerment presupposes and fortifies Indigenous women's way of being in the world.

Both processes of empowerment lead to development of their self-determination as Indigenous women in transnational movements. Self-determination is understood in the way that Tuhiwai Smith (1999, p. 116) explains in her work, 'a political and social justice goal of the new agenda of Indigenous activity, toward the development of global Indigenous strategic alliances'. As a nation, at the Nomadic Feminist Nations Zero-Risk, Indigenous women carry out the processes of Decolonisation, Transformation, Mobilisation, and Healing as mapped out by Tuhiwai Smith (1999, p. 117). We must keep in mind that the result of self-determination is a way of being in the world, an alternative way from the heteropatriarchal and capitalist world-system. This way of being in the world is expressed in their political identity, an artistic expression of their existence. These spaces of enunciation are a territory of decolonisation but also a space of new forms of social construction outside of the hegemonic heteropatriarchal capitalist power.

In the same way, in these symbolic lands, it is possible to create a Circle of Trust as sovereign speakers. In the Circle of Trust, Indigenous women can write a new regime of truth, in the words of Michel Foucault (1978), since they can use, as a collective, the methods to transform, produce and distribute their own system of enunciation. In this way, they will be able to change the hegemonic regime of truth and produce a new politics of truth (Foucault 1978). Their own regime of truth, among other things, consolidates their emancipation as a counter-hegemonic resistance group.

These nomadic spaces of enunciation make it possible to travel the way of the transformation of consciousness *in* itself into consciousness *for* itself, which presupposes the surpassing of the native's subaltern consciousness and the constitution of identity pride. Identity pride implies a level of reflective self-awareness about identity, becoming an expression of the evolution of their consciousness. It is a positive and self-affirming force that wants to put into practice their mode of self-enunciation, self-representation, and where the fact of being Indigenous Women appears re-signified.

Before concluding, I would like to honour the memory of all those brave Indigenous women who made these spaces possible, such as Ingrid Washinawatok El-Issa (1957–1999), Esmeralda Brown (1952–2019) and many others Indigenous women leaders around the world. We have these spaces of enunciation because of them. Eskerrik asko ('thanks' in Basque) to all Indigenous women ancestors who made it possible for us to be here today. They are here with us forever.

Narrative #3: waaseyaa'sin Christine Sy, 'Anishinaabe womxn at the sugar bush in Occupied Anishinaabewaki'

I come to the theoretical underpinnings of this conversations with some anxiety around the term 'Indigenous feminist transnationalism' and wonder about its helpfulness for my people, the Anishinaabe, on the ground, in everyday life. Yet, I fully realise that the local and global are always in relationship, as is theory with practice, and both inform Indigenous life in gendered ways under imposed settler-state borders. I've spent a lot of time reflecting on the process of coming-to-consciousness about a global Indigeneity, considering the impacts of globalisation on Indigenous peoples, particularly womxn, in our local contexts (Kuokkanen 2008), Indigenous internationalisation and how settler states, such as Canada and the US, also interfere in the lives of Indigenous peoples elsewhere.[4] While so much of this coming to consciousness has been prompted by interpersonal exchanges and learning in public spaces, Carol J. Williams (2012), Joseph Bauerkemper and Heidi Kiiwetinepinesiik Stark (2012), Chantal Fiola (2013),Yi-Chun Tricia Lin (2016), Hokulani K. Aikau, Arvin Maile, Mishuana Goeman, and Scott Morgensen (2015), and Corinnee L. Mason (2018) help me to think about transnationalism and Indigenous peoples, including through a gendered lens which focuses on womxn, Indigenous feminist transnationalism, and transnational feminism. I am committed to growing Anishinaabe understanding of ourselves as gendered, politicised, economic, and historicised subjects in a global world, under imposed border and settler states. At the same time, I am motivated to re-activate knowledges about Anishinaabeg womxn's land-based relationships across historical, political, and social-economic contexts. An Anishinaabe feminist transnational lens allows space for this complexity.

As a shorter contribution to an anticipated monograph chapter on Anishinaabe histories of the sugar bush – the place where Anishinaabeg harvest maple sap and produce syrup and sugar – I'm thinking about mapping as a method whose visual capabilities reveal Anishinaabe feminist transnational possibilities. Specifically, I revisit an earlier mapping of historical Anishinaabe sugar bush womxn at sugar bushes. I identify areas of inquiry that will activate the map epistemologically (that is, via spatial orientation, Indigenous place names) through a historicisation of shifting relationships with the sugar bush that are informed by both Anishinaabe governance, as well as settler-state (and global) impositions. This is achieved through querying the sameness and difference between Anishinaabeg womxn within our Anishinaabe nation and between Canada and the US. It may also be achieved by contextualising of Anishinaabeg sugar bushing within a broader global history of sugar.

In broader research inquiring how sugar bushing could be understood as a form of Anishinaabe womxn's economic sovereignty, I examined published traditional stories, published oral reminiscences, archived ship manifests, and living oral histories, memories, knowledges, and experiences of sugar bush work with thirteen Anishinaabeg in both Canada and the US. Missing from these areas of investigation were many of the documented names of Anishinaabe womxn who had participated in sugar bush work between 1800 and 2014 as well as the place locations of the sugar bushes they worked. Naming is important as an Anishinaabe epistemology, research process, and act of decolonisation. Naming, re-naming, and removing names is also a tool of colonisation. Under and through settler colonialism, Indigenous womxn have been physically removed from the land in terms of our complex relationship with it and are often rendered invisible or marginal, dehumanised, or misrepresented in documentary sources and elsewhere. Because of this, it was imperative for me to, at a minimum, bring together the Anishinaabe sugar bush womxn that existed in the sources I examined but did not utilise. Similarly, it was crucial to locate the womxn in place, on the land – specifically in the sugarbushes they worked. I wanted to see all these womxn together; I wanted a document where readers could see Anishinaabeg womxn together in shared practice, across our territory. I decided the best method to do this was to collate the information and transcribe it onto a map.

We began with an image from Google maps (see Figure 13.1), Ojibwe thought and names informed by Charles Lippert and Jordan

ANISHINAABEWAKI

Canada

USA

international border
that bifurcates
Anishinaabe territory

20
19 gichi-zaagi'igan
(Lake Ontario)

18

waaseyaagami-wiikwed
(Georgian Bay)

waabishkiigoo-gichigami
(Lake Erie)

16 17

Waabanong
(East)

15

13

naadowewi-gichigami
(Lake Huron)

11 14
12

10

anishinaabewi-gichigami
(Lake Superior)

boojwiikwed
(Green Bay)

mishigami
(Lake Michigan)

animbiigoo-zaaga'igan
(Lake Nipigon)

9

8 7

6

5

4

3

2

1

manidoo-ba zaaga'igan
(Lake manitoba)

0   km   300

1. Gaa-gwe-kwekojiwang,
   Ebb n' Flow, Manitoba
2. White Earth, Minnesota
3. Leech Lake, Minnesota
4. Ottertail Point, Minnesota
5. Mille Lacs, Minnesota
6. Lac du Flambeau, Wisconsin
7. Partridge Lake,
   Vilas County, Wisconsin
8. Lac Vieux Desert, Michigan
9. L'Anse, Michigan
10. Omanitigwe'aawii Ziibing
    Manistique, Michigan
11. Goulais Mission,
    Lake Superior, Ontario
12. Bois Blanc Island, Michigan
13. Batchewana Village,
    Lake Superior, Ontario
14. Sugar Island, Michigan
15. Garden River, Ontario
16. M'Chigeeng, Ontario
17. Wikwemikong, Ontario
18. Shawanaga, Ontario
19. Waawshkegemonki
    Curve Lake, Ontario
20. Alderville, Ontario

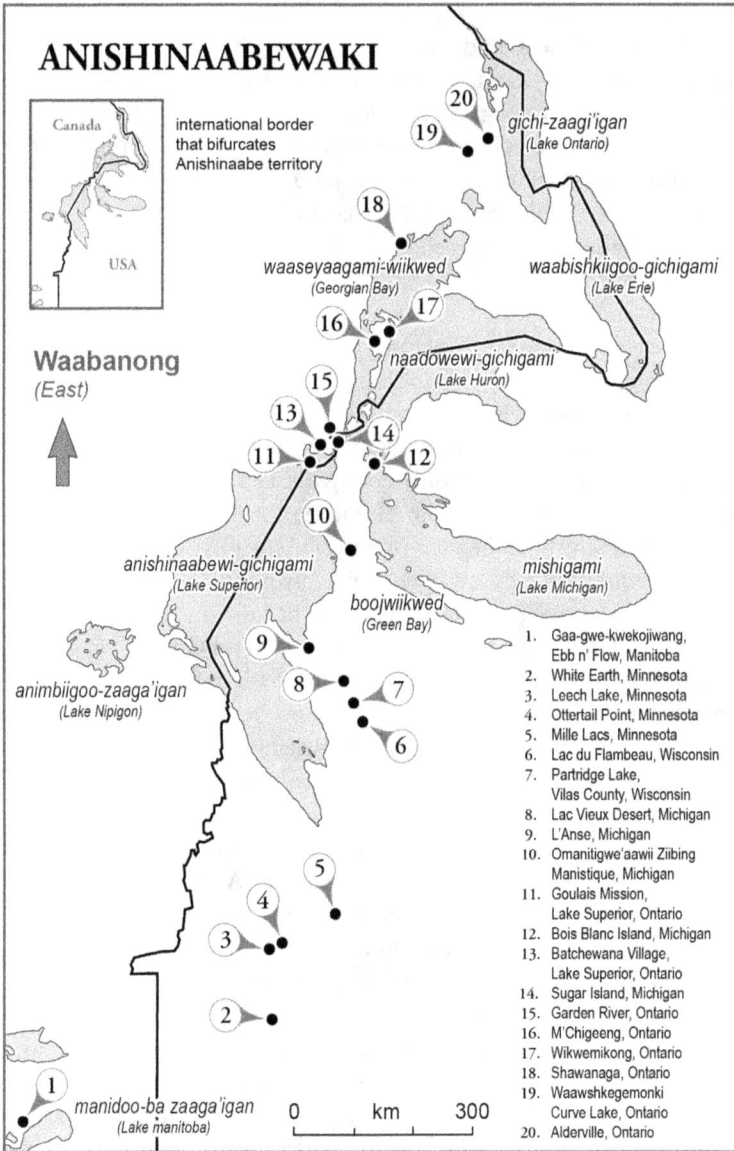

Figure 13.1 Anishinaabe map
Source: Based on map created by Brigitte Evering

Engels from *The Decolonial Atlas*, and the data from my research. From this, my friend and fellow Indigenous Studies scholar, Brigitte Evering, created a map documenting forty-two Anishinaabeg womxn engaged in sugar bush work at twenty different sugarbush locations (Evering & Sy 2019, pp. 314–319). This map is simple and beautiful – an aerial view of a land mass where the lakes and watershed are coloured royal blue and the land is coloured in various shades of dark green. Oriented towards the east, the map is in accordance with Anishinaabe directional primacy. Anishinaabe names for several lakes are indicated and include gichi-zaagi'igan (Lake Ontario), waaseyaagami-wiikwed (Georgian Bay), waabishkiigoo-gichigami (Lake Erie), naadowewi-gichigami (Lake Huron), mishigami (Lake Michigan), anishinaabewi-gichigami (Lake Superior), animbiigoo-zaaga'igan (Lake Nipigon), boojwiikwed (Green Bay), and manidoo-ba zaaga'igan (Lake Manitoba). Anishinaabewaki, which is the word Anishinaabeg use to describe the physical world we live in that is our home, becomes recognisably politicised vis-à-vis a line, coloured bright yellow, that runs top to bottom and through four of five major lakes. This line, which can be seen on Google images and which we have left un-named, represents the international border that bifurcates Anishinaabe territory and demarcates Canada and the US, the settler states that occupy Anishinaabewaki.

Twenty white markers, numbered consecutively, denote places where womxn worked the sugar bush throughout Anishinaabewaki. In the part of Anishinaabewaki that is occupied by Canada and where there are treaties that govern Canada-Anishinaabe relations, these sugar bush sites are: Gaa-gwe-kwekojiwang, Ebb n' Flow, Manitoba (1); Goulais Mission, Lake Superior, Ontario (11); Batchewana Village, Lake Superior, Ontario (13); Garden River, Ontario (15); M'Chigeeng, ON (16); Wikwemikong, ON (17); Shawanaga, ON (18); Waawshkegemonki Curve Lake, Ontario (19); and Alderville, Ontario (20). In the part of Anishinaabewaki that is occupied by the US and where there are treaties that govern US-Anishinaabe relations, these sugar bush sites are: White Earth, Minnesota (2); Leech Lake, Minnesota (3); Ottertail Point, Minnesota (4); Mille Lacs, MN (5); Lac du Flambeau, Wisconsin (6); Partridge Lake, Vilas County, Wisconsin (7); Lac Vieux Desert, Michigan (8); L'Anse, Michigan (9); Omanitigwe'aawii Ziibing

Manistique, Michigan (10); Bois Blanc Island, Michigan (12); and Sugar Island, Michigan (14). Many of these places today are known in Canada as First Nations (that is, reserves) or, in the US, as reservations. However, naming them as such suggests modern historical markers and borders that foreclose consideration of Anishinaabeg womxn's temporal-spatial relationships with place that are long-standing and fluid.

Further, as stated above, naming Indigenous womxn is an important political, historical, and Indigenous feminist project, particularly given the ways settler states, historians, patriarchal and capitalist ideologies de-centre, misrepresent or erase Indigenous womxn from the record (Alia 2009; Sy 2021, pp. 188–189, 193–194). This said, research by, for, and about Indigenous peoples requires considerations beyond the need to name such as relationality, accountability, and ethics. It also requires care for the intimacies and implications that come with bringing forth names from the archive and/or the living into the public domain. For the present project whose audience is global, I don't identify the Anishinaabe sugar bush womxn associated with these places. Bringing the names beyond the dissertation, and symbolically beyond Anishinaabewaki, for a global audience, requires a consideration of relational ethics process. For example, the names need to be re-introduced first to a wide Anishinaabe audience with the intent of benefitting Anishinaabeg; living Anishinaabeg womxn must be given the opportunity to say if they want their name publicised on a wider platform. The map is generative without these names because the many places where Anishinaabeg womxn have been documented as carrying out the sugar bush harvest is made visual. In many cases, if not most or all, the womxn are more than individual workers of a finite production. Identified womxn in these places would be doing this work alongside other unidentified womxn. Also, the womxn doing this work and who have this relationship with the sugarbush would be living links in the intragenerational and intergenerational transmission of this relationship with place and the work carried out here.

The map, for me, is a powerful and stunning visual representation of documentary, photographic, oral, and living evidence of Anishinaabe womxn engaged in sugar bush work throughout Anishinaabewaki. The map is contextualised within a historical present that erases, invisibilises or marginalises Anishinaabeg womxn's presence on the land and in land-based relations that produce more life. It supplants nation-building narratives of the romantic and economically charged settler maple syrup industry and masculinist or patriarchal tropes of Anishinaabeg man-on-the-land. It also begins to re-introduce land-based relational histories to both non-Anishinaabeg and Anishinaabeg that affirm Anishinaabeg womxn's primacy. Finally, in quite unexpected and interesting ways, the very present yellow line portraying the settler state border provokes the potentiality of an Anishinaabe feminist transnational analysis. The border itself prompts queries. However, it is the visual output portraying Anishinaabeg sugar bush womxn in the sugar bush throughout our territory, on both sides of the border, that compels a consideration of the possibilities of Indigenous feminist transnational inquiry regarding Anishinaabeg land-based relational life prior to, during, and despite settler–colonial occupation. When I look at this map, to me, there is so much life here and so much room for more life.

The starting point for inquiry from a transnational feminist lens often begins with some engagement with the global. However, in an Indigenous feminisms roundtable discussion of the transnational, Kanaka 'Ōiwi scholar Hokulani K. Aikau references a key principle in the University of Hawai'i Indigenous Politics, which emphasises localising struggle 'before scaling up the analysis to a regional or global scale' (cited in Aikau et al. 2015, p. 85). She states:

> When Indigeneity is placed at the centre, when we turn our attention in a material rather than a metaphorical way to the lands upon which we stand, to 'āina, then we are able to challenge the fundamental legitimacy of the nation-state structure. If we acknowledge that the sovereignty of the land continues to persist and is Indigenous, then we have to challenge the legitimacy of the United States. This kind of approach asks us to pay attention to work with, and be accountable to the ways in which global processes play out on Indigenous bodies in the places where we live rather than just in those places where we work. This relates to the conversation yesterday about what is the global, what is the local, what are the relationships between them – for us this is clear: place matters. (Cited in Aikau et al. 2015, p. 86)

Centring Indigeneity in transnational feminisms requires beginning with local place before, or while, embarking in regional, national, international or global analytics.

In the same discussion, Towanda Seneca scholar Mishuana Goeman considers Indigenous conceptions of geography (including both land/water and bodies) in relation to transnational feminisms, grounding her knowing in the fact that her community and the Haudenosaunee nation is 'spread across what is now known as Canada and the US' (cited in Aikau et al. 2015, p. 93). Where Aikau emphasises the local and place, Goeman focuses on myriad meanings and possibilities of land and water. She begins with an 'Haudenosaunee model of analysis that works toward decentering settler nation-state formations' without diminishing the material realities of such formations and asks,

> what forms of analysis or actions can take place by centering Indigenous conceptions of land as connected, rather than land as disaggregate parcels at various European-conceived scales, [e.g., reservations, nation-states, continents, hemispheres] which is a project of accumulation ... And what if we position land and water as always connected? (Cited in Aikau et al. 2015, p. 94)

Aikau and Goeman exhibit a shared interest in unsettling the normativity of the settler nation-state, evidenced in their respective articulations of the Indigenous local and place and land in the multi-scalar as an Indigenous feminist contribution to feminist trans-nationalism. They provide a foundation through which I can revisit my map of Anishinaabeg sugar bush womxn at the sugar bush and embark on sketching out questions relative to an Indigenous/Anishinaabe feminist transnational query. Some of these questions include:

- What are the epistemological significances of womxn's names and place names identified?
- What stories of Anishinaabeg life, and Anishinaabeg womxn's holistic relationships with the lands and waters through the sugar bush are carried with each womxn named in this map? What stories are carried from/through each place identified on this map?
- Who is not named here? Who is yet to be named?

- How can womxn's relationships with the sugar bush, and the lands and waters, be historicised?
- What/how are the relationships between womxn on this map?
- Was there a collectivity or network of Anishinaabeg womxn's sugar bushing? What possibilities arise from the creation of a sugar bush womxn's collectivity or network today? What are the possibilities of/from this across different kinds of land-and-water based relationships (that is, ricing, berry-picking, etc.)?
- What were the gendered impacts of the Canada–US border on Anishinaabeg land and water-based relationships and what were the impacts on Anishinaabeg womxn? How was this specific to the sugar bush?
- How did the Anishinaabeg womxn come to 'have' sugar bushes to participate in this work? How did this shift through various historical periods? How were Anishinaabeg womxn displaced/alienated/dispossessed of their relationships with sugar bushes? How might this be restored? Is restoration of these relationships something of important to Anishinaabeg generally or Anishinaabeg womxn specifically?
- How did living under different social-political-economic or military conditions shape womxn's relationships with the sugar bush?
- Sugar – in the form of sugar cane – is a global commodity often associated with enslavement, exploitation, economic migration and coloniality. In the form of beet sugar, it is considered a commodity in modern industry. What is the relationship between these global histories of sugar and Anishinaabeg womxn's sugar bush work?
- How can Canadian and US imperialism have impacted Anishinaabeg sugar bushing and sugar bushing of other Indigenous nations? How might it impact a mass restoration of such practices?
- What/how are the differences that exist between Anishinaabeg sugar bush womxn across places, the border, and other sites of differences (for example, class, access to knowledge, land, material/economic/social resources)?
- How might Anishinaabeg womxn's sugar bushing persist despite the settler nation-state? How might modern heteropatriarchal or masculinist associations with land-based/sugar bush work that exist within Anishinaabeg communities today shape the possibility of Anishinaabeg womxn reclaiming these relationships?

- What does it mean to view a map and say that the imposed settler border and the nation-states matter/do not matter to the enduring and ongoing presence of the Anishinaabeg Nation, and Anishinaabeg womxn's relationships with lands and waters, such as the sugar bush?
- How does the border and the respective nation-states of Canada and the US archive, document, preserve or gather knowledge/information/sources about Anishinaabeg womxn and what are the implications of this for knowing Anishinaabeg womxn and/or future archival commitments into the future?

Narrative #4: Alex Wilson, 'Coming in to ourselves as relations: queering (as transnational practice) as medicine'

My home, where I wrote this paper, is located in the traditional territory of the Swampy Cree in northern Manitoba, Canada. Our people recognise the land, water, sky and other living beings as our relatives, and understand that we must be responsible and accountable in these relationships. This sense of relationality is expressed in our family name, Wassenas, which links us to light.

As a professor in the Department of Educational Foundations at the University of Saskatchewan, my work has focused on Indigenous land-based education. This chapter draws on experiences of the land and of Indigenous peoples in the regions in which I have worked, studied, and lived. However, our experiences parallel those of Indigenous peoples throughout the Americas and across the globe who, like us, have continued to learn from, care for, protect, and be sustained by their relationships with the land for millennia.

Throughout most of history, the land has been the primary site of learning and source of knowledge for Indigenous peoples across the world. We have learned that to survive, we must take care of the land and of the many human and more-than-human beings who are here with us. As Inuk advocate and climate activist Siila Watt-Cloutier (2020) has stated, the land has taught us that we cannot just take from nature – we must also give back. This is a fundamental ethic in land-based education.

In Canada, land-based education is inseparable from Indigenous sovereignty and resistance movements. Today, land-based education is integrated into the programming of many First Nations and other schools in Canada where Indigenous students form a significant proportion of the student body. As will be clear from the discussion (later in this paper) of the Indian Residential School system, this was not always the case. Much of the initial momentum for the reintroduction of Indigenous land-based learning into educational programming came in the early 1970s, when First Nations leaders demanded more control of education in their communities (Kirkness 1984). The movement has continued to grow since then, and land-based educators have developed formal and informal collaborative networks through which they share knowledge, practices, pedagogy, and resources. The value of Indigenous land-based education has been recognised internationally, with, for example, organisations such as the United Nations Educational, Scientific and Cultural Organization (UNESCO) now integrating it into programming at their schools.

The expansion of Indigenous and non-Indigenous students' access to land-based education is encouraging. At the same time, however, I have seen that colonial practices and mindsets – in particular, heteropatriarchy – are sometimes replicated in land-based activities, distorting and displacing traditional Indigenous knowledge and life ways. These have included teachings and practices that disempower and exclude Indigenous women and 2SLGBTQI+[5] people.

In Cree cosmology and stories, the Weesageechak (or, as some know it, Orion) constellation is recognisably queer, constantly shifting its shape and state of being. Indigenous knowledge systems are grounded in our cosmologies, and Weesageechak has helped us understand, on a deep level, the biodiversity and implicit order of life. Weesageechak represents a continuity of energy that is about love, the energy that maintains and sustains life.

My home is on the shores of Atikameg, which translates as 'whitefish lake' (named so because that fish could be harvested in these waters), but in English is called Clearwater Lake, because its water is perfectly clear. The region is part of the Saskatchewan River Delta, one of the largest inland deltas in North America, home to old-growth boreal forests, peat moss, and waterways that connect with the more than 110,000 lakes in the province. Cree people have lived in this region for tens of thousands of years, moving when the ice ages arrived and returning when they receded.

More recently, in what feels like a blink of the eye, a lot has changed. Once colonial forces realised that there were resources in our region that they might be able claim and exploit for profit and power (as justified by the legal fantasy of *terra nullius* and authorised by the Doctrines of Christian Discovery), they – and their capitalist ideology and practices – moved in. One of their first actions was to map our territories, flattening the land and waters we lived with to tidy two-dimensional arrays of squares, recording their inventory of local resources they could use to assess the economic value of any given section of our territory. The colonisers' cartography was strikingly different to the cartography used by Cree elders in a recent mapping project undertaken by Opaskwayak Cree Nation to support community members' reconnection with the land. The elders developed a map of their traditional territory, tracing routes that they and their ancestors had travelled, identifying different sites at which they had camped or harvested, and sharing Cree place names for these sites, which described their relationships with the land at that place. Our elders' cartography connects physical space, human bodies and kinship structures that extend well beyond human relationships.

To make room for capitalist claims and enterprises, the colonial government established a system of 'reserved lands' for Indigenous people. Indigenous people were forcibly relocated to small, confined tracts of land within their traditional territories. The reserves were located on sites deemed valueless by the colonial government, and the structure, layout, and design of the reserve communities, right down to the blueprints of the houses into which Indigenous people were moved, did not support the traditional lifeways that had enabled us to survive and to thrive. Legal prohibitions were put in place to restrict our movement, limit our access to our traditional lands and limit our access to our traditional foods. A resident of the reserve could only go out on the land if they secured an official 'Permit to Leave Reserve' from the government's representative. In my home community of Opaskwayak Cree Nation, trappers were given a muskrat quota card, which recorded, for each year, the area and zone in which an individual was permitted to hunt, the number of muskrats they were allowed to trap, and, at the end of the season, their total catch that year. Nimoosum (my grandfather) Charlie Wilson was issued a muskrat quota card but Nookum (my grandmother) Beatrice Wilson, who was equally a part of the family, was not. This is one of many examples of how Cree women were erased and silenced by colonial policy.

As many Indigenous people and their allies continue to remind us, water is life. In our territory, however, we now hear that 'Water is megawatt or kilowatt hours, and that equals dollars.' The huge network of life that we have travelled along and stewarded for centuries and is now endangered, subject to the reckless neoliberal and corporate policies and practices of parties such as Manitoba Hydro, SaskPower, Ducks Unlimited, Husky Oil and phosphate-spewing commercial farming operations.

Throughout our colonial and postcolonial history and continuing in the neocolonial present, these activities have impacted the land, and, in a parallel process of dominion, regulation, exploitation and extraction, impacted Indigenous people. This has been especially true for Indigenous women and Two Spirit and queer people, who have been repeatedly and multiply marginalised.

Nearly a century and a half after the fur traders and settlers' arrival in the traditional territory of the Swampy Cree, the consequences of their irresponsible relationship with the land and waters are in plain sight. Ordinarily, winter in our region is bitterly cold. The ground is covered by a deep layer of snow, and we do not see the grass until April. In recent years, however, our region, like other northern regions, has felt the effects of global warming. A seemingly endless line of logs was harvested from old growth boreal forests ('virgin forest' as they are called, imposing heteropatriarchal language on the land) in our traditional territory. A strong global market for these centuries-old trees exists because of the texture of their wood, which has unusually long and strong fibres. Chopped down, the trees will be pulped and processed at a paper mill, and then used to produce SPK (special kraft paper) packaging for bulky, heavy materials such as pet food or concrete mix.

What happens to the next generation of trees when all their Elders are cut down or killed? Like us, trees live in families and communicate. Without Elders to guide them, how does a new generation of trees understand how to grow and survive? Ikea, the largest consumer of wood in the world, harvests and grows trees in the boreal forest zone in Finland. Images of the corporation's plantation show what happens when the next generation of trees has no Elders and no continuity of knowledge or lifeways. As trees, they now stand as individuals, seemingly not in relation.

These trees' experience parallels that of the generations of First Nation children who were forcibly removed from their families, communities, and lands, and sent to residential schools. The residential schools were run by Christian churches, funded and mandated by the federal government, and established to assimilate (or, at the very least, 'de-Indigenise') Indigenous children. Epistemicide – undoing Indigenous ways of learning and knowing – was embedded in the schools' practice and policy. The first school was opened in the 1800s, and the last was not closed until 1997. In spite of the fact that the schools no longer exist, the goal of assimilating Indigenous people still drives policy and practice in many institutions and organisations, including many classrooms within the current mainstream education system, where pedagogy and curriculum typically do not support Indigenous children's relationships with the land and land-based knowledge systems.

My father once explained that the Cree term used to describe youth who had been in residential schools and later returned to their community could be translated as 'people who don't know how to behave'. The relentless ontological violence of the residential school system had stripped them of their understanding of self. Our recovery from the residential school experience has also involved an ontological shift, one in which, rather than understanding oneself to be an individual self, we have recovered our understanding of self as self-as-relations. We are our relationships.

Queering is one way to repair this ontological shift. Sarah Hunt and Cindy Holmes (2015: 156) describe queering as a 'deconstructive practice focused on challenging normative knowledges, identities, behaviours, and spaces thereby unsettling power relations and taken-for-granted assumptions'. My friend Dr Kalani Young offers a succinct definition of queering that draws our attention to the healing potential of the process. Queering, she told me, is about 'transforming poison into medicine' (Young 2018, as cited in Wilson et al. 2021).

The term decolonisation is often used to describe how we might undo or repair the impacts of Canada's colonial history and present-day neocolonialism. Rather than hang our future on undoing the past, we can choose instead to embrace the radical and reconstructive potential of queering. We can reclaim and reassert our queer cosmologies; our intimate relationships with the land and with the beings who share the land with us; land-based knowledge and ways of being that nourish, animate, sustain life, and enable our survival, sustainability and wellbeing; and the diverse possibilities of who we, as humans, are and who we might become.

As a Cree Two Spirit person, my own identity development and the identity of most of my Two Spirit peers skipped what seemed at the time to be a requisite step to empowered adulthood for LGBTQAI+ youth. We did not come out. Then, coming out was typically configured as a bold declaration of an individuated identity, a willingness to continue declaring that identity even if it resulted in the loss of family, place, or community. My peers and I had a different experience. Rather than come out, we came in. We re-centred ourselves in the traditional knowledge, practices, and lifeways of our people, found strength in our families and communities, and were sustained by our (and their) sense of self-as-relations.

Over the last several years, it has become clear that human-made climate chaos is steadily depleting the planet's capacity to sustain human life. As Siila Watt-Cloutier (2020) has stated in a recent Climate Atlas of Canada documentary, 'Indigenous wisdom is what the Western world needs to heal, to understand and to get back into creating a more sustainable world. Indigenous knowledge is the medicine the world seeks.' Other Indigenous women within Canada and across the globe are also sharing their understanding of our relational responsibilities to the land, recognising that 'Indigenous sovereignty is climate action' (Idle No More 2019) and working to generate change.

Conclusion

Through these accounts of Indigenous womxn's projects, the roundtable tells stories of transnational Indigenous feminisms: land-based learning and building a sustainable community; land-based knowledge documenting, archiving, and political mobilising;

engendering a digital transnational Indigenous activist scholarly community for transnational Indigenous knowledge dissemination and production; or caring for sugar bush, a marae, a territory. With these four profound and enriching testimonies that narrate divergent transnational Indigenous feminist projects, we must ask what a full contour of transnational feminisms from the Fourth World might look like. Carlson, Juanena, Sy and Wilson provide us glimpses of Indigenous feminist border-crossing projects and the possibilities of global Indigeneity. This forum is but one gesture to push, widen, and Indigenise feminist inquiries transnationally.

These rich narratives offer lessons for all to re-think and re-frame feminist/womanist/humanist projects. At the same time, they beg for more. There needs to be more telling of the transnational collaborative projects by, for, of, and with Indigenous womxn and their communities against heteronormative regimes and gender violence of all forms, against corporate exploitation, against mindless destruction of ancestral grounds on Indigenous lands. These stories have implications for all of humanity. What concerns the Indigenous peoples concerns the whole humanity. In 'Age, Race, Class, and Sex: Women Redefining Difference', Audre Lorde states, 'we have no patterns for relating across our human differences as equals. As a result, those differences have been misnamed and misused in the service of separation and confusion' (2007, p. 115). Indigenous womxn and their communities have shown the world otherwise. They provide more than patterns, a roadmap of relating across all differences, across all nations, human and all, as shown in the four narratives. What we capture indicates, indeed, a much larger narrative intimating decolonial possibilities of making another world that could take lessons from transnational Indigenous feminist practices and thoughts.

Notes

1 Lesbian, gay, bisexual, transgender, queer, asexual and intersex and the plus signifies a number of other identities (LGBTQAI+).

2 For example: AWID's 10th International Forum, Bangkok (Thailand 2005); AWID's 11th International Forum, Cape Town (South Africa 2008); AWID's 12th International Forum, Istanbul (Turkey 2012);

IIFB Working Group on Indicators, Security of rights to territories, lands and natural resources, Nairobi (Kenia 2010).

3 I will write Indigenous Women in capital letters when referring to their political identity, as opposed to 'Indigenous women' in lower case only as a collective.

4 Key undocumented moments come from exchanges with or learning from Columbian Canadian surgeon-activist Manual Rozental (2008), Palestinian activist and legal researcher Suha Jarrar-ban (2009), and a Kanaka Maoli Uber driver whose name I don't know (2019). For instance, it has been surprising for me to learn, on more than one occasion, that some Indigenous peoples outside of Canada and the continental US, had thought, before meeting me, that the Indigenous peoples of Canada no longer existed.

5 Two Spirit, lesbian, gay, bisexual, transgender, queer and intersex. The plus signifies a number of other identities (2SLGBTQI+).

References

Lin, Y. T. (2016). Transnational Indigenous feminisms: Why transnational? Why now? *Lectora: Revista de dones i textualitat, 22*, 9–12.

Lorde, A. (2007). Age, race, class, and sex. In Scott, K., Cayleff, B., Donkey, S. & Lara, I. (Eds), *Culture: An Intersectional Anthology for Gender and Women's Studies* (pp. 16–22). Berkeley: Crossing Press.

Smith, L. T. (2012). *Decolonizing Methodologies: Research and Indigenous Peoples*. London: Zed Books.

United Nations (General Assembly). (2007). United Nations Declaration on the Rights of Indigenous Peoples. www.un.org/development/desa/indigenouspeoples/declaration-on-the-rights-of-indigenous-peoples.html

Wagner, S. R. (2001). *Sisters in Spirit: Haudenosaunee (Iroquois) Influence on Early American Feminists*. Summertown: Native Voices.

Narrative #1

ABC. (2015). Prime Minister Tony Abbott's interview with the ABC Goldfields Esperance. *ABC Goldfields Radio*. www.abc.net.au/local/videos/2015/03/10/4194973.html

Carlson, B. (2013). The 'new frontier': Emergent Indigenous identities and social media. In Harris, M., Nakata, M. & Carlson, B. (Eds), *The Politics of Identity: Emerging Indigeneity*. Sydney: University of Technology Sydney E-Press.

Carlson, B. (2021). Internet users: Learning to trust ourselves. *Australian Feminist Studies, 36*(107), 9–25.

Carlson, B. & Berglund, J. (Eds). (2021). *Indigenous People Rise Up: The Global Ascendancy of Social Media Activism.* New Brunswick: Rutgers University Press.

Carlson, B. & Day, M. (2022). Colonial violence on dating apps. In Arden, H., Briers, A., & Carah, N. (Eds), *Conflict in My Outlook* (pp. 72–74). Brisbane: University of Queensland Press.

Carlson, B. & Dreher, T. (2018). Indigenous innovation on social media. Media International Australia, October. http://journals.sagepub.com/pb-assets/cmscontent/MIA/MIA_CFP_Indigenous_innovation_in_social_media.pdf

Carlson, B. & Frazer, R. (2016). Indigenous activism and social media: The global response to #SOSBLAKAUSTRALIA. In McCosker, A., Vivienne, S., & Johns, A. (Eds), *Rethinking Digital Citizenship: Control, Contest and Culture* (pp. 115–130). Lanham: Rowman and Littlefield International.

Carlson, B. & Frazer, R. (2018a). *Cyberbullying and Indigenous Youth: A Review of the Literature, Commissioned by the Aboriginal Health and Medical Research Council of NSW.* Sydney: Macquarie University. https://researchers.mq.edu.au/en/publications/cyberbullying-and-indigenous-australians-a-review-of-the-literatu

Carlson, B. & Frazer, R. (2018b). *Social Media Mob: Being Indigenous Online.* Sydney: Macquarie University. https://researchers.mq.edu.au/en/publications/social-media-mob-being-indigenous-online

Carlson, B. & Frazer, R. (2021a). Anger, hope and love: The affective economies of Indigenous social media activism. In Carlson, B., & Berglund, J. (Eds), *Indigenous People Rise Up: The Global Ascendancy of Social Media Activism* (pp. 48–64). New Brunswick: Rutgers University Press.

Carlson, B. & Frazer, R. (2021b). *Indigenous Digital Life: The Practice and Politics of Being Indigenous on Social Media.* London: Palgrave McMillan.

Castells, M. (2015). *Networks of Outrage and Hope: Social Movements in the Internet Age.* Cambridge: Polity.

Clarke, A. (2015). How a single Facebook post inspired thousands to stand up for Indigenous rights. *Buzzfeed.* www.buzzfeed.com/allanclarke/how-a-single-facebook-post-inspired-thousands-to-stand-up-fo

Dennis, J. (2019). *Beyond Slacktivism.* Cham: Springer International Publishing.

Deschine Parkhurst, N. (2021). From# Mniwiconi to# StandWithStandingRock: How# NoDAPL Movement disrupted physical and virtual spaces and brought Indigenous liberation to the forefront of people's minds. *Indigenous People Rise Up: The Global Ascendancy of Social Media Activism,* 32–46.

Duarte, M. E. (2017a). Connected activism: Indigenous uses of social media for shaping social change. *Australasian Journal of Information Systems*, 21, 1–12.

Duarte, M. E. (2017b). *Network Sovereignty: Building the Internet Across Indian Country*. Seattle: University of Washington Press.

Dreher, T., McCallum, K., & Waller, L. (2016). Indigenous voices and mediatized policy-making in the digital age. *Information Communication and Society*, 19(1), 23–39.

Harlow, S. (2011). Social media and social movements: Facebook and an online Guatemalan justice movement that moved offline. *New Media & Society*, 14(2), 225–243.

Hedgpeth, D. (2020). 'Jim Crow, Indian style': How Native Americans were denied the right to vote for decades. *The Washington Post*. www.washingtonpost.com/history/2020/11/01/native-americans-right-to-vote-history/

Moeke-Pickering, T., Rowat, J., Cote-Meek, S., & Pegoraro, A. (2021). Indigenous social media activism using Twitter: Amplifying voices using# MMIWG. *Indigenous People Rise up: The Global Ascendancy of Social Media Activism*. New Brunswick: Rutgers University Press, pp. 112–124.

New Matilda. (2015). In Andrew Bolt's world, Black is white and peaceful protest is war. *New Matilda*. https://newmatilda.com/2015/05/04/andrew-bolts-world-black-white-and-peaceful-protest-war/

Petray, T. (2011). Protest 2.0: Online interactions and Aboriginal activists. *Media, Culture & Society*, 33(6), 923–940.

Timberg, C., Harwell, D., Reiley, L., & Bhattarai, A. (2020). The new coronavirus economy: A gigantic experiment reshaping how we work and live. *Washington Post*. www.washingtonpost.com/business/2020/03/21/economy-change-lifestyle-coronavirus/

Watson, M. (2015). The Herald Sun has dismissed 4,000 Indigenous rights activists as a 'Selfish Rabble'. Junkee. https://junkee.com/the-herald-sun-has-dismissed-4000-indigenous-rights-protestors-as-a-selfish-rabble/54833

Wilson, A., & Zheng, C. (2021). Shifting social media and the Idle No More movement. In Carlson, B., & Berglund, J. (Eds), *Indigenous Peoples Rise Up: The Global Ascendency of Social Media Activism* (pp. 14–31). New Brunswick: Rutgers University Press.

Narrative #2

Cavarero, A. (2005). *For More than One Voice*. Stanford: Stanford University Press.

Foucault, M. (1978). *Vigilar y castigar: Nacimiento de la prisión.* Madrid: Siglo.

Foucault, M. (1990). *Tecnologías del yo.* Barcelona: Paidós.

Foucault, M. (1991). *'La función política del intelectual. Respuesta a una cuestión', Saber y verdad.* Madrid: La Piqueta, DL.

Galtung, J. (1969). Violence, peace, and peace research. *Journal of Peace Research,* 6(3), 167–191.

Galtung, J. (1990). Cultural violence. *Journal of Peace Research,* 27(3), 291–305.

Gilligan, J. (1997). *Violence: Reflections on a National Epidemic.* New York: Vintage Books.

Said, E. W. (1996). *Cultura e Imperialismo.* Barcelona: Anagrama.

Smith, L. T. (1999). *Decolonizing Methodologies: Research and Indigenous Peoples.* London: Zed Books.

Narrative #3

Aikau, H. K., Arvin, M., Goeman, M. and Morgensen, S. (2015). Indigenous feminisms roundtable. *Frontiers: A Journal of Women Studies,* 36 (3) 84–106.

Alia, V. (2009). Inuit women and the politics of naming in Nunavut. In Monture, P. A., & and McQuire, P. D. (Eds), *First Voices: An Aboriginal Women's Reader* (pp. 101–105). Toronto: Inanna.

Bauerkemper, J. and Kiiwetinepinesiik Stark, H. K. (2012). The trans/national terrain of Anishinaabe law and diplomacy. *The Journal of Transnational American Studies,* 4 (1), 1–21.

Evering, B. and Sy, W. C. (2019). Map, place names, and sugar bush womxn, c. 1800–2014. In Sy, W. C. (Ed.), *Following Ininaahtigoog Home: Anishinaabeg Womxn Iskigamiziganing* (pp. 314–319). PhD dissertation, Trent University.

Fiola, C. (2013). Transnational Indigenous feminism: An interview with Lee Maracle. In Dobson, K., & McGlynn, A. (Eds), *Transnationalism, Activism, Art* (pp. 162–170). Toronto: University of Toronto Press.

Kuokkanen, R. (2008). Globalization as racialized, sexualized violence: The case of Indigenous women. *International Feminist Journal of Politics,* 10 (2) 216–233.

Lin, Y. T. (2016). Transnational Indigenous feminisms: Why transnational? Why now? *Lectora: Revista de dones i textualitat,* 22, 9–12.

Mason, C. L. (2018). Transnational feminisms: Challenges and possibilities. In Hobbs, M., & Rice, C. (Eds), *Gender and Women's Studies: Critical Terrain,* 2nd ed. (pp. 709–723). Toronto: Women's Press.

Sy, w. C. (2021). On being with (a photograph of) sugar bush womxn: Towards Anishinaabe feminist archival research methods. In Lien, S., & Wallem, H. N.. (Eds), *Adjusting the Lens: Indigenous Activism, Colonial Legacies, and Photographic Heritage* (pp. 186–204). Vancouver: UBC Press.

Williams, C. (Ed.). (2012). *Indigenous Women and Work: From Labor to Activism*. Urbana: University of Illinois Press.

Narrative #4

Hunt, S., & Holmes, C. (2015). Everyday decolonization: Living a decolonizing queer politics. *Journal of Lesbian Studies*, *19*(2), 154–172.

Idle No More. (2019). Indigenous sovereignty is climate action. Video. https://idlenomore.ca/indigenous-sovereignty-is-climate-action/

Kirkness, V. J. (1984). *Indian Control of Indian Education: Over a Decade Later*. London: Mokakit Indian Education Research Association.

Watt-Cloutier, S. (2020). Our planet in peril. Video, YouTube. www.youtube.com/watch?v=sZcs0gcnXxc&t=73s

Wilson, A., Murray, J., Loutitt, S., & North Star Scott, R. (2021). Queering land-based education. In Russell, J. (Ed.), *Queer Ecopedagogies: Explorations in Nature, Sexuality, and Education* (pp. 219–231). Berlin: Springer.

Index

EU authorised representative for GPSR:
Easy Access System Europe, Mustamäe tee 50,
10621 Tallinn, Estonia
gpsr.requests@easproject.com